The Emergence of Classes in Algeria

Westview Special Studies
in Social, Political, and Economic Development

Gordon Donald, *Credit for Small Farmers in Developing Countries*
John S. Gilmore and Mary K. Duff, *Boom Town Growth Management:
A Case Study of Rock Springs—Green River, Wyoming*
Marnia Lazreg, *The Emergence of Classes in Algeria: Colonialism and Socio-Political Change*
Donald R. Mickelwait, Mary Ann Riegelman and Charles F. Sweet, *Women in Rural
Development: A Survey of the Roles of Women in Ghana, Lesotho, Kenya, Nigeria, Bolivia,
Paraguay and Peru*
Elliott R. Morss, John K. Hatch, Donald R. Mickelwait and Charles F. Sweet, *Strategies for
Small Farmer Development: An Empirical Study of Rural Development Projects in
Gambia, Ghana, Kenya, Lesotho, Nigeria, Bolivia, Colombia, Mexico, Paraguay
and Peru*
Paul Shankman, *Migration and Underdevelopment: The Case of Western Samoa*

This book seeks to determine the impact of colonialism on the evolution of social classes in Algeria from 1830 to the present, and to
analyze the relationship between classes and political and economic
development. Colonialism is viewed as a mode of production which
resulted in the distortion of the indigenous socio-economic configurations and led to a particular form of political alliance culminating
in the creation of the F.L.N. The evolution of the latter, the achieve-
ment of independence, and the establishment of a new power structure are examined in the light of class antagonisms. The Algerian
form of socialism is interpreted as the outcome of the struggle between the petite bourgeoisie and the technocracy. The role of the
Party, of the bureaucracy, and of ideology in a selected number of
political measures indicated the existence of a specific pattern of
social development which may not be grasped by the conventional
tools of analysis. The major conclusion of the book is that societies
such as Algeria present the observer with a reality for which a new
mode of theorizing is needed.

Marnia Lazreg was born in Mostaganem, Algeria. She holds a
licence-ès-lettres from the University of Algiers and a Ph.D. in Sociology from New York University. She has taught at Brooklyn and
Hunter Colleges and is now an Assistant Professor of Sociology at
the Graduate Faculty Center, New School for Social Research in
New York.

The Emergence of Classes in Algeria

A Study of Colonialism and Socio-Political Change

Marnia Lazreg

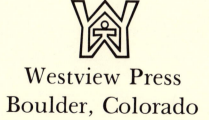

Westview Press
Boulder, Colorado

Copyright © 1976 by Marnia Lazreg.

Published 1976 in the United States of America by
   Westview Press, Inc.
   1898 Flatiron Court
   Boulder, Colorado 80301
   Frederick A. Praeger, Publisher and Editorial Director

Library of Congress Cataloging in Publication Data

Lazreg, Marnia
   The Emergence of Classes in Algeria

   Bibliography: p.

   1. Social classes—Algeria. 2. Algeria—Politics and government. 3. Socialism in Algeria. I. Title.
HN810.A6L37   301.44'0965   76-7955
ISBN 0-89158-107-3

Printed and bound in the United States of America.

To the memory of my father.
To my mother.

Contents

Tables and Figures

Acknowledgments

This book is the result of a long-standing commitment to understanding socio-political changes of which I was both a member and an outsider. In the nine years that I have been away from Algeria, I have received invaluable help from Algerian friends working within and outside the government structure. On my yearly trips, they spent hours discussing issues and events with me; without them it would have been impossible to grasp the meanings of a complex and fast-changing social reality. Their help does not mean, however, that anyone other than myself is responsible for the interpretations offered in this study.

I am indebted to Professors Wolf V. Heydebrand, Carolyn Etheridge and David Greenberg for their extensive comments and suggestions on an earlier draft. Barney Rosset read the manuscript and generously helped with his advice at the editing and publishing stages of this book. Last but not least, I am grateful to Mark Woodcock for reading and editing the manuscript. Most of all I thank him for his encouragement and moral support.

Introduction

On 3 July 1962 one of the bloodiest colonial wars of the
twentieth century ended: Algeria recovered her national sovereignty from the French and set out to mold from the ruins
of the past what it claimed was to be a socialist society.
During the first three years of independence, this experimentation with socialism occurred amid internal political
strife and external threat, especially from Morocco, which
laid claim to part of the Algerian territory. Within this framework, the coup d'état of 19 June 1965 ousting Ben Bella and
bringing to power Colonel Houari Boumédiène, was hailed by
some as a welcome move. It put an end to what had been
considered an irrational if not a mindless socialist policy,
which had allegedly resulted in economic waste and administrative inefficiency. Yet, Colonel Boumédiène, the new leader
of Algeria, continued to refer to his government as socialist.
Algerian socialism was seen as specific to the social and historical conditions of the country. Boumédiène's commitment
to socialism is illustrated by the maintenance of the worker-
managed agricultural estates formerly owned by French

colonists and nationalized by Ben Bella's government. It is also exemplified by the implementation of an agrarian reform that places limits on large landholdings and encourages the creation and productivity of small-sized farms. In the industrial sector, this socialism is characterized by the strengthening of both private and state roles through a liberalization of investment procedures and the establishment of numerous national corporations. The state is a major or equal shareholder with native or foreign investors in these corporations.

Boumédiène's government began operating under the mottoes of profitability, administrative efficiency and social welfare. All three goals are general enough to be pursued by any type of government, socialist or capitalist. They acquire a special importance for Algeria, however, because they are stated to be part of a unique socialist endeavor meant to signify the end of privilege, social inequality, and the exploitation of man by man. There is on the one hand a contradiction between the continuous assertion of socialism as a goal that inspires and determines policymaking and on the other hand the disparities in income distribution, styles of life and modes of thinking of individuals and groups that do not conform to a socialist culture.[1] It is precisely this contradiction that prompted the initial reflection behind this study.

As an Algerian who grew up at a time when colonial rule was challenged and finally overthrown, I am both sensitive to and interested in understanding the dynamics of the contradictions between ideology and concrete reality. In the case of Algeria, the objection may be made that the gap between the rhetorical and the existential levels is explicable in terms of the transition from a colonial to an independent social formation still in search of its political identity. It is true that post-colonial Algeria is only fourteen years old and no definite conclusion can be drawn about its ultimate social, political and economic structures. However, it is also true that the present determines the future and must be analyzed in its own terms, not with reference to a vague and elusive concept of transition. Vital decisions that affect the lives of millions of individuals are taken everyday in most Third World societies. These decisions are taken as part of a general system in which old patterns of doing things cut across, but may not necessarily supersede new ones. In the name of transition we tend to forsake serious analysis of existing reality and subsume unique developments under general laws. Thus, both the Left and the Right use this concept to legitimize inconsistencies and contradictions. The Left explains away non-socialist behaviors and structures within avowedly socialist societies as passing phenomena of maladjustment. The Right views authoritarianism and repression as necessary evils of "modernization." Meanwhile, little is done to determine just where the transition begins and where it ends. In fact, it could be argued that for some Third World countries such as Algeria, the transition period began with colonialism and ended with its defeat.

The social-political configurations that emerge after a society achieves its formal independence can be viewed as unique occurrences already bearing the imprint of that society's identity. A society may be socialist or capitalist, a mixture or a variation on the two, but it is not transitional. With this in mind, it is proposed that social contradictions in Algeria be viewed as part of a larger process located in the country's historical past.

How was Algerian society structured before the French colonized it? What were the effects of French domination on the evolution of indigenous social groups? What is the impact of colonialism on the present power relations and political orientations? Two concepts acquire a major importance in answering questions of this kind: the *colonial factor* and *social class*. Nineteenth-century Algerian society developed within the context of a settlement colony which entailed distortions of a cultural, political and economic nature. The concept of social class in its Marxian meaning encompasses these three dimensions and thus provides the opportunity to analyze the different impacts of colonialism on Algerian society. The clash between two cultures resulted in the French determination to break up the existing social relations in order to facilitate colonial hegemonic rule. The process through which Algerian groups restructured themselves and engaged in a nationalist political practice constitutes the first clear example of the specific effect of colonialism on social change. The second and perhaps more significant example is illustrated by the shape and direction of socio-political action that occurs after the physical presence of the colonists is removed: Antagonisms and contradictions develop more freely, yet the colonial past weighs more heavily than before, ever present in its absence.

In this study, the impact of colonialism on the process through which social groups restructured themselves and emerged as full-fledged classes is examined from a historical and structural perspective. A preliminary chapter discusses the theoretical issues involved in the study of Third World social structures. It also specifies the applicability of the concept of class to the Algerian social reality. Chapter Two presents a historical overview of Algerian social structure under Turkish colonial rule. Chapter Three investigates the changes that affected the property structure and the relations of production in the French colonial era. Chapter Four analyzes the process through which nationalist leaders acquired power and used it partially to promote class interests. Special attention is given to the 1962 political crisis when a military confrontation occurred between two groups of nationalist leaders and resulted in the formation of the first government of the independent Algerian republic. Chapter Five examines the articulation of the interests of an emergent dominant class. The analysis centers on the state control of workers' management of agricultural and industrial enterprises, the evolution of the workers' union, the creation of national corporations and the revision of the Code of Investments offering guarantees to private investors. Chapter Six deals with the ideological orientation of the dominant class. Speeches made by the President of Algeria and official documents such as the Tripoli Program and the Charter of Algiers receive special attention. Chapter Seven examines the relationship between class and party, while Chapter Eight studies the relationship between class and bureaucracy in order to determine the latter's share in political power.

---

1 Although it is undeniable that the living conditions of Algerians have qualitatively and quantitatively improved, trends towards greater disparities of income are becoming more and more obvious. Statistics show that 5% of Algerian households receive 28% of the national income. See Secrétariat d'Etat au Plan, A.A.R.D.E.S., *Enquête sur les Budgets Familiaux*, no. 1, July 1973. p. 84.

1
Theoretical and Methodological Context

To understand the social structure of post-colonial Algeria it is necessary to refute the basic assumptions that, first, Algerian society is in a state of transition toward socialism[1] and, second, Algerian society is involved in a process of nation-building and cultural revival in which the collective search for unity overrides class cleavages.[2]

Regarding the first assumption, the imputation of transiency is inadequate for reasons discussed in the Introduction to this study. Furthermore, this view posits a definite model of socio-economic development which Algeria is alleged to approximate, regardless of the existing reality which may and often does invalidate that model. The assumption rests on the existence in Algeria of certain structures which are informed by a socialist ideal, namely, workers' self-management in agriculture and the role played by the state in heavy industry. In fact, the part of the economy that is socialized (worker-managed) is limited and has not

1

been expanding since 1963.³ State intervention in industry may be seen as a matter of circumstantial necessity rather than as a tribute to the ideal of socialism. It was not possible for nations like Algeria, which acquired their political independence after a protracted war and within the context of an already constituted world economy, to leave the development of their industry to groups that have remained relatively small and ill-equipped in both capital and skills. The state is in a better position than any single class to mobilize the necessary resources to promote industrialization.

It is difficult at this point to determine the nature of Algeria's socio-economic system. The difficulty lies in the complexity of the struggle between the nationalistic drive to control its own resources and the desire to industrialize in a short period of time. Population growth and unemployment further compound the issue and expose the contradictory nature of this struggle. While the future remains open to speculation, the present can be analyzed in terms of the relationship between old and emerging structures and the nature of the transformation of the former into the latter.

The second argument, according to which new nations such as Algeria are better understood if studied in terms of cultural revival and nationalism, is likewise misleading. First, it identifies the ideology of nationalism with its socio-economic base. In other words, it assumes that the nationalist orientation is the fundamental element in terms of which all socio-political phenomena must be explained. It also assumes that the construction of a national economy is the overriding interest of both leaders and led without specifying the form and content of this economy and its possible effects on the social structure. In Algeria, the desire to industrialize at a rapid pace has led to a form of economic organization which is not labor-intensive, and which has therefore resulted in an increased gap between the employed and the unemployed and a subsequent increase in immigration to France.[4] It is possible to view nationalism as a "class phenomenon instead of a supra-class mechanism."[5] The national *élan* ought perhaps to be analyzed in terms of the objective conditions under which leaders create new institutions and the interests which these institutions reflect.

Finally, the emphasis on post-colonial national unity rather than class emergence betrays an elitist and an evolutionist bias. It is taken for granted that national "elites" are best equipped to deal with the task of economic reconstruction and that the "masses", stricken by some "political inertia,"[6] can only wait for the elite to improve the conditions under which they live. There is the implicit assumption as well that new nations exhibit a simple structure which will get more complex as their economies become more diversified. Berque's focus on nationalism as a factor of unity further assumes that the phenomenon of political independence has the effect of merely restoring the pre-colonial values rather than transforming the structures inherited from the colonial era. The pre-colonial order is implicitly identified with cooperation, communal bonds and community of faith. In reality, the Algerian pre-colonial era was characterized by a specific network of relations of property and appropriation which, although cast within a seemingly communal framework, was marked by some degree of inequality in the ownership of the means of production.[7]

Cultural revival as a factor that overrides class cleavages denotes a conception of the world in terms of essence rather than existence. In the Algerian case, it consists in positing that a renewed interest in Islam, a specifically non-Western philosophy, precludes any apprehension of the Algerian social structure in class terms because Islam emphasizes the values of sharing, brotherhood and community. By the same token, it is implicitly recognized that Algerian society has an "immutable and impenetrable" essence that is inherent in the "monolithic bloc" of Islamic civilization.[8] This means that Algeria's Islamic character gives it a specificity that is irreducible to non-Islamic societies. Although the Algerian specificity is undeniable, it cannot alone explain all socio-political phenomena. It is, for example, unable to account for the July 1962 crisis and/or the 1965 coup d'état.

The emphasis that Berque places on the study of cultural revival and nation building as fundamental characteristics of newly independent societies is overstated and fails to eliminate the need for class analysis. This need has been recently emphasized by students of Third World societies. Wallerstein points out that it may be difficult to study African societies in terms of class. Nevertheless, "the reality of class is not lessened by the very real resistance to class analysis, nor by its rarity as a political phenomenon."[9] However, in his attempt to demonstrate why and how a class analysis of African societies should be undertaken, he introduces an overdetermining international dimension. He maintains that "in peripheral areas of the world economy . . . the primary contradiction is between the interests organized and located in the core countries and their local allies on the one hand, and the majority of the population on the other."[10] Although the capitalist world economy has undeniable consequences on the shape and content of Third World structures, its importance should be specified. It cannot be taken for granted that there are and there will always be "local allies" of foreign capital. Nor can one overlook the fact that some classes in the "peripheral" areas are fiercely nationalistic insofar as they try to minimize the political effects of foreign capital, while at the same time attempting to meet the demands made upon them by the laboring classes. This is precisely the case in Algeria. It would be depriving the Algerian social classes of their specific dynamics to study them only as epiphenomena dependent on a struggle located beyond their national boundaries. Struggles between international actors are likewise affected by antagonisms and conflicts occuring at the national level. For these reasons, this study will focus primarily on the internal dynamics of social classes.

The external dimension is implicitly present in the types of policies and decisions promoted by the classes in power, although to be adequately understood these would require a separate study.

MARXIST AND NEO-MARXIST CONCEPTIONS OF CLASS

Wallerstein's interpretation of the concept of class raises the problem of its applicability to non-Western societies that have yet to achieve industrialization. A review of Marx's treatment of social classs and of some of the selective ways in which the concept has been elaborated upon by neo-Marxists will make it possible to assess the applicability of a class model to post-colonial societies.

Although it did not result in a specific definition, Marx's treatment of class hinges on three main elements: 1) relation to the means of production; 2) consciousness of one's class position and interests; and 3) political organization to promote class interests.

The ownership of the means of production gives rise to unequal social relations between those who own capital and those who merely own their labor power. In other words, the process of production determines the mechanism of distribution and autonomy at work. The inequality of the distribution of products within the capitalist mode of production is a reflection of the inequality in the "distribution of the instruments of production."[11] Thus, the ownership of the instruments or means of production determines the distribution of individuals into two main classes: the capitalists and the workers. This, however, is an "objective" division which may be necessary but not sufficient to qualify a group of people as members of a class. A class "in-itself" will become a class "for-itself" only if the individuals engaged in the process of production develop a consciousness of their objective situation as members of a class with common interests. The consciousness of an identity of interests is assumed to lead to a "community," a "political organization"[12] which would promote those interests through the "class struggle".

Considering that Marx often referred to social groups as classes without necessarily demonstrating or indicating that they fulfill the criteria mentioned above, it becomes important to investigate the nature of these criteria and their relationships. It has been suggested that we view one criterion as a crucial indicator of the existence of class division within the "pure" capitalist mode of production while the other two remain contingent upon the social formation studied. Thus, Poulantzas considers the ownership of the means of production as essential to the study of class, whereas "class consciousness" is dismissed as a "Hegelian reminiscence".[13] As to political organization, it is seen as incidental rather than essential. This kind of interpretation is made possible by the distinction that is established between structure and class. Marx's concept of the means of production and political organization is identified with structures of a social formation, and class with the "global effect of structures in the field of the social relations of production."[14] It is further specified that the "relations of production when conceived of as structure are . . . not social classes."[15] "Social classes are not, in fact, an 'empirical thing' whose structure would constitute the concept; they connote social relations, social wholes, but they are their concept just as the concepts of Capital, Wage Labor, Surplus Value constitute concepts of structures and relations of production."[16]

It must be noted here that the relationship between structure and class is in effect seen as a relationship between the signifier and the signified within the sign-system that serves as a model to a structuralist approach to social phenomena. Thus, social structures constitute the Saussurean "langue", while classes make up the "parole" or speech.[17] The distinction between language and speech, although meant to transcend the classical mind/body opposition, merely transfers it to a narrower domain, namely, the sign unit. In other words, "every phenomenon carries with itself both superstructure and infrastructure, both culture and nature, both meaning and raw material."[18] Within this frame of reference, it becomes intelligible for Poulantzas to conceive of class as being both a concept (i.e., the signified) and a sort of "acoustic image" (i.e., the signifier) that "connotes social relations, social wholes".[19] This coexistence of superstructure and infrastructure within the same unit of discourse necessarily leads to a fusion of both form and content. Thus, Poulantzas indicates that classes are also structures insofar as they serve as a "frame of reference" (*cadre référentiel*)[20] for social relations. In other words, classes constitute both the structures and the effect of structures on the social relations of production. This means that classes are the result of a given arrangement of economic and political structures while at the same time they circumscribe the relations between owners and producers. The implication is that although classes may not be directly observable entities, their existence is nevertheless present at the level of mediation between the means of production and the social relations of production.

Within this context, the subject's consciousness of his class position is irrelevant. Likewise, the distinction between class in-itself and class for-itself may be dismissed as a "Hegelian reminiscence".[21] Consequently, the Marxist criterion of organization which identifies a class for-itself is conceived of as the "overdetermining level" of the "political superstructure."[22] In other words, the diachronic dimension of class is transformed into a synchronic category where "the political struggle between classes is the central point of the transformation process which has nothing to do with a diachronic historicist process 'acted' upon by an actor, the class as a subject."[23] It follows that a class may exist at one level of the relations of production within a given social formation and be absent at another. This is what Poulantzas refers to as the "under-determination" of some classes as a result of the "dominance of a mode of production over others."[24]

Despite its structuralist character, this interpretation of class is not without relevance for this study. It provides a descriptive device which makes the analysis of the Algerian modes of production easier. The fact that Poulantzas' approach is ahistorical cannot affect this study adversely because its descriptive categories befit the Algerian colonial situation. Under French rule, the dynamics of the Algerian social structure were arrested in both space and time. Any change that affected the indigenous society originated from the colonial superstructure.

Poulantzas' reading of Marx points to two areas of investigation:

First, on a methodological level, the existence within a given social totality of several modes of production with specific structures points to the possibility of setting up criteria of class derived from the various structures involved. In other words, class could be defined in terms of the dominant mode of production. In the Algerian case, this means that the state-capitalist mode of production may be used to define class not on the basis of the ownership of the means of production but according to the mode of appropriation of labor. This, however, does not cancel the structural effect of the existence of a pure capitalist mode of production. This is why it is here assumed that the appropriation of labor power represents the combined effects of the two modes of production more adequately than their ownership and control. More concretely, this means that the Algerian administrators of state corporations and the emerging national entrepreneurs display a similarity of interests in the face of a growing proletariat and a large peasantry. They are more partners than adversaries, as is exemplified by the creation of "mixed" corporations in which state and private capital are combined.

Second, the related issue of the number of classes that exist in a given society is seen by Poulantzas as being a function not only of the relations to the means of production but also of the combination of the various modes of production.[25] The implication is that a multiplicity of classes may not result from a multiplicity of criteria. This is due to the fact that the various modes of production that coexist in a given society are united by individual owners and/or controllers. The relationships between these individual owners, therefore, override the number of the modes of production in which they partake. In the Algerian case, the coexistence of three modes of production does not necessarily mean that the social structure is made up of three classes, as will be discussed later.

OPERATIONALIZATION OF "CLASS"

In his *Introduction to the Critique of Political Economy,* Karl Marx notes that, on the methodological level, the "real subject retains its autonomous existence outside the head just as before; namely, as long as the head's conduct is merely speculative, merely theoretical. Hence, in the theoretical method, too, the subject, society, must always be kept in mind as the presupposition."[26] The presupposition to be kept in mind in attempting to elaborate an operational definition of class is precisely the nature of the society under investigation. Only twelve years ago, Algeria was a colony. As such, it was referred to as an asymmetrical society because of the coexistence of a highly modern economic sector owned by the French colonists and a poorer and non-mechanized sector owned by the indigenous population and often referred to as "traditional".[27] Today, it is characterized by a combination of public, private and self-managed (i.e., socialized) types of economic organization.

In order to avoid mechanically equating social classes with these types of economic organization, it is perhaps more fruitful to use Poulantzas' conception of a social formation as being made up of several modes of production of unequal importance which, in their interaction, affect the social relations of production unequally. What is needed here is a concept that captures what is common to the three modes of production that exist in the Algerian social formation. That concept is the mode of appropriation of labor.

The workers who are involved in the socialized part of the economy do not participate in the management of the finances of the enterprise (which they theoretically manage themselves), nor do they market the product of their labor.[28] In fact, for the former colonist a director and a management committee have been substituted who extract the same surplus out of the workers. The latter receive a fixed wage often incommensurate with the amount of work supplied. Yet, the recent draft of the National Charter made public in a special issue of *El Moudjahid* in May 1976, maintains that "work must be paid according to its quality and quantity." In the public and private sectors of the economy, the product of labor is appropriated through the same method of wage distribution.

The difference between these three types of economic organization lies in the agents who control labor. In the socialized and public sectors, control is exercised by the state. In the private sector it is exercised by private individuals or corporate groups. It must be pointed out that the state also engages in joint ventures with private partners, thereby functioning as a corporate entity for the pursuit of profit. Under these circumstances, it becomes obvious that private ownership of the means of production may not be a significant criterion in a definition of the concept of class.

Contrary to Djilas, who equated the control of the means of production with their actual ownership, it is here suggested that the right to dispose of the means of production either through private ownership or administrative control be viewed as a criterion.[29]

This suggestion is based on the notion of property that was prevalent in pre-colonial times. Then, private ownership of land was a recognition of the actual working of that land. If a land was not exploited or "revived", it was considered "dead" and free to be owned through being worked.[30] By extrapolation, it may be argued that when the Algerian state appropriates the means of production in the name of the people, it is in effect taking upon itself to manage them, since their former "owners" (the colonists) abandoned them when the country achieved its political independence. Likewise, the Algerian individuals who own land have, in fact, as a result of historical circumstances (of which colonialism and its notion of individiual property are a major part), appropriated the right to exploit the land, thereby fusing exploitation with ownership. In the first instance, the right to control the means of production is derived from revolutionary legitimacy; in the second case, it is derived from private ownership.

To sum up, class may be defined, in the Algerian case, in terms of the appropriation of the means of production and the mode of appropriation of labor power. Class consciousness is not taken here as a defining criterion because the manifestation of this concept is contingent upon the availability of channels that permit the expression of class interests and legal provisions regarding the freedom to organize politically. In the absence of these conditions, it seems more fruitful to seek manifestations of class consciousness in a sphere other than political associations and demands. Class consciousness may be studied through concrete activity, such as workers' takeover of colonists' estates, workers' denunciation of individuals or government agencies who appear to have impeded the functioning of self-management and/or strikes.[31] This kind of consciousness cannot be confused with what Lenin referred to as "embryonic" consciousness because the activities mentioned here are not spontaneous disturbances of the status quo. Instead, they are goal-oriented and reveal an awareness and appreciation of conflicting interests and power relations.[32]

Although there are three types of economic organization in Algeria, there are only two modes of appropriation of the means of production: the private and the state-controlled. The socialized sector which is theoretically separate from the public sector is empirically confounded with it, as was pointed out earlier. It was also indicated that these three types of economic organization have one element in common, namely, the appropriation of labor power through wage allocation.

If class is defined according to the mode of appropriation of the means of production and labor power, it is clear that Algerian society is composed of four main classes: 1) those who appropriate labor power. Within this class three factions emerge: a) the state administrators and controllers of the means of production; b) the new entrepreneurs who are encouraged by the state to create industries that would supplement the government's efforts in these areas. The latter are theoretically controlled by the former. However, when they become partners as in the establishment of "mixed companies," the notion of control loses its significance. Antagonism between the two factions may occur as the new entrepreneurs' dynamic growth finds itself stunted by the restraints of a nationalistic economic policy.[33] c) The large landowners, some of whom happen to be members of the state apparatus.[34] 2) Urban and rural wage labor; 3) individuals in the liberal professions and small businessmen who constitute an intermediate class; and 4) peasants who own small plots of land.

THE DOMINANT CLASS

The focus of this study will be on the emergence, as a class, of those who control the means of production. The determination of the process through which this class emerged, the manifold manifestations of its existence as such and its relations to other classes constitute matters for investigation.

This class, which will be referred to as the dominant class, has been subject to contradictory interpretations. It has been analyzed as a *"classe politique."*[35] a "political elite"[36] or a "bureaucratic class."[37] As pointed out earlier, the notion of a political elite assumes more than it is able to demonstrate. As indicated above, it takes for granted that elites and non-elites share the same goals, and at the same time it does not satisfactorily explain conflict when it occurs among members of the elite.[38] Thus, in accounting for the lack of cohesion and consensus among the Algerian "elite", Quandt advances such arguments as differences in time of recruitment in the elite, family, school and political socialization.[39] These are useful but secondary variables which still do not explain why, once independence was achieved, intra-elite conflict became sharper than in the period just preceding the start of the revolution.

The notion of a "political class" presents a methodological shortcoming. It places the concept of class at the level of the superstructure, therefore detaching it from its historical moorings and encapsulating it in the present. Besides, this formulation assumes that there is some degree of homogeneity and coherence among members of the class. In reality, up to 1965, Algerian politicians were conspicuously heterogeneous and conflict-ridden and therefore did not exhibit any consciousness of kind. Furthermore, to maintain that a "political class" exists in Algeria is to equate playing a role in government with determining the policies of that government. Finally, political power alone is not a sufficient condition for a social category to be called a class.

The conception of a "bureaucratic class" leaves unexplained the actual relationship between state power and state apparatus. This conception is similar to Djilas' characterization of the Russian social structure which appears to be neither consistent nor precise. Indeed, Djilas refers to the "new class" as the "political bureaucracy" whose members are not bureaucrats but "political leaders" who hold an "administrative monopoly". Furthermore, although the members of the new class are not bureaucrats, "only a special stratum of bureaucrats, those who are not administrative officials, make up the core of the governing bureaucracy."[40]

The equation of the bureaucracy with a class rests on the assumption that the expertise of the bureaucracy is indispensable to the maintenance of the state, be it socialist or capitalist. As Weber put it: "Under normal conditions . . . 'the political master' finds himself in the position of the 'dilettante' who stands opposite the 'expert', facing the trained official who stands within the management of administration."[41] However, Weber also asserted that the "ever-increasing 'indispensability' of the officialdom, swollen to millions, is no more decisive for this question"[42] (i.e., power of the bureaucracy). To equate indispensability with power is in effect to uphold an elitist model of society. Indeed, the underlying assumption is the same, namely, that those who are best trained wield power. Besides, to view bureaucracy as a class is to obscure the relationship between the bureaucrats' class attachments and their input in the political process, as is discussed in Chapter eight.

The following are proposed as indicators of the objective existence of the dominant class: 1) control[43] of the ownership of the means of production; 2) dominant[44] role in economic organization and distribution of surplus value; 3) dominant role in ideological elaboration; and 4) dominant role in political decision making.

The control of the means of produciton will be studied through the process of nationalization of agricultural and business enterprises and the containment of self-management as a type of economic organization that was spontaneously set up by Algerian workers after independence.

The use of ideology as a tool of class domination will be studied through an analysis of the coup d'etat of 1965, which ended the struggle between two factions of the dominant class. The faction led by Ben Bella included Marxist individuals who pushed for giving a share to peasants and workers in the control of the means of production, as was exemplified by the government endorsement and codification of self-management. The faction led by Boumédiène was more concerned with economic efficiency and the building of a strong state aparatus. It will be shown how the ideology elaborated by one faction will be kept and manipulated by the other faction in order to maintain its dominance over workers and peasants.

The specific choice of the economic organization that characterizes Algeria will be studied as a reflection of the interests of the dominant class. Since 1965, this class has built a state apparatus ostensibly meant to promote the interests of the people. However, the economic branch of this apparatus is organized in such a way that it evolved interests that appear to be opposed to the people's, in that state managers and individual producers represent the antithetical goals of general and private interests. Considering that the Algerian state was built on the ruins of the colonial bureaucratic structure and that it is guided by norms borrowed from the French capitalist state apparatus, it is predetermined to operate as a capitalist state.[45] It is legitimate, therefore, to conceive of the Algerian bureaucratic structure as a formal capitalist structure which "guarantees the economic interests of certain dominated classes which may eventually be contrary to the short term interests of the dominant classes but are compatible with their political interests and their hegemonic domination."[46]

The creation of state corporations by the Algerian government may be in the interests of the workers who are not, in this way, faced with private owners of the means of production. But, in the long run, these corporations maintain the existence of the dominant class whose continued control over the workers is thereby secured. Besides, the granting since 1966 of specific guarantees to indigenous investors is a further indication that the interests of the dominant class are not identical to the workers'. The latter stand in the same relation to the industrial entrepreneurs as producers to owners.

On a theoretical level, the purpose of this study is to investigate through a concrete case the specifications that must be brought to the Marxist conception of class when used in a society with its particular social and historical characteristics. It is also hoped that some of the shortcomings of various studies done on Algerian society will be avoided. A quick glance at the relevant literature reveals either a conspicuous neglect of the changes that have affected the class structure since 1962 or a nominalist conception of social class.

Thus, W. Quandt's concern with the identification of the members of the Algerian government confines him to a description of the socio-political background and functions of what he refers to as the "political leadership".[47]

Pierre Bourdieu's treatment of the social dislocations that resulted from the French policy of displacing widely dispersed peasants and grouping them into better controllable villages is merely a description of a social problem created by a brutal colonialism.[48] Indeed, Bourdieu does not analyze the impact of the structure of the peasantry as a class and its relation to other classes. Whenever he touches upon classes, as in his pre-independence study of Algerian workers, he does so within essentially a Weberian perspective.[49] Classes are defined by several dimensions such as occupation, career stability, type of activity and degree of qualification or education. These criteria belong in effect to the sphere of distribution rather than production and thereby describe rather than explain unequal relationships between producers. This approach is insufficient in that it takes for granted that which is problematic, namely, explaining why one economic sector is more profitable than another and determining the impact of socio-economic differentials on the socio-political relations between owners and producers taken as a totality.

Writing before the independence of Algeria, Fanon warned against the danger of having a national bourgeoisie arise after political freedom is achieved.[50] This class would be alien to the needs of peasants and workers and would be economically dependent on the former "mother country," exhibit no initiative to industrialize and, in effect, live a parasitical life in a fashion similar to the colonists it has merely replaced. In his speculations, Fanon did not foresee the rise of a class that would be intent on becoming as little dependent as possible on European powers and as highly ambitious in its plans for industrialization as the Algerian dominant class has turned out to be.

The mechanism or process by which a new class arose after independence has received little attention. Consequently, Chaliand's[51] and Clegg's[52] attempts to explain the lack of expansion of self-management to all spheres of economic life and the non-participation of workers in political decisions in terms of a class struggle between the working class, the peasantry and a newly emerged middle class remains more an assertion than a demonstrated fact. This may be due to the lack of a definition of the concept of class that takes into consideration the specific characteristics of the Algerian social structure.

In fact, Clegg uses the Marxist definition in terms of "relations to the means of production" and the "existence of distinct forms of consciousness". Without determining the nature of and the relationship between these criteria, he comes up with five classes, each corresponding to a separate form of consciousness: the peasantry, the sub-proletariat, the working class, the "traditional bourgeoisie" and the "new middle class". The unspecified notion of "form of

consciousness" results in a contradictory assertion according
to which the workers form a class but their action (i.e.,
spontaneously taking over agricultural and industrial enterprises abandoned by the French colonists after independence) is "not a conscious praxis"[52] because they could not
prevent the state from controlling them at a later stage.
This contradiction reveals that the author in effect divorces
class from consciousness and equates the latter with the
workers' ability to stand up to the state, without any
attention given to whether it was possible to adopt such a
stance.[54]

It may be argued that the workers did indicate consciousness
of their objective situation in the social structure by re-
opening farms and industrial concerns without waiting for
the state to take action on their behalf. The notion of un-
conscious praxis is a contradiction in terms since praxis is in
itself conscious activity. This contradiction is a manifestation
of the lag between theory and reality and points to the need
for a re-evaluation of concepts elaborated in specific societies
at a given stage of their historical development.

A more recent study focuses on the imputed specificity of
the Algerian model of economic development which it relates
to the class nature of the state. Although it provides a good
analysis of the Algerian economic structure, it fails to
examine the mechanism whereby changes in the composition
and functions of the various social classes corresponded to
changes in economic policy.[55]

A Word of Caution

The terminology borrowed from Western sources and used in
this study is not entirely adequate. For example, the concept
"bourgeoisie" or "bourgeois" does not in the Algerian case
have the same meaning that it conveys within a European
context. For the purposes at hand, these terms are used to
refer to a class that aspires to play the same role as its
European counterpart but which does not have the same kind

of economic power. It was not deemed appropriate to employ instead the term middle class because in Algeria there is no truly articulated upper class to distinguish it from. The landlords who benefited from colonial domination did not form an aristocracy in socio-political terms.

2

The
Algerian Social Structure under
Turkish Domination

The Algerian mode of production before 1830 displayed a few similarities with the pre-capitalist economic formations described by Marx. However, because Algeria had been under Turkish rule from 1519 to 1830, its social structure was affected in such a way that it cannot be reduced to any specific pre-capitalist formation. Indeed, the Turkish regime had detrimental effects on the Algerian system of property, but it did not destroy it as did the French at a later period.

The Turks established feudal relationships of a peculiar kind with the Algerian population. The latter, while retaining some degree of autonomy, was compelled to produce enough to enable the Turks to perpetuate the conditions of their domination.

HISTORICAL BACKGROUND

The history of the Maghreb of which Algeria is a part is characterized by various invasions. Romans, Vandals, Byzantines, Arabs, Turks and Frenchmen swept over this

northern part of Africa. The longest-lasting influence, however, has been the Arabs who penetrated the area in three
successive waves in the seventh, eighth and eleventh
centuries. They established a religious bond with the Berber
populations with whom they lived in a symbiotic relationship.[1]

The Middle Ages of the Maghreb are not very well known.[2]
Arab and Berber dynasties succeeded each other, and their
kingdoms reached a high peak of development between the
ninth and eleventh centuries. Since then, periods of decay
set in on the three kingdoms which roughly correspond to
what are today Morocco, Algeria and Tunisia. Internecine
conflicts and intermittent Portuguese and Spanish attacks
at the end of the fifteenth century contributed to the
weakening of the area. The conditions were ripe for
occupation by the Turks.

The Turkish Occupation of Algeria

In the sixteenth century, the Spanish kingdom of Ferdinand
the Catholic undertook what was termed an "African
crusade,"[3] attacking the Muslim Maghrebin shores to take
hold of the major forts, thereby acquiring supremacy over
the strategic southwest of the Mediterranean. Algiers, then "a
municipal republic administered by a bourgeois oligarchy
under the protection of the Thaaliba," (an Arab tribe),[4]
responded by soliciting the services of a renowned Turkish
corsair, 'Aroudj (also named "Barbarossa"), to deliver it
from the Spanish incursions. Barbarossa's successes prompted
him to seek to establish his own sovereignty over the areas he
wrested from the Spanish occupation. But he perished in
1518. His brother, Kheir-eddine, fulfilled his goals, and being
aware of his inability to retain alone the re-conquered
territory, he presented it to the Turkish Sultan, Selim, who
immediately appointed him *pasha*, bestowed upon him the
title of *beylerbey* (emir of emirs), and dispatched an army of
2,000 janissaries and 4,000 volunteers to Algiers.

Thus, Algiers became the Regency of Algiers, which later included most of the territory known today as Northern Algeria.

Turkish Social Structure

Turkish domination over Algeria was characterized by the rule of the military caste of the janissaries, referred to as the *odjak.* Soon the janissaries entered into conflict with the corsairs' corporation, the *Taifas of Rais,*[5] who prided themselves for their exploits on the high seas and were contemptuous of the janissaries, whom they contemptuously referred to as "the oxen of Anatolia".

In 1671, the *Taifa* took upon itself to abolish the position of *pasha* of the Regency and elect a *dey* instead. This move was meant to make Algiers more independent from Constantinople. The continuous struggle for power between the *Taifa* and the janissaries ultimately ended with the victory of the former who subsequently acquired the right to elect the *deys.*

The Regency was divided into three districts or *beyliks,* each governed by a *bey* appointed by the *dey* of Algiers for a three year period from among those Turks who could afford to be the highest bidders for the function. *Beys* were helped in their administration by a military task-force and civilian *caids* whose functions were to control the tribes, fix and collect the various taxes on land, crops and cattle.[6] The Turkish authority, however, did not extend to the entire Algerian territory. In fact, it became effective only at tax collection time, when troops set out to visit the Arabo-Berber tribes to get the *dey's* tribute.

The increasing role played by the janissaries in public affairs and the material and legal privileges they secured for themselves accounted for their conflicts with the corsairs. The latter counteracted the janissaries' bids for power by supporting the *beylerbey.* It is reported that the corsairs enjoyed a great popularity among city dwellers because they contributed to their wealth and commercial activity.[7] The corsairs sold slaves and the goods they seized from the ships they attacked. By 1568, they were made to accept the janissaries in their corporation. This decision contributed to the decline of the *Taifa* toward the end of the eighteenth century.

There do not seem to be any significant differences between the *Taifa* and janissaries in terms of social background. The janissaries were recruited among poor people from Anatolia, Albany and other Turkish provinces, whereas the corsairs[8] were usually people who had left Asia at an earlier date and had been operating off the shores of North Africa before the janissaries arrived. As an organized army, the janissaries were more necessary to the *dey* to maintain the Turkish presence in the hinterland. They could, therefore, compete for power more efficiently. They soon formed a new aristocracy which, in effect, had a caste outlook based on racial origins. To be a Turk was a prerequisite for membership. The higher officers along with the *dey* and his staff received land privileges from a territory considered public domain and controlled directly by the Treasury. The Turks never worked the lands thus obtained. These were usually taken care of either by tribes (as part of the forced labor they were subjected to) or by hired peasants, referred to as *khammes*, who kept one-fifth of the land's yield.

The origin of this public domain is not known with accuracy. It has been speculated that it may be a perverted form of the primitive communal property of antiquity.[9] However, it may also be the result of the old Islamic notion that, in conquered territory, the individual has only the right to work (not to own) the land, in return for which he pays a tax called the *kharaj*. In fact, in Algeria, land was no longer considered land of conquest, but the *kharaj* tax was maintained.[10] Part of the public domain was also used to secure the allegiance of some tribes, as will be seen in more detail later.

The new military and maritime aristocracy was open in its lower stratum to the descendants of Turkish fathers and Algerian mothers, the *khurghuli*. The Moors, refugees from the Spanish inquisition, constituted a bourgeoisie which was organized into corporations with the monopoly of local industry. They were prohibited from engaging in military activity. The wealthiest among them used to invest in the corsairs' ships and share in their profits.[11] The Jews (*Kiboussines*), especially those who emigrated from Spain at the same time as the Moors, were also part of this bourgeoisie. They were mostly traders who would secure export licenses from the Regency. Other social and/or ethnic groups were confined to specific activities such as butchers, millers or construction workers.

Outside the main urban centers, the social structure was tribal. The hinterland was dominated by competing local groups. Those who cooperated with the Turkish central authority were known as *Makhzen*. Among them were re-cruited administrative aides to the provincial governors. Their link to the central authority did not prevent the *Makhzen* tribe leaders from taking the side of the impoverished tribes against the Turkish state during their frequent rebellions. However, because of the nature of their position vis-à-vis the Turks, Makhzen tribes often entered in conflict with either the religious confederations or the rest of the tribal population or *R'ya*.

THE ALGERIAN PROPERTY STRUCTURE

Mode of Production

Although the social structure described above was prevalent in the cities before 1830, it must be pointed out that pre-capitalist Algeria did not exhibit a clear-cut separation between town and country. There were towns and fortified places that formed centers for the neighboring tribes. In this sense, Algeria retained the imprint of her Roman past.[12] The form of the social structure in the country was determined by its specific mode of production with its original system of ownership. It is important to identify this social structure because it has been either genuinely misunderstood or deliberately distorted.[13] Thus, French military men and colonial administrators saw the Algerian form of property either as feudal or communal, depending on the purpose the interpretation was to serve. Algerian land ownership was claimed to be communal when French immigrants needed land and the only way to acquire it was to declare that the indigenous population lived under a "communal regime" that was "an obstacle to progress".[14] It was dismissed as feudal whenever the colonists needed labor which they could get only by detaching small farmers from the networks of rights and duties that linked them to well-off landowners. The latter were referred to by the colonists as the "local aristocracy" and attacked for curtailing the freedom of the small and landless peasants.[15]

In fact, pre-capitalist Algeria was neither feudal nor communal. Neither was it made up of nomadic tribes roaming through vast stretches of land, as has been claimed. It was customary for Algerian tribesmen to leave part of their land fallow in order to avoid exhausting it and move on to cultivate new plots within a given territory.[16] The fact that some of these tribesmen often lived in tents which were more functional because they permitted greater mobility in view of ever-receding plots was interpreted by French colonists as a sign of a generalized nomadic life style.

The structure of Algerian property was composed of three categories: *arsh* (private but non-alienable property); *melk* (equivalent to private alienable property); and *habus* (or land donated for religious or cultural purposes).

Arsh designates both the tribe and the land which tribesmen share according to their material capacity to cultivate it.[17] Each member has a plot which he works with equipment and

Algerian Property Structure

Arsh	Part of the tribal land recognized as the private property of the individual or family who works it	Cannot be sold
Melk	Private property acquired by contract	Can be sold, but custom forbids selling it
Habus	Property donated to religious foundations or cultural institutions	Cannot be sold

cattle that he owns. When the owner of a plot dies, his land is inherited by his male descendants only.[18] If the deceased has no heirs or if the latter are unable to develop his property, the land is returned to the community, which then redistributes it among its members. For this reason, there was a continuous process of readjustment of plots according to need and ability, which led to the erroneous notion that land was redistributed every year according to the mood of the *caids* (i.e., tribe administrators).

Individual plots were not fenced in order to leave more freedom of movement to those who worked their lands in common and to provide open space for the tribe's cattle. The lack of fences reinforced the idea among French colonists that there was no private ownership of the land. Under the *arsh* system of ownership, no written title to a plot was required. It was understood that all land belongs to

God and that a Muslim can only have a usufruct on it. At the same time, however, the right to usufruct is obtained through work, so that if a tribesman started cultivating a plot that was previously fallow, it became his and was passed on to his heirs. The original character of the *arsh* form of property lies precisely in the fact that the labor one invests in the land makes one its owner.

Melk, the second form of property, implied the idea of sovereignty.[19] Indeed, whereas *arsh* property was based on the right to work, *melk* property is associated with the right to own. In this sense, it is closer to the European conception of private property. Under the *melk* system, plots are often fenced and their owners have written titles to them. If no document is available, "notoriety is sufficient to certify the long-standing possession of the land, and nobody ever thinks of doubting such a right to property."[20]

However, this kind of property is still different from the European type. Indeed, although an heir to a *melk* is not prohibited from selling it, there are certian restrictions. For instance, he must secure the consent of *all* his co-inheritors; and if this condition is fulfilled, he would have to transcend the opprobrium that befalls any individual who sells the land of his forefathers. Land for sale is first proposed to members of the tribe in order to preserve the integrity of its territory. Only if no tribesman can buy it is the land sold to outsiders. The *melk* system of ownership shows how the individual's right, even when it is held sovereign, is set in a communal framework.

Melk property was found either interspersed with *arsh* land or as a predominant system, depending on the geographical area. For example, in the Mitidja Valley, *melks* were the predominant form of property. Several *melks* would form a *haush,* which would take the name of the man who owns the largest of them,[20] but which implied no greater sovereignty.

Along with *arsh* and *melk* forms of property, *habus* was the last original feature of the Algerian ownership system. This represents "the thing whose ownership is reserved to God, with the intention that the use should benefit his creatures."[22] *Habus* usually consists of a donation to a religious or charitable organization. "Once consituted, the property became inalienable in the hands of the recipient mosque or foundation, with the intention that the product, in rents, crops, or other income, should benefit in perpetuity the particular cause involved."[23]

Sometimes the donor's family retains the right of usufruct on the *habus* through the generations stipulated by the donor.[24] This practice was meant to avoid the confiscations which the Turkish government often resorted to. The retaining of the usufruct over *habus* property hid an indirect form of appropriation of labor. Indeed, the members of the religious or cultural community who invested labor in the donated property did so on grounds that ultimately the *habus* is theirs. *Habus* property was more common in the town than in the rural areas, possibly because their management needed a bureaucratic structure that was available in urban centers only. City *habus* consisted of buildings, suburban gardens and nearby farms. Rural *habus*, on the other hand, were made of land in the custody of "great families" who traced their ascendancy to the founder of Islam. The labor necessary to work these lands was provided by the community. There are only partial data on the size of this type of property. It is estimated that there were between 40,000 and 50,000 hectares of rural *habus*, although the figure may have been as high as 75,000 hectares.

Turkish Form of Appropriation of Labor

The combination of *arsh* and *melk*, individual right to cultivate and own land along with the communal preservation of these rights, made for a specific system of property. When inscribed in the larger context of Turkish domination, this property system takes on an even more original dimension.

It was indicated earlier that the Turkish *dey* had secured control over a vast public domain estimated at 146,693 hectares divided into two main parts: first, the property of the *dey*, the *beys* and their dependents; and second, the property called *azel*. The former were among the best lands and were cultivated either by neighboring tribesmen or landless peasants, the *khammes*. *Azel* lands were used to reward staff members for services rendered and to compensate some tribes who were willing to raise the *bey's* cattle. It also happened that *azels* were conceded to farmers on condition that they produce a given quantity of grain and that in return they would pay a reduced tax.

Most importantly, *azels,* along with partial tax exemptions, were granted tribes who paid allegiance to the *bey* and helped him levy taxes on their more recalcitrant fellow tribesmen. Often *azel* would simply mean the right to levy taxes ceded by the *bey* to some tribe. Tribes who benefited from a land or tax *azel* were *makhzen.*

ALGERIAN TYPE OF PRE-CAPITALIST FORMATION

The communal development of *arsh* land, the inalienable character of *melk* property, along with kinship relations within tribes, have often obscured the fact that, in effect, the whole property system was based on the recognition of the right to own land either by formal contract or through labor.

The identification of this particular property structure is made easier if it is compared to the pre-capitalist economic formations described by Marx.

Pre-capitalist Economic Formations

Marx distinguishes between the Asiatic, Germanic and Ancient types of property. In the Asiatic type, "there is no property, but only individual possession."[25] It is the community that is the real owner of the land. The individual is an organic member of a self-sustaining community that combines agriculture and craft manufacture. Part of the surplus labor is appropriated by "the higher community which ultimately appears as a person."[26]

The Ancient form of property is characterized by the separation of common land from private property. Common land is the State property, or *ager publicus*. Due to the war-like organization of this type of community, production is centered in the city. Only a citizen "is and must be a private proprietor."[27] In this sense, the *ager publicus* "appears as the particular economic being of the State, by the side of the private owners."[28]

In the Germanic type, "the property of the individual does not appear mediated through the community, but the existence of the community as mediated through . . . the independent subjects."[29] The *ager publicus* here is also distinct from private ownership, but it serves as a supplement to it. Indeed, the Germanic *ager publicus* consists of "hunting grounds, common pastures or woodlands, etc."[30] In contra-distinction with the ancient type of property (as exemplified by the Romans), production is based in the countryside rather than in the city.

Types of Pre-capitalist Economic Formations

Type	Property Form	Ager Publicus	Production Base	Relationship between Town/Country
Asiatic	Communal	Communal	Town and Country	Undifferentiated
Ancient	Private	State-controlled	Town	Urbanization of countryside
Germanic	Private	Communal	Country	Separate
Algerian	Private possession Private ownership	Communal and State-controlled	Town	Ruralization of town

Figure 1. *Pre-Capitalist Algerian Social Structure*

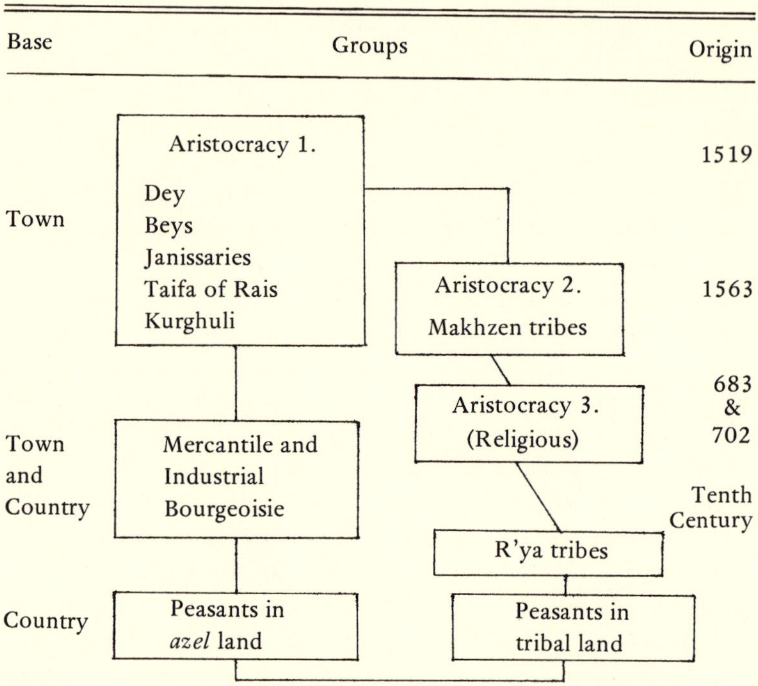

Base	Groups	Origin
Town	Aristocracy 1. Dey Beys Janissaries Taifa of Rais Kurghuli	1519
	Aristocracy 2. Makhzen tribes	1563
	Aristocracy 3. (Religious)	683 & 702
Town and Country	Mercantile and Industrial Bourgeoisie	Tenth Century
	R'ya tribes	
Country	Peasants in *azel* land	
	Peasants in tribal land	

In comparing pre-capitalist Algeria to these three types of economic formations, Galissot[31] speculated that in those areas where *melk* property was predominant, as in the Mitidja Valley, the Algerian socio-economic structure was of the ancient type. On the other hand, wherever *arsh* property dominated *melk* property, Algeria approximated the Asiatic type of economic formation. Besides, wherever *melk* and *arsh* coexisted in such a way that *arsh* was a mere supplement to *melk*, Algeria was closer to the Germanic type. Clearly this kind of interpretation is based on the identification of communal work with communal ownership. It is also based on a simplified reading of Marx's analysis of pre-capitalist economic formations.

Marx's classification took into account four factors which had to be related in a specified way. Each mode of production was studied in terms of the existence of common land (*ager publicus*), private property, town and country. Therefore, before claiming that pre-capitalist Algeria was of a Germanic or Ancient type, it is necessary to check every component of each type against the real situation. It becomes apparent, then, that the Algerian economic formation was similar to the Germanic, Asiatic and Ancient types in form more than in content. Indeed, insofar as in some areas *melk* property seemed to predominate over *arsh* property, one could think of a similarity with the Ancient model. Likewise, in areas where *arsh* lands are predominant, a similarity exists with the Asiatic model. However, insofar as *arsh* property amounted to legal possession and *melk* was not exclusive of community rights, pre-capitalist Algeria is reducible neither to the Ancient nor to the Asiatic or Germanic models. Indeed, whereas in the Asiatic model the relationship between town and city is undifferentiated, the ruralized city was a major factor in tribal Algeria. On the other hand, whereas the Germanic model is characterized by the existence of land proprietors who live in isolation from their tribes, there is no evidence that the Algerian owners of *melk* lived away from their tribes.

The inadequacy of forcing the Algerian reality to fit accepted models becomes even more evident when this reality is looked at in its entirety, namely, when the Turkish super-structure is taken into account. Galissot suggested that the Turkish domination combined with the tribal mode of economic organization to form a special mode of production referred to as "command feudalism."[32] This type of feudalism is seen as somewhat different from the accepted European feudal model in that it encompasses both town and country. The European model was country-based and gradually evolved an antagonistic relationship between town and country, whereas it is claimed that the Algerian type of feudalism was based on the subordination of the country to the town. But this kind of analysis overlooks the social and economic implication of the Turkish presence and rule.[33] Apart from those who collaborated with the new regime (i.e., the *Makhzen* tribes), the indigenous aristocracy stood in an exploited-exploiter relation to their Turkish counterpart. Interaction between the two was with very few exceptions[34] minimal and prejudice against non-Turks was endemic. Besides, the Turkish monopoly of public functions—mint, arms manufacture, water mills and control over external trade—compounded the unequal relationship between Turks and Algerians and gave it an added colonial dimension.

As pointed out earlier, the Turkish aristocracy secured for itself an *ager publicus* which resembled the Roman type in that "to be a member of the community remains the precondition for the appropriation of land . . . "[35] The Turkish *ager publicus* was a way of safeguarding the exclusiveness of the Turkish community by providing it with economic self-sufficiency and maintaining its power over the indigenous population by using part of this public domain as compensation for a pledge of allegiance. Therefore, insofar as the Turkish public domain did not benefit the entire Algerian community, and insofar as its extension was possible only at the expense of the indigenous tribes, the Turkish socio-economic organization cannot be conceived of as the coordinating factor that accounts for the final form of the total mode of production (i.e., "command feudalism").

To the extent that ground rents and taxes were imposed by an aristocracy on a peasantry that also had to submit to military duty, pre-capitalist Algeria was feudal. But, insofar as there existed an alien and an indigenous aristocracy with divergent interests[36] and unequal powers, the comparison to European feudalism cannot be pushed any further.

The conditions of production prevalent in Algeria from 1519 to 1830 display similarities with but are not reducible to those described by Marx. Reliance on labor as a pre-condition for the appropriation of land under its *melk* or *arsh* form, along with the recognition of the individual's right to work, make for the distinctive character of this society at the tribal level. However, the Algerian mode of production combined feudal and colonial features that account for the particular form of the social structure. Thus, a Turkish aristocracy made up of administrators and military men held the monopoly of political and economic power. Subordinated to it was another aristocracy (*makhzen*), local in character and deriving its power over a given territory by virtue of its allegiance to its Turkish counterpart.

There were variations in the degree of power wielded by the *makhzen* tribes. The more they depended for their wealth on the lands and other benefice imparted to them by the *beys*, the closer they were to the Turkish government, to the point where they became confounded with it. A third aristocracy was comprised of religious leaders who generally opposed Turkish rule.[37]

A mercantile and industrial bourgeoisie formed the intermediary class between the various aristocracies and the peasantry.[38] Active but tightly controlled by the Turkish government, who ultimately retained trade monopoly, this bourgeoisie had no privileges. Its distinctive feature was its link with the countryside where it owned land. Besides, it was made up of alien ethnics, namely, the Moors and the Jews.[39]

The peasantry was composed of the landless individuals who sold their labor power to landed tribesmen or to the *beylik*. This peasantry did not form a cohesive social class because of the fragmented nature of their material conditions and the fact that individual behavior and action was still circumscribed by the framework of the tribe or clan.

Nevertheless, there were periodic peasants' revolts which, however, tended to "dissolve in inconsequential violence or to get diverted into local conflicts, particularistic groupings or mysticism and superstition."[40]

When looked at from a static point of view, this social structure appears as a hierarchy of power and privilege. But, as was pointed out earlier, the actual situation was different. The dynamics of Turkish domination were such that what is here labelled aristocracy was but the inorganic conditions for the perpetuation of the Turkish presence. The fragility of this system will be demonstrated by the relative ease with which it collapsed under the French cannons.

3

The
Algerian Social Structure
under
French Domination

After more than three hundred years of subjection to Turkish rule, Algerian society fell into the grip of a new colonizer. Soon after they invaded Algiers, the French embarked upon a policy aimed at systematically destroying Algerian society for the purpose of realizing capital accumulation. It is necessary to review in detail the process through which such a destruction was carried out in order to understand the conditions under which Algerian society attempted to restructure itself before the war of liberation and after independence.

HISTORICAL BACKGROUND

An apparently frivolous incident caused the French to land in Sidi Ferruch, west of Algiers, on 14 June 1830.[1] The *dey* Hussein had struck the French consul with a fan in April, 1827, to express his disappointment with the French government's unwillingness to honor a debt contracted almost thirty years before. This incident brought about a three-year French embargo of Algiers, and a series of Turkish counterattacks on French shipping.

By June 1830, the French were ready to send a Force of 37,000 men to take Algiers. The weakness of the Turkish regime, rent with dissensions and palace intrigues, made this task easy. On 5 July 1830 the *dey* was forced to capitulate, and Maréchal de Bourmont announced that Algerians of "all classes" would be guaranteed their freedom to worship, to own property and to trade. At the same time, he permitted his troops to ransack the city.

Resistance to the French came first from Western Algeria where it was led by the Emir Abd-El-Kader, a member of the religious aristocracy. The Emir's successful defense compelled the French to recognize temporarily the independence of a state he created in northwest Algeria. This was little more than a truce, however, because Abd-El-Kader would ultimately be defeated.

In a letter to the Minister of War, the French Maréchal Bugeaud explained the purpose of the limited peace treaty he was about to sign with the Emir: "Is it not preferable to have our own undisputed territory, trade freely with the rest of the country and establish a colony that will serve as a model of civilization for the rest of Africa? That is how we can conquer a new nation of consumers for our industry and commerce."[2] The economic motive for the French conquest of Algeria accounts for the various colonial policies and their far-reaching impact on the indigenous social structure. Algeria was not only meant to be a new market for French goods, it was also meant to become a settlement colony.[3] This required that advantages be granted to the French expatriates, especially in the form of land, "the raw material of colonization."[4] Algeria, however, was not a vacant territory.[5] The distinctive character of the Algerian form of property provided the advocates of colonization with the opportunity to impose the French notion of property. The net effect was to dispossess the indigenous population of its land, and not, as de Bourmont declared on his arrival in

Algiers in 1830, to liberate them "from Turkish subjugation."6

The history of French colonization in Algeria is characterized by a contradiction between the economic motives and goals of the colonists and their political justifications. This contradiction was reflected in the various forms of administration to which Algeria was subjected.

The Colonial Forms of Administration

Between 1830 and 1834, Algeria was under exclusively military rule. Initially, the military administration was superimposed on the Turkish one.7 "Bureaus of Arab Affairs" were created to serve as liaison between the French command and the Algerian administrators. These Bureaus were composed of interpreters, judges, technical advisers and intelligence officers. Their frequent contacts with the Algerian population gave them a more realistic view of prevailing socio-economic conditions. They sometimes resisted pressure by the civilian colonists systematically to expropriate the tribesmen.

In 1834, Algeria came officially under the administration of a Governor General appointed by the French Ministry of Defense. On 18 April 1845, the territory was divided into three zones, civil, "mixed" and Arab. Civil territories were those having a majority of Europeans "which would permit an organization of all public services". The "mixed" territories referred to those areas where the European population was a minority and where, therefore, it was not possible to have a "complete" administrative organization. The Arab territories included areas where only Arabs lived, and these were placed under military rule. The civil territories would later be divided into full communes (or *communes de plein exercice*), organized after the French model, and "mixed communes". The latter were administered by municipal commissions (rather than councils), comprised of civilian and military Europeans along with token "Muslims" and Jews.8

The French Revolution of 1848 had repercussions on the administration of Algeria. The institution of universal suffrage enabled the colonists to be represented in the Constituent Assembly. Furthermore, the 1848 Constitution declared Algeria to be an "integral part of the French territory." Between 1852 and 1860, a Ministry of Algeria and the Colonies was created. The Minister, who resided in Paris, was anxious to "govern from Paris and administer [in Algeria] ". This administration by remote control was abolished under Napoleon III, who installed a Governor General and a military deputy-Governor in Algiers.

The tribal insurrection of 1871, followed by a series of revolts in 1876, 1879 and 1881, gave the colonists an excuse to attack the military for its inefficiency and to demand control over the "Arab territories." They also began an official, systematic policy of settlement by encouraging immigration from Alsace-Lorraine and Southeastern France. Between 1879 and 1881, the military administration was practically abolished. The colonists practiced a policy of administrative assimilation with a particular frenzy.[9] All Algerian affairs were to be handled by French ministries in Paris, under the guidance of the colonists' representatives.

Between 1898 to 1900, colonial Algeria acquired a separate legal status and financial autonomy through the creation of the "Délégations Financières," with authority on budget spending. The Algerian representation at these Assemblies (as well as on the municipal councils and the *Conseils Généraux* at the district level), were such that the colonists' control was ensured.[10] From 1900 to 1962, Algeria was continuously under civilian rule, except for a brief period in 1958 when the military, four years after the start of the Revolution, attempted a *putsch* in an effort to keep Algeria French. These shifts in forms of government were accompanied by debates as to whether Algerians ought to have political rights. At the same time, each administration made its contribution to the destruction of the Algerian legal system and social fabric.[11]

DESTRUCTION OF THE ALGERIAN PROPERTY SYSTEM

The most important act of sovereignty that the French government took was the destruction of the indigenous property system. Three major decisions put an end to the Algerian form of property. These were the 1844-46 ordinances, the 1863 *senatus consultum* and the 1873 law, amended in 1887.

The 1844-46 Ordinances

Following what it believed to be the norm in Islamic countries, namely, that all land ultimately belonged to the *beylik*, the French colonial administration considered itself heir to the Turkish state. The administration declared the expropriation of all land that appeared to be uncultivated.[12] Thus, the 1844 ordinance declared that all uncultivated lands in specified areas would be classified as vacant if nobody could prove right of ownership. Regarding the *habus* property, it claimed that the "perpetual rents have lost their primitive utility and constitute today an obstacle to the development of industry; the time has come to declare it (*habus* property) resalable at the legal monetary interest rate".[13] In other words, *habus* property was abolished.[14]

The 1846 ordinance merely specified the conditions enunciated in the ordinance of 1844. Thus, property titles to the seemingly uncultivated lands were to be filled in within a three-month period; otherwise, property rights would become void. Titles dated after 5 July 1830 (date of the French invasion) were to be rejected. The last clause indicates that land speculation was rife, especially between 1830 and 1844, as a result of the exodus of Algerian landowners who abandoned their fields to seek refuge in nearby towns or in the mountains.[15] French colonists moved in on tribal land, hoping that their newly acquired property would be legalized. Indeed, the 1846 ordinance was partly intended to check what was held to have been a spontaneous peasant movement to take possession of portions of the former Turkish public domain. The most telling result of these two ordinances was best summarized by the Commandant-General of Algiers: "Almost all of the natives have actually ignored the 21 July 1846 ordinance, which explains why so few of them have filled out the required forms. Today, great is their surprise when they are told that for want of complying with it they have lost their property rights."[16]

Indeed, out of 168,203.59 hectares in the Mitidja Valley, 131,672.45 were expropriated. Of the remainder, 11,511.74 hectares were left to their owners, while the rest was in litigation.[17] Those among the indigenous population who lost their rights had their land annexed to the public domain. In compensation, they received small concessions as a "purely gracious favor and not as the recognition or homologation of a right."[18] The recipients of these concessions acquired the curious name of "Arab colonists". In order to promote individual property, concession titles spelled out the share of each member of the recipient family. Another stipulation of the concession act required that plots be marked by hedges or ditches at all times.

The communities thus expropriated were relocated in poorer areas. For example, 81 families in Algiers province were given 326 hectares for cultivation and 121 hectares of marsh land for pasture.[19] The tribal communal pastures had become the property of the French state. Algerian individuals were mere occupants of specified portions of it, if at all. Tribesmen could no longer extend their cultivation by reclaiming brush land. The 1846 ordinance classified as uncultivated those lands kept fallow according to the agricultural method of the time. As a result, the indigenous population lost even more territory. Further, the fields that were cultivated by their owners in 1846 were not always recognized as such. "The Commission for Transactions and Divisions was instructed by article 24 of the 21 July 1846 ordinance to give the natives whom it deemed worthy of interest the portions of the land they cultivated at the time of the investigation."[20] In other words, the recognition of the right to a concession on one's own property was predicated upon some undefined attitude toward the French administration.

The 1863 Senatus Consultum and the 1870 Law

If the 1844-46 ordinances found their theoretical justifications in the identification of all property rights with the Islamic Turkish state, the *senatus consultum* of 1863 and
the 1870 law were based on the even more debatable distinction between *arsh* and *melk* forms of property. The
1863 *senatus consultum* was meant to redress the inequities of 1844-46. However, it resulted in similar abuses.
It defined *arsh* as collective property and undertook to make
an inventory in order to determine the proportion of *melk*
and *arsh*. At a later stage, it proposed to distribute the
inventoried *arsh* property among individual members of the
tribes. The desire to create individual property of the
European kind was unmistakeable. However, the *senatus
consultum* (undertaken by Napoleon III, who dreamed of
creating an Arab kingdom) was also meant to protect the
indigenous population's right to property. In practice,
however, this meant the creation of reservations for the
tribesmen whose abstract right to property was thus
recognized. Land was divided into three categories:
1) "collective" cultivation land; 2) collective pastureland,
declared "the property of the tribes who could exploit it
permanently and traditionally"[21]; and 3) *melk* land. *Azel*
land was also considered tribal property. Collective land was
declared inalienable until individual property was constituted.

Severely criticized by the advocates of colonization, the
senatus consultum nevertheless failed to protect Algerian
property. Its peculiar interpretation of the concepts of
arsh and *melk* and the distorted and haphazard application
of its instructions led, in effect, to generalized expropriations. Thus, *azel* lands, which had already been appropriated
by the public domain administration prior to 1863, were not
given back to the tribes. Furthermore, the inventory itself
was inaccurate and hasty. Field measurements, for example,
were made by firing a shot and calculating from the time
it took to hear the shot's report![22] The classification of

inventoried land was also inadequate. *Melk* property was classified as *arsh* and vice versa. Even so, the results of the *senatus consultum* surprised the promoters of colonization in that a high proportion of land was found to be *melk*. Indeed, 2,840.531 hectares were classified *melk* and 2,859.505 hectares *arsh*.

The application of the law establishing individual alienable property was opposed by the military establishment, which was traditionally in conflict with the civilian administration.[23] The colonists' counterattack resulted, on 1 May 1870, in an amendment to the *senatus consultum* prohibiting indigenous co-proprietors from opposing the individual sale of a plot. All *melk* were subject to mortgage procedures, and French law alone applied to transactions with Europeans or Jews.[24] This amendment had the effect of enabling French colonists to settle among the tribes, whose land they could now purchase.

The 26 July 1873 law constitutes a third historic measure in terms of the destructuring of the tribal organization of Algeria. This law was a revision of the 1863 *senatus consultum*. It undertook to determine the individual property of the tribesmen, and to enforce the use of French law in *all* land transactions, not only between Algerians and Europeans, but among Algerians as well.[25]

In effect, the application of this law backfired. Aimed at determining and fixing individual property in the hope that inalienable property would disappear, it actually resulted in exposing the very structure of the Algerian system of ownership. Each tribesman was found to possess a specific portion of the territory on which he lived. The accurate calculation of each individual's property (based, paradoxically enough, on the Muslim law of inheritance) led to the unsettling discovery that some owned fractions with a six, seven, or even an eight-digit denominator.[26]

Under these circumstances, breaking the structure of in-alienable property did not result in very much land for sale. However, it did allow the administration to carry out its policy of *cantonnement* (i.e., reservations) by establishing an arbitrary minimum of land for each individual. This was set at an average of 3 hectares in Western Algeria.[27] It was customary for a speculator to buy one share and subsequently invoke Article 827 of the French Civil Code, which stipulates that "if real estates cannot be conveniently divided, a licitation sale must ensue."[28] By these means, the process of liquidation of *melk* property began.

The seemingly liberal content of the 1863 *senatus consultum* was completely circumvented by the opening of "collective" land to sale. This was done by the 1887 law. This and the previous law naturally affected the new land inventory. It is reported that investigators received a commission on each new plot they could extract from the tribal communities. The most significant result was a dramatic increase in sales. Between 1885 and 1889 an average of 1,087 judicial sales, 343 licitation sales, and 666 seizures occurred.[29] The laws fulfilled their purpose in that they "delivered the natives' land to the French market," as the President of the Court of Algiers put it.

STRUCTURAL CONSEQUENCES OF PROPERTY LAWS

Changes in Individuals' Relations to Property

Taken as a whole, these laws started, accelerated and con-solidated the process of destructuring Algerian society. This process will be examined on three levels: 1) the level of the individual's relation to property; 2) the structural level; 3) the institutional level.

The first consequence of the 1846 ordinance was a sharp de-cline in cattle breeding because of the expropriation of cattle lands, so that the "natives were compelled to give up this traditional form of their activity."[30] At the same time, the

the seasonal migrations of herds from the South to the plains in the North had to cease, severely curtailing the intense commercial activity that had been a concomitant of the moves. Those who could no longer feed their herds as a result of restricted pastures sold them and sought work with the new European landowners. Those who were granted concessions on the territory that used to be theirs "started reclaiming what was left for them. They extended their reclamation to the nearby mountains up to now used for grazing. But . . . their concessions were so shrunken that almost everywhere they did not have enough land to meet their need in grain."[31]

This forced transformation of the means of production inevitably led to the alienation of what had been, up to then indivisible property. Sales became more and more frequent. Those who could not sell their fields rented them out to Europeans. Gradually, the peasant who had once owned his land became a *khammes* or sharecropper on it, prompting the military administration to report that "this was a development in the process of being generalized" and that instead of "decreasing every year it seems to become more intense with the help of the Administration."[32] Those without land to rent hired their services out to the colonists. Those who were unable to adapt to their new material situation emigrated to remote areas within the country or abroad, notably to Morocco and Syria.

A by-product of the application of French laws to Algerian property was the institution of usury. The need to borrow money to pay taxes and legal fees, a result of the registration of one's property or suits against the administration for expropriation and/or sequestration, attracted unscrupulous usurers and land speculators. All the literature, whether sympathetic or hostile to colonization, has denounced the effects of usury. Loan rates were as high as 120%, and repayments were often scheduled on a weekly basis.[33] The *Service des Affaires Indigènes* noted in 1879 that "all of the tribal middle classes are collapsing under the weight of usury; they are deeply in debt, and the good crops will only be a temporary remedy for them. They are rushing towards their ruin."[34] The effect of usury became all the more crucial when a series of calamities befell the country between 1865 and 1872.[35] Significantly enough, "epidemics took the highest toll in those areas that had already been ruined by the war and requisitions."[36]

Institutional Changes

The policy of *cantonnement,* along with the importance attached to money as the medium for all exchange, resulted in the breakdown and ultimately the disappearance of those tribal institutions that had helped individuals whenever crops were bad. Thus, the largest families within the tribes could no longer provide the peasants with emergency services as before when they themselves were affected by the new changes in the system of property. Furthermore, the appropriation of *habus* estates by the French administration resulted in the abolition of the *zawias* as provident institutions which used to advance grain to the poor peasant, returnable only if the next crop was good.[37]

At the same time, another traditional practice, the storing of grain in tribal silos, declined or disappeared because of the large-scale exports of wheat to France, especially during the Crimean and Italian wars. The need for money compelled Algerians to "sell their crops before they were harvested and their wools before they were shorn"[38]

Structural Changes

The radical change in the structure of Algerian property naturally affected the social organization of the tribes. The process of dislocation was completed by administrative measures aimed at replacing kinship tribes by locality tribes. Indeed, fractions from different tribes were combined to form a single *duar,* or fractions of the same tribes were divided up in a small number of *duars.*[39] It was not uncommon that parts of the same tribe came under different communal jurisdictions.

Consequently, by exploding the territorial and administrative unity of the tribe and by "introducing into the native world the perturbing element of the European village, colonization left the old tribal concepts nothing but sentimental bonds betweeen individuals conscious of their belonging to the same community."[40]

The Aristocracy

This dislocation of the tribal organization necessarily reflected on the composition of the social groups that made up the tribes. The religious and *Makhzen* aristocracies were affected differently, depending on whether they rallied to the French military or to the leader of the Algerian resistance, Emir Abd-El-Kader. It is important to note that, by and large, the religious aristocracy fought on the Emir's side, whereas the *Makhzen* aristocracy fought against him. Many tribes drifted to one side or the other, depending on their ability to withstand a protracted war. In general, the war cost the religious and warrior aristocracy their economic and social power. After the Algerian resistance was broken, tribe rebellions were punished with land sequestration.[41] Combined with a new regulation forbidding tribes from using forests and an increase in taxation, these sequestrations completed the process of impoverishment of the tribal aristocracy.

The colonists' appetite for land accounts for the hostility they fostered against the Algerian "great families," whom they also referred to as the "feudal lords." However, the decadence of these families was cause for alarm among some Frenchmen who were more concerned with social control. Thus, it was stated that "while pursuing these ghosts, we have completely disorganized the indigenous society so that when we need to act on it we find that we have no grasp over it; we are faced with isolated individuals." As a result, "we are without intermediaries either to make our intentions known and implement our orders or to assess the needs and moods of these people."[42]

Some have suggested that the old aristocracy was displaced by a new one composed of those who fought in the ranks of the French army, those appointed to serve in the military administration, and those who acquired land as a result of the 1873 law.[43] In fact, during the first phase of its administration, the military attempted to reconstruct the Turkish administration by keeping the same posts and titles and by securing material advantages to cooperative tribesmen. However, they depreciated the actual authority of their indigenous auxiliaries and soon transformed their functions into mere honorary titles. Those hired to serve in the supervisory administrative corps (i.e., the *Bureaux Arabes*) as interpreters, clerks and Islamic lawyers, acquired more social importance in the eyes of tribesmen because of their access (although limited) to the new power holders. The depreciation of the old functions of *agha* and *caid* was compounded by the appointment of non-aristocratic individuals to fill them whenever the administered tribes rebelled.

The New Caids

Thus, a whole new group, often referred to by Algerians as the "shepherds," came to the fore. They were often illiterate people who received a meagre income and had no job security, in that they were appointed and dismissed at will. To survive, these functionaries exerted their limited and borrowed power to extract more surplus from the communities they helped administer. They did so with a vengeance, often displaying callousness and cruelty, especially if appointed to communities with which they had no social ties and to whom they, therefore, felt no responsibility.

They could by no means be identified with a rising aristocracy. Pressured by their employers to levy an ever-increasing number of taxes, unable to make a decent living and denounced by the local population, they were the epitome of the failings of the colonial regime. They were blamed by the colonists who objected to the military administration and by the Algerians who objected to heavy taxation.[44]

In 1898, the French government ordered the military to "strengthen the authority of the native chiefs and to appoint at the head of tribes and villages only those natives who have a real hereditary influence over their countrymen or notables whose prestige was beyond any doubt."[45] At the same time, no positions were to be given to "former unknown collaborators, letter carriers or servants whose sole merit was to be devoted to the functionaries they served."[46] However, giving administrative positions to the old aristocracy did not restore its socio-economic power and prestige.[47] Some of its members did take the positions offered, but these were in the lower ranks of the bureaucratic hierarchy. Those who did so facilitated their sons' integration in the colonial system in that they provided them with a French education. The new groups which acquired more land (see table 1), especially in areas that the colonists had not yet penetrated, were less of a new aristocracy than a "rural bourgeoisie." The decline of what is often referred to as the "rural middle class" does not appear to constitute a significant change in the Algerian social structure.[48]

Table 1.[49]. *Comparative Structure of Landed Property*
(Cheliff Valley)

Owners		Size (in hectares)						
	5	5-10	10-20	20-50	50-100	100-200	200-500	500+ 1000+
Algerians	613	120	83	52	18	15	8	0 0
Europeans	289	100	102	99	52	38	31	5 2

The Bourgeoisie

In urban centers, the small traditional bourgeoisie which prided itself for its Islamic spirit, refined lifestyle and hostility to French culture gradually became a marginal social category. In its place there emerged a new social category comprised of businessmen, exporters of farm produce, brokers, wholesale and retail grain and tobacco dealers, oil manufacturers, landlords and inn keepers. Intellectuals, i.e., professors and teachers, Islamic judges, lawyers and interpreters represented a fraction of this category. This was a "pseudo-bourgeoisie" because its élan was stunted by the all-powerful French bourgeoisie in whose shadow it was, in a sense, permitted to exist.

Khammes and Wage Labor

Among the rural workers, famers and wage laborers were two new social categories.[51] The institution of farming was introduced by French colonists as a more economical alternative to the sharecropping system. The latter could become expensive, especially if the *khammes* worked on good land. The farmers who were hired by individual colonists and private companies were contracted by the year only and had to pay their ground rents in money. They formed 3.12% of the active rural population.[52] Rural wage labor was comprised of seasonal, semi-permanent and permanent workers. The seasonal workers' wages varied from 1.50 francs a day to 1.75 for men and 0.50 francs for women and children. Permanent workers were paid 360 francs a year. The introduction of farming and wage labor did not create a privileged group of people, as the promoters of colonization often argued.[53] In fact, calculations based on the wage rate per hectare of land worked demonstrated that wage labor created a situation that was less "advantageous than that of the small proprietor who was able to cultivate 10 hectares of land every year."[54] The condition of the sharecropper worsened as a result of the introduction of mechanisation in agriculture. He was no longer an associate in the production of the fields he worked on and soon became a wage laborer, hiring his services as a seasonal worker on a colonist's land, while fulfilling the function of a sharecropper for a landowner.

Below the *khammes* existed a whole new category of men who lived off the charity of their relatives and friends. They often had a minuscule plot of land on which they grew fava beans and raised chickens and a few goats. Their number was estimated to be 1,386,510 at the turn of the century. This rural proletariat was a concern to the local administrators who regretted that it "[would] some day cause us serious embarrassment."[55] The situation was correctly seen as related to the generalized pauperization of the indigenous society, with this increasing proletariat falling relentlessly downward and threatening to sweep the whole colonial structure in its wake. Hence, an administrator's remark that this "fall of the indigenous people into the proletariat constitutes a grave danger for the future; it will deprive us of our most powerful means of action on the vanquished race, the fear of sequestration, and will open in the colony a social question all the more fierce in that it will be coupled with racial and religious antipathies."[56]

This rural proletariat was reinforced by a newly-formed industrial proletariat. The building of railroads, the opening of the canning industry and clothing manufacture among others attracted an increasing number of workers of both sexes. This army of laborers did not benefit from the labor laws applied in France. In fact, the 1892 and 1893 laws on working hours and personal security were declared non-applicable to Algeria,[57] otherwise "we would soon see in every *duar* a new species of round, fat and heavy-jowled philosophers who, poking fun at our sentimental humanitarianism, will say when asked who made their leisure possible: we are the victims of work."[58] With the rise of industry and the expansion of trade, the old handicraft corporations declined. Leather and copper craftsmen along with wood workers and weavers all but disappeared as independent producers and swelled the ranks of wage labor.

CONCLUSION

The French colonization of Algeria had irreversible consequences on the social structure of that country. The desire to make a settlement colony out of an already populated area led to a policy of driving the indigenous people out of the best arable lands. Although occurring three centuries later, the process of destructuring a pre-capitalist society in order to set up a capitalist apparatus bore striking similarities to the rise of primitive accumulation in 16th century England. The French law of 1844-1846 secured for the colonial administration the Turkish public domain, just as the English "landlords and capitalist appropriators of surplus value" took hold of "state lands."[59] The French decision to seize *habus* estates was the counterpart of the English oligarchy's appropriation of the Church lands. The 1863 *senatus consultum* delivered to the colonists communal and *arsh* lands in the same manner as the "Acts for Enclosure of the Commons" did to the British landlords.[60] Besides, in breaking down the tribal structure and replacing its traditional unit with the commune, the French achieved the same result as the English landlords who engaged in the "clearing of estates," whereby peasants were "hunted and rooted out."[61]

The only difference is that the French colonists thought of but did not need to burn down the *gurbis* (small dwellings) of the peasants. The 1873 law that made property alienable, combined with collective and nominal sequestrations,[62] the introduction of usury and a timely series of droughts, succeeded in achieving similar effects. The same "idyllic methods of primitive accumulation" performed "under circumstances of reckless terrorism,"[63] set capitalist colonization off from the Turkish occupation of Algeria.

The deep structural transformation that ensued for Algerian society was accurately summarized by a French administrator:

In the Arab society such as we found, economic fluctuations being continuous, the wheel kept turning and everyone, in his turn, provided that the crop was good and that he managed to get a couple of horses, enjoyed an annual share drawn on the collective property. Therefore, at the heart of this chaos there were guarantees for work and some feeling of equality. This will be no more, after the introduction of the individualization of property. Once the land is definitively appropriated, inequality begins with the landowners on one side and the proletariat on the other, as in our civilized societies.[64]

Indeed, land expropriation, the rise of capitalist agriculture and the expansion of monetary economy[65] resulted in the pauperization of the tribes. Aristocracy and peasantry were equally affected: the former lost their power, prestige and wealth, whereas the latter lost their right to produce. From the ruins of the old *Makhzen* and *R'ya* tribes arose a group of landowners who paradoxically benefited from the laws that were meant to serve the colonial establishment.[66] Scattered, dependent on the colonists' goodwill to keep their property and lacking in power, they did not displace the old aristocracy. In the face of the generalized proletarianization of the old society, their wealth appeared out of proportion.[67]

The most significant development was the emergence of a social category of intellectuals and professionals[68] trained in French schools and a growing rural and urban proletariat, uprooted, alienated from its native land and forced to adapt to new economic conditions. To this new environment they soon reacted with new methods. Thus, as early as 1900, longshoremen went on strike.[69] Moreover, although colonization created the material conditions for classes to develop, it could not provide the necessary political channels for antagonisms to unfold. Instead, classes were as yet only incipient, and the struggle remained necessarily focused on the unequal relationship between colonizer and colonized which took on religious and racial overtones.

The superimposition of an alien social entity obeying the logic of capitalistic colonialism and requiring the destruction of all those forms of the indigenous social life which stood between man and his transformation into a commodity, differed in content from the Turkish domination. As state earlier, the Turks maintained the indigenous social structure intact while deriving their income from it.[70] The French, on the contrary, could only exploit the indigenous population by breaking down its very foundations. This process of systematic social destructuring was, on the ideological level, meant to open the French society to the "natives." But the contradiction was that the colonial society could not be opened to the "natives" without destroying itself. The result was that the series of political reforms made between 1871 and 1920 exacerbated more than they encouraged the Algerians, especially the French-trained intellectuals and professionals. Indeed, to become a French citizen, one had to renounce one's religious status. To participate in the political life of one's province, one had to be elected by a "second college" of a limited number of voters chosen on the basis of their ownership of property and sympathy toward the new regime.[71]

The contradiction lay in the economic exploitation and political expediency which reminded some of "Sparta living under the spell of danger from the Helots and increasing it by the very means employed to dispel it."[72] In fact, the very process that destroyed kinship unity within the tribes brought about among the Algerians the consciousness of a community of fate which ultimately transcended divisions of a socio-economic and ideological nature.

4

The Dynamics
of
Incipient Classes

The colonial policy of primitive accumulation of capital created the material conditions for the development of indigenous incipient classes. The latter's interests were both predicated upon and mediated by the political moves of the colonial administration. By expropriating the Algerians, the colonists relegated them to a subsistence economy, while at the same time holding up to them the promise of political participation. In this sense, the colonial administration created a situation whereby Algerians fought for access to a political sphere divorced from their own economic conditions. They were made to aspire to a political life based on their own exploitation.

This contradiction between French political structure and Algerian economic oppression is at the roots of the nationalist movement in Algeria. By displacing the emphasis of the struggle from the economic to the political, Algerian nationalism was to some extent a political response to political oppression. However, the nationalists' demands were related to the general economic situation of Algeria and evolved accordingly. The nationalists were by no means a homogenous group of individuals. They held divergent views on the future of Algeria and defended divergent interests. The evolution of the nationalist movement reflects the process of formation and structuration of social classes. This process will be studied through the expression of differing conceptions of the means to achieve political freedom and the means to govern the independent Algerian state. It is necessary, therefore, to analyze the process through which political groups and parties were formed, how they were affected by the Revolution, and how they crystallized after independence. This analysis will cover the period extending from 1900 to 1965.

DEVELOPMENT OF INCIPIENT CLASSES

The Young Algerians

After the last insurrection led by Bou Amama in 1881, disapproval of the French colonial policy was expressed in a peaceful fashion through the available channels. The first expression of political interests came in the early 1900's from the "Young Algerians," who, inspired by the "Young Turks," were eager to revamp Islam with French culture. Their goal, in effect, was to acquire *droit de cité* e.g., full membership in French society just like the French citizens of Algeria. Consequently, their demands included the abolition of special tribunals, the "natives' code," a penal code applied to Algerians only, the suppression of taxes known as "Arab taxes," political participation in local institutions and representation in the French parliament.

In return for the drafting of Algerians in the French army, the Young Algerians asked for French citizenship, which the jurists of the Second Empire had thought incompatible with Islamic civic status. Indeed, the 1865 *senatus consultum* stipulation that "the Muslim native is French; nevertheless, he will continue to be regulated by Islamic law,"[1] was not applied. It was held that the principles of Islamic law were "contrary to our laws and mores relating to marriage, repudiation, divorce and children's civic status."[2] Therefore, to become French citizens, Algerians had to relinquish their religious status. This issue was all the more debatable in that Algerian Jews (initially also considered "natives" by the French) had been granted full citizenship by the Crémieux Decree of 1870 and foreigners born in Algeria by the 1889 law.

The Young Algerians were mostly people in the liberal professions, although they also included some teachers and members of "practically all the strata of Muslim society."[3] They were opposed by another group, *El Haqq* (justice), more intent on Islamic revival than achieving equal rights with the French. *El Haqq* was comprised of small landowners, shopkeepers and teachers. They demanded social and administrative reforms, especially the improvement of the peasants' economic condition and guarantees against land expropriation. Contrary to the Young Algerians, the *Haqq* group was staunchly opposed to both the draft and the idea of extending French citizenship to Algerians. Thus, whereas the Young Algerians were the spokesmen for what was called the new "elite," *El Haqq* defended the rights of the peasants. However, it also rallied those among the Young Algerians who were opposed to giving up their Islamic status in order to obtain French citizenship.

The logic of colonization was such that *El Haqq* was deemed less serious than the Young Algerians. The latter were the object of severe criticism in the colonial press. It was remarked that "assuming that their intentions are beyond any doubt, it is legitimate to fear that their demands meet with success because the Europeans might very well be the victims."[4] Governor Lutaud correctly assessed the strength of the Young Algerian movement when he declared that it "does not deserve a severe judgment, nor does it justify overly pessimistic prognoses."[5] Nevertheless, the prevailing attitude toward the movement was dictated by the warning that "admission of the natives to political rights would enable the Young Algerians to start a nationalist movement directed against the French occupation."[6]

L'Etoile Nord-Africaine and the Ulemas

The early 1920's were marked by a drought and increased economic difficulties which led to famine and a quickened pace of immigration to France. As a result, political opposition took on a new character. A new group emerged in Paris in 1926 under the name of *L'Etoile Nord-Africaine* (The North African Star). The Secretary General, Messali Hadj, was a former member of the French Communist Party who was later influenced by Islamic revivalism. Messali was the first Algerian industrial worker to voice a political opinion in a public forum and the first Algerian to call for the independence of Algeria. He was also the Algerian leader most harassed by the French police.[7] He served as a mentor to the generation of nationalists who started the armed struggle although they rejected his authoritarian style of leadership.

Apart from the *Etoile Nord-Africaine,* opposition was organized around the heirs of the Young Algerians, often referred to as the *Assimilationistes,* and the *Ulemas,* an Islam-oriented group. The *Assimilationistes* were soon dominated by the personality of Ferhat Abbas, who was perhaps the most articulate advocate of the political assimilation of Algeria to France. He later became one of the most prominant figures during the revolution. He once stated that "our generation is intellectually French, although it has retained its religion, its language, its mores, and above all it does not conceive of any framework to political life other than the French."[8] Like their predecessors, the *Assimilationistes* had a well-to-do social background and had received a French education. Their faith in assimilation to the French nation, however, gradually eroded as time passed. Unlike the Young Algerians, they had better opportunities to voice their demands. Indeed, they had benefited from political reforms which the colonial administration had made following World War I.

For example, the Algerian electoral body was extended to include 421,000 people; the number of municipal councillors grew from 930 to 1,549, and the general counsels increased from 8 to 29.[9] The advent in the early thirties of the *Front Populaire* in France brought about a draft bill that would enable the Algerians to become French citizens without relinquishing their Islamic status. This bill, known as the *Blum-Violette* bill, was rejected in 1938 by the French Senate after heated debates, thereby dealing a severe blow to the *Assimilationistes*.

Conversely, the *Blum-Violette* bill meant a victory for the third opposition group, the *Ulemas*. The latter's aim was the renovation of Islam through the development of science and the fight against superstition and uncritical thought.[10] Their slogan was, "Islam is my religion, Arabic is my language, and Algeria is my country." Led by Sheik Ibn Badis, the *Ulemas* pushed for a program of education, the abolition of religious confederations, blaming them for distorting Islam and calling them vehicles of obfuscation and ignorance, and the search for an Algerian identity. Thus, Ibn Badis once declared that "we do not want assimilation, nor do we want independence."[11] The *Ulemas'* main purpose was a "house-cleaning" which would prepare the country for nationalism.[12]

The M.T.L.D. and the U.D.M.A.

The idea of nationalism gradually made its way through the various opposition groups, especially the *Assimilationistes*. This may be due to the economic condition of Algeria during World War II. The declining grain production was aggravated by war requisitions for troops in Germany and Italy. At the same time, sheep and goat herding decreased from 6,406,000 in 1939 to 2,053,000 in 1946, thereby contributing to the ruin of small peasants. Furthermore, wages lagged behind prices while the indigenous population (despite a high mortality rate) increased from 6,121,000 in 1936 to 7,600,000 in 1948. Parallel to this, urban centers attracted a continuous flow of rural people in search of jobs. Between 1936 and 1948, population increased from 13% in 1936 to 16.4% in 1948. Between 1930 and 1940, a major change occurred in the structure of property, as shown in Table 2.

Thus, the trend since 1930 was for the number of landowners to decrease (20%) while the number of rural workers increased (29%). At the same time, the categories of *khammes* and *métayers*[13] were the main casualty of the war, which produced a "real mutation in the social structure."[15]

Table 2. *Changes in Property Relations*[14]

| Categories | Numbers of Property and Non-property Owners | | | | |
	1930	1938	1940	1948	1954
Landowners	617,544	549,395	531,600	537,800	494,500
Métayers	634,600	713,000	–	132,900	60,400
Khammes	50,711	55,600	–	–	–
Day Workers	428,032	462,467	–	448,100	375,500
Seasonal Workers	–	–	–	35,800	77,100
Permanent Workers	–	–	–	–	108,800
					1,438,300

Given these socio-economic developments, it was not surprising to see indigenous political movements display a more determined spirit. Thus, in an anti-colonial manifesto, Abbas renounced his assimilationist approach:

> It is enough to examine the process of colonization in Algeria to realize how the policy of assimilation, automatically applied to some and denied to others, has reduced Muslim society to utter servitude . . . This colonization can have but one concept, that of two mutually alien societies. Its systematic or disguised refusal

to allow the Muslim Algerians into the French community has discouraged all those who have favored a policy of assimilation already extended to the aborigines.[16]

Abbas called for an autonomous Algerian State with a separate constitution but having close ties with France. DeGaulle's answer to the request was the creation of a mixed commission to investigate the process of integration of 50,000 to 60,000 Algerians in the French *cité*.[17]

In response, Abbas formed the *Amis du Manifeste et de la Liberté*, (A.M.L.) a front that gathered all political groups in the hope of wresting more radical concessions from the French government. Soon Messali's followers managed to establish their preeminence within the A.M.L., but their domination was cut short by the 8 May 1945 massacre. During a demonstration in Sétif (Eastern Algeria), apparently staged for the release of Messali from jail, shots were fired which resulted in brutal repression by the French army that left 45,000 dead, according to the Algerian official figure. It has been argued that Messali was then preparing for an armed uprising and realized at the last moment that he could not carry it out.[18]

The severity of the 1945 repression had the double effect of radicalizing the younger members and making the older P.P.A.* members more cautious about the use of open confrontation with the French.[19] Another consequence of the Sétif massacre was the dismantling of the A.M.L. A new party was formed under the name of *Union Démocratique du Manifeste Algérien* (U.D.M.A.) in 1946 with Abbas as its leader. At the same time, Messali founded the *Mouvement pour le Triomphe des Libertés Démocratiques* (M.T.L.D.). Both Abbas and Messali prepared lists of candidates for the 1948 elections to the newly instituted Algerian Assembly whose membership was to include 120 Frenchmen and 60 Algerians.

---

*See footnote no. 7.

The French Administration tampered with the election and jailed 30 members of the M.T.L.D. (who would later become the leaders of the revolution).[20] These new arrests were made among the younger members of the M.T.L.D. who had already formed a paramilitary organization, the *Organisation Spéciale* (O.S.), to "fight colonialism by all means."[21] However, the French police succeeded in destroying the O.S. in March 1950, thereby dealing a second blow to the M.T.L.D.

The Creation of the C.R.U.A.

A congress of M.T.L.D. nationalists held in April 1953 debated the issue of the reconstruction of the O.S. and voted down Messali's request for larger powers. The opposition to Messali came mostly from the members of the Central Committee (the *Centralistes),* whereas the rank and file supported him. Single-handedly, Messali dissolved the Central Committee at a congress held in Belgium in mid-July, 1954, which elected him president for life. In response, the *Centralistes* expelled Messali and his followers from the M.T.L.D.

The sources of the conflict between Messali and the *Centralistes* have not been thoroughly investigated in the literature. The usual explanation is given in terms of a personality conflict. This seems inadequate in view of the many other personality conflicts that occurred in the history of Algerian nationalism and does not shed any light on the opposition which would later develop between the M.T.L.D. and the F.L.N. It has been suggested that before the split occurred between *Centralistes* and Messalists, the former were moving toward more legalistic means of action and away from revolutionary programs. "They represented a non-proletarian leadership in the P.P.A., all of them latecomers to party membership."[22]

In order to put an end to the stalemate, two *Centralistes* and two members of the now defunct O.S. formed a *Comité*

Révolutionnaire d'Unité et d'Action (C.R.U.A.). The
C.R.U.A. then appointed a committee of twenty-two
individuals to prepare for the armed struggle. A steering
committee was elected to make the necessary arrangements
for arms supplies and military organization. A *Front de
Libération Nationale* (F.L.N.) was constituted with the
stipulation that it was open to all political groups. The ideal
was to make the F.L.N. a "nation-party."[23]

Interpretation

Before analyzing the meaning of the conflicts that
characterized the F.L.N. during the revolution and immediately after the independence of Algeria, it is necessary to
interpret the political movements just described.

First, it must be pointed that, more often than not, the
literature on the Algerian Revolution is confined to a
chronological report of events. Quandt made an effort at
presenting a rational framework within which one might
make sense out of the complex historical sequences.
However, his theoretical approach and his choice of the categories of analysis led him to simplify the reality and
ultimately accept ready-made explanations. Thus, Quandt
divides the leaders of the various political movements into
three categories: the Liberals (i.e., the *Assimilationistes*),
the Radicals (i.e., the *Centralistes*), and the Revolutionaries
(i.e., the members of the C.R.U.A.). The differences between
the three groups are seen in terms of social background,
political socialization and time of entry into the movement.

His findings indicate that there is no significant difference
between Liberals and Radicals in terms of their social
background and their family political socialization. Indeed,
they both tended to come from economically or socially
privileged segments of the Algerian population. School
socialization on the other hand was more important for the
Radicals than for the Liberals. The former, because they were
younger, found an existing political climate, whereas the

latter, in a sense, contributed to creating it. It was, therefore, natural that the Radicals be involved in politics during their student years, whereas the Liberals only derived from school a sense of differentness and separateness from French students.[24] The Revolutionaries were found to differ from both the Liberals and Radicals on their educational levels and their social backgrounds. The Revolutionaries were not lawyers, doctors or pharmacists. Several of them were at one time or another workers in small industries or on farms. Others were involved in commerce, union activities or teaching. Some of them had even started a career in the French army. Unlike the Liberals and the Radicals, the Revolutionaries had divorced themselves from the legal political process early in their political careers.

This description of the recruitment of the Algerian political men during the pre-independence era is useful in that it permits the identification of key background variables. However, it is insufficient if one tries to understand the liberation movement in its entirety and the specific form of government to which it gave rise after independence. Thus, the antagonism between the C.R.U.A. members and those they referred to as the "politicos" (i.e., *Assimilationistes* and *Centralistes*) must be interpreted as a sign of struggle between differing world views, even if these were not explicitly spelled out.[25] What has often been taken as a lack of ideology in the F.L.N. could be seen as a deliberate setting aside of any concern about the specific form of the future Algerian state for the purpose of achieving unity behind the nationalist flag.

It was necessary to acquire a framework within which class antagonisms could unfold without being stunted by a colonial superstructure.[26] The fact that the colonial administration had in its first fifty years set out to annihilate the Algerian aristocracy did not mean that it erased aristocratic values and aspirations. In effect, the colonial factor contributed to an ossification of values held by Algerians, as was described by Fanon.[27] In this sense, values acquire a life of their own, although the material base that supports them is undermined. This may account for the fact that "in Algeria one finds many men of modest social origins who hold quite bourgeois beliefs."[28] Thus, to rely heavily on the socio-economic background of political actors in the pre-independence era may result in imposing limits on one's ability to comprehend social processes in their totality.

THE WAR OF NATIONAL LIBERATION

The F.L.N., Sole Party

In response to the creation of the F.L.N., Messali set up a *Mouvement National Algérien* (M.N.A.), which the F.L.N. made it one of its "early and enduring tasks to destroy."[29] Considering that the F.L.N. made it a policy to be open to all political groups, provided that they agreed on the principle of national independence and operated within the Front, it is unclear why it sought to annihilate the Messalists rather than reach an agreement with them. There is simply not enough reliable information available to determine the nature of this irreconcilable opposition. The fact that Messali was supported by the rank and file who happened to be proletarian could be indicative of an ideological conflict between the F.L.N. and the M.N.A. The F.L.N. found it easier to rally the members of the U.D.M.A. and those of the M.T.L.D. Indeed, the "politicos" were considered more skilled than the founders of the F.L.N. in wielding political rhetoric and conducting negotiations.

On 1 November 1954, the F.L.N. launched its first attack against the colonial regime by burning French property. In the summer of 1955, the "Declaration of the Sixty-One," a manifesto expressing the position of the *Assimilationistes,* recognized the "idea of an Algerian nation".[30] The F.L.N. was thereby implicitly accepted as a party struggling for the restoration of the sovereignty of the Algerian nation. The *Centralistes* who had been jailed when the F.L.N. started its nationwide operation followed suit as soon as they were released in 1955.

The First F.L.N. Congress

The unity achieved over the "national idea" barely hid the conflicts caused by differing political orientations, as was demonstrated at the first congress held by the F.L.N. on 26 August 1956. Despire French counterinsurgency techniques, the congress met in Algeria in the Soummam Valley to give the F.L.N. a political platform. The congress included only members who were involved in the struggle within Algeria (the "internals"). It is not clear whether those outside of Algeria were not invited or were unable to attend. However, the debate at the congress centered around whether the struggle should be directed from within the country while an external group would provide diplomatic support and arms supplies, or whether it should be under the leadership of a group based outside of Algeria. It was decided that the interior ought to have supremacy over the exterior. Likewise, the political leaders were to have precedence over the military ones. Besides, the direction of the struggle was voted to be collective.

It is sometimes argued that this congress, in effect, meant that the internal leaders, under the guidance of a young revolutionary, Abane Ramdane, seized the direction of the Revolution.[31] The antagonism between "internal" and "external" leaders has often been interpreted as reflecting the antagonism between Arabs and Berbers. This interpretation, in ethnic terms, is of limited value. There were Berbers in both groups. In fact, ethnicity in Algeria is not a clear-cut issue if one takes into consideration the history of the area, which was marked by a series of invasions during which different races mingled more than they simply co-existed. It is not surprising, therefore, that ethnicity has been identified with personality differences, which nevertheless "had only little influence in the broad lines of the politics of the F.L.N. and should not, therefore, be overestimated, as it has often been in some articles."[32]

Institutions of the Revolution

The importance of the Soummam congress lay in its giving the Revolution two major institutions, the C.N.R.A. (or *Conseil National de la Révolution Algérienne*) and the C.C.A. (or the *Comité de Coordination et d'Exécution*). Commenting on the congress, Ben Bella declared:

> ... it brought it [the revolution] a bureaucratic apparatus and red tape that gradually divorced it from the realities of the struggle. Above all, it made the mistake of introducing in the managerial organs political personalities who had, at all times, fought against the idea of an armed struggle and who, after 1 November, did not hesitate to publicly disavow our action. Confusion, contradiction, the absence of firm principles thus set in at the head of the F.L.N. Our capture[33] a few months later enabled leftist or conservative politicians to lead a revolution for which they were unprepared.[34]

However, for other F.L.N. members,

> ... the congress of the Soummam was a second November 1. Up until then, I was afraid of dying for fear the organization of the revolution might collapse. After 1956, I had no fear, since solid structures were rapidly set up.[35]

The composition of the C.N.R.A. reflects the open character of the F.L.N., in that it included seventeen former C.R.U.A. members, five *Centralistes,* two *Assimilationistes* and two individuals known for their ties with the *Ulemas.* However, the split between the external and internal leaders is made evident in that out of the seventeen top personalities eight were from the exterior and seven from the interior.[36]

The second organ of the revolution, the *Comité de Coordination et d'Exécution* (C.C.E.), was recruited exclusively among the internals. Its membership included two former *Assimilationistes.* The role of the C.C.E. was to make

decisions between meetings of the C.N.R.A. It must be noted
that the membership of both organs kept changing at least
partially as some leaders were killed and new men had to
replace them. In the course of the Revolution, the C.C.E.
made two major moves with long-range effects. First, it de-
creed an eight-day strike of all the employed indigenous
population and all the Algerian students enrolled in French
schools and colleges. Second, it adopted urban guerrilla
warfare as a supplement to the struggle in the countryside.
This led to the "Battle of Algiers," which opposed French
paratroopers to urban guerrillas and the indigenous
population of Algiers. "The Battle of Algiers" in turn
resulted in the quasi-annihilation of the urban political cells
and forced the C.C.E. members to flee to Morocco and
Tunisia.

Consequently, the split between the internals and the
externals became even sharper. Indeed, now that the C.C.E.
had to operate from outside Algeria, the *wilayas* (military
zones) acquired more autonomy with respect to the conduct
of the war. Such autonomy increased over the years as the
French army installed electrified wires at the Moroccan and
Tunisian borders in an effort to cut arms supply routes.
Reflecting on this situation, Ben Bella claimed that

> ... abandoned, deprived of arms, the *wilayas* suffered
> from a deterioration that could have been prevented. They
> closed in on themselves as they had no links with the
> exterior and sometimes with one another; they lived
> autarchically in regions they started to look upon as fiefs
> and where some commandants ended up acquiring feudal or
> gang leaders' attitudes.[37]

The G.P.R.A.

The responsibility for this state of affairs, according to Ben
Bella, lay with a "bureaucratic apparatus which, [because it
was] involved in international activity and personal rivalries,
no longer gave enough attention to those who carried the

struggle at the base."[38] This bureaucratic apparatus took the name of *Gouvernement Provisoire de la République Algérienne* (G.P.R.A.) on 16 September 1958, with Ferhat Abbas as Prime Minister. The membership of the G.P.R.A. was a combination of former *Centralistes* and *Assimilationistes* and the four hijacked leaders, now jailed in France, as honorary members. Apart from being unable to check the internal leaders, the G.P.R.A. was at odds with the troops of the National Liberation Army stationed at the Moroccan and Tunisian borders. As these troops found it almost impossible to cross mined fields to get into Algeria, the military command became involved in the politics of the G.P.R.A. These military men were generally contemptuous of the "politicians" and were sometimes unwilling to implement their decisions. Thus, Colonel Boumédiène, then Chief of Staff, accused the G.P.R.A. of not living up to the spirit of the C.N.R.A. and, along with two aides, refused to endorse the Evian Accords, which ended the war with France in 1962.[39]

An investigation of the socio-economic background of the military men shows that they differed from their colleagues who started the revolution only in that they were slightly more educated.[40] Besides, they were younger than the "politicos" and the leaders of the revolution. This means that they did not come to the revolution through a political channel. In this sense, they had some affinities with the later recruits, namely, students, teachers and professionals.[41] However, the ideological orientation of the military was somewhat populistic and directed to the peasantry which supplied the army with men.

The Tripoli Congress

The third meeting of the C.N.R.A. in 1961 provides another instance of conflict between men of differing ideologies. The meeting was held in Tripoli, Libya, for the purpose of drafting a new F.L.N. program to be implemented after independence along with the appointment of the members who would be in charge of the application of this program. A Political Bureau was to be formed in order to prepare for the installation of the new government.

It is claimed that the program, known as the Tripoli program, was drafted under Ben Bella's direction by M. Harbi, a Marxist, M. Yazid, a former *Centraliste,* and M. Lacheraf, a Sorbonne professor.[42] The program presents a brief analysis of Algeria's socio-economic condition since its colonization and sets forth in an outline form the political and economic orientation of the future state: agrarian reform, economic planning, nationalization of minerals and energy sources, credit and foreign trade, development of literacy and building of public facilities, etc.[43] The program opens up with a short class analysis of Algerian society. It describes the National Liberation Movement as having been supported by

> ... the poor peasants, the chief victims of colonialist seizures of land, segregation and exploitation ... the urban proletariat, a relatively small group and the teeming sub-proletariat ... another intermediate social category ... which is composed of artisans, menial and middle-rank workers, functionaries, small shopkeepers and certain members of the liberal professions, all of whom together make up what might be called the lower middle class. This group has frequently taken part in the fight for liberation and contributed political staffs ... a relatively unimportant middle-class, composed of businessmen, wealthy merchants, managerial personnel and a few industrialists. These last two social categories have participated sporadically in the movement, perhaps from patriotic conviction or perhaps from opportunism. Exception must be made for flagrant administrative feudalists and certain traitors who have sold themselves body and soul to colonialism.[44]

The program also underlines the fact that "it is in general the peasant and worker who have been the active base of the movement and have given it its essentially political character."[45]

The Congress adopted the program "unanimously, without a single modification."[46] However, the vote on the members of the future Political Bureau was more difficult to achieve. In fact, the Congress adjourned in total confusion with members undecided on the group to choose. There were three groups competing for power: first, Ben Bella, who got support from two of his former jail companions, M. Khider and R. Bitat; second, the G.P.R.A., which was supported by the F.L.N. chapter in France (the *Fédération de France du F.L.N.*); third, three military leaders (from *wilayas* 2 [North Constantine], 3 [Kabylia] and 4 [Algiers] who had blamed Boumédiène for not adequately supplying them with arms.

The July 1962 Crisis

Before entering Algiers on Independence Day, the G.P.R.A. (which was weary of the army as an organized body) made public a decision dissolving the Staff and dismissing Boumédiène as its head. This decision enabled Ben Bella to strike an alliance with Colonel Boumédiène, who then marched on Algiers, after defeating *wilayas* 3 and 4 and convincing *wilayas* 1 (Aurès) and 2 to join him. In the complex and still little known process of alliances and counteralliances that took place during this crucial period, certain socio-political patterns emerged. The members of the ex-C.R.U.A. (the committee that started the armed struggle) and the military were equally divided in their attitudes toward the G.P.R.A. and the Political Bureau. However, the ex-*Assimilationistes* were anti-G.P.R.A., whereas the ex-*Centralistes* were mostly pro-G.P.R.A. As to the latecomers to the revolution, they were either neutral or pro-G.P.R.A.

Viewed from a larger historical perspective, this pattern may be interpreted as the resurgence of the older distinction between the assimilationists and the nationalists, except that at this particular juncture both groups operated within a nationalist framework. What may seem puzzling is the equal split between the ex-C.R.U.A. members and the military. Within the former, personalities came to be associated with specific ideologies.

Indeed, a member of the Congress, explaining why he joined Ben Bella's group, declared: "The G.P.R.A. included too many anti-socialists and counter-revolutionary types who would have let the poor remain poor. They would have helped the city dwellers and ignored the peasants. Ben Bella seemed to express 'our' ideas, and we also thought that the myth of Ben Bella could be used."[47] This statement made by one participant in the 1962 political crisis may not be sufficient to interpret the crisis in ideological terms. On the other hand, to state that "political conflict was primarily an extension of divisions created within the elite by divergent patterns of political socialization" is not only an insufficient but also inadequate explanation. This argument ignores the role of the dynamics of the revolution in affecting the political outlook of individuals who, regardless of their political background, were involved in a common struggle for national liberation.

Although a complete evaluation of Quandt's thesis that the revolution acted as a divisive rather than a cohesive factor is beyond the scope of this chapter, it is nevertheless important to comment on it. To say that "the failure to adopt means of resolving intra-elite conflicts was due to the fact that differences were not based on clearly recognized class, regional, confessional or communal ties but rather resulted from a combination of *historical accidents* [emphasis mine] which had produced men whose views of politics differed significantly,"[48] is empirically wrong. Indeed, the fact of colonization was not accidental, nor were its consequences. The colonization of Algeria had the effect of levelling down some classes and creating the material conditions for others to arise. The conflicts that broke out at the end of the struggle for decolonization must be sought in those very conditions rather than in an immaterial historical happenstance. The fact that members of the

G.P.R.A., when interviewed, stated that the 1962 crisis was not ideological but personal may not necessarily reflect the reality. If it is true that revolution does not inevitably bring about unity, it is also true that it cannot simply act as a temporary framework for warring factions to join their efforts in fighting a common enemy and subsequently disintegrate.

It is important to realize that the very process of decolonization gave rise to the G.P.R.A. Before 1954, there were political organizations but no national government to participate in. The creation of a provisional government with a bureaucratic structure and the division of labor that this entailed was a significant development in the experiences of the ex-M.T.L.D., U.D.M.A. and C.R.U.A. members. It is, therefore, incorrect to assert that the 1962 crisis repeated the pre-war conflicts among the three groups. Rather, it seems that the G.P.R.A. structure gave rise to an oligarchy keen on perpetuating itself after independence was achieved. Hence, the G.P.R.A.'s members' refusal to vote on the formation of a Political Bureau that signified the destructuring of the G.P.R.A. It also happened that this government was, in effect, politically dominated by ex-*Centralistes* whose intellectual outlook was different from most former C.R.U.A. members, as indicated in Table 3 below. Besides, the G.P.R.A. had recruited, over the years, individuals whose political outlook was as moderate as theirs. This explains why during the crisis these recruits were opposed to the creation of a Political Bureau and in favor of maintaining the G.P.R.A.

To accept the argument that there were no ideological elements at the core of the 1962 conflict, it is important to determine what is meant by the explanation that the crisis revolved around differences in personal styles of individual members of the G.P.R.A. and the Ben Bella group.

Table 3.1. *Social Composition of the G.P.R.A.*[49]

GPRA					Number of Individuals				
	Peasant	Land-owner	Worker	Shop-kpr.	Civil Srvt.	Teacher	Lib. Prof.	Mil.	No answer
1st			3	2	2	1	5	1	4
2nd		1	3	1	2	1	3		3
3rd		1	3	1	2	1	1		3

Table 3.2. *Education Background of G.P.R.A. Members*[50]

Govts.	Number of Individuals			
	Grade School	High School	College	No Answer
1st GPRA	8	2	9	
2nd GPRA	7	2	4	
3rd GPRA	7	3	2	

It is a characteristic of Algerian culture that the individual is often seen as part of a group, his family, his village, his tribe. Although the latter no longer exists as a structure, its name and its past assets and liabilities are still kept in the collective memory. In a conflict involving two individuals, reference is often made to the opponent's group so that the conflict takes on the character of a virtual struggle between larger entities. Thus, it may not be impossible, by extrapolation, that the crisis between the *Assimilationiste*-dominated G.P.R.A. and the Ben Bella group unfolded as a struggle between the social categories to which the two opponents belonged, although it has been interpreted as a personality clash. In this case, the *Assimilationistes* represented the well-off, educated social category intent on using independence to establish and consolidate its power, whereas their opponents stood for the less educated or self-made men. Although they did not have an explicit ideology, the latter identified with the peasantry and were concerned with social justice, as the Tripoli Program indicated.

As for the ex-*Centralistes*, those among them who rallied to the Political Bureau instead of seeking refuge in a cautious neutrality may have done so for tactical reasons. However, it is not inconceivable that they had been genuinely radicalized by the revolutionary process, as was stated by a participant in the 1962 Congress.

INDEPENDENCE

The First Ben Bella Government

The composition of the first Algerian government and the vissicitudes of the first (and last) National Constituent Assembly helped crystallize the July crisis on specific issues. An amended list of candidates to the National Assembly was drawn up by the Political Bureau in September 1962. The choice of candidates reflected a desire to reduce the number of the ex-*Assimilationistes* and *Centralistes,* as well as those recruited by the G.P.R.A. during the revolution and the military leaders who had favored the provisional government. Table 4 summarizes the composition of the Assembly. Two elements emerge from this table: a high proportion of military men and a low proportion of workers.

Deputies differed in their conception of the role of the Assembly. In general, those used to French politics, such as Abbas and those ex-members of the C.R.U.A. opposed to Ben Bella, "felt that the Assembly should operate as a check on the powers of the Party and of the executive."[52] On the other hand, the military, some former *Centralistes* and C.R.U.A. members in favor of Ben Bella, thought that the Assembly's role should be limited, given the fact that the Party was too weak to exercise any effective control over it.

Table 4: *Composition of the National Constituent Assembly*[51] *1962*

Military	18%
Liberal Professions	18%
Commerce	14%
Teachers	12%
Agriculture	11%
Workers	7%
Cadres, Employees, Civil Servants	10%
Students	10%
Total	100%
N:	194

They also felt that "legalism" was a sterile endeavor when what was needed was to build a Party. Opposition to the government during the first year of the Assembly was expressed by the ex-*wilayas* 3 and 4. Indeed, 72% of the 81 deputies who represented these areas were in opposition to the government, as against 12% of the deputies from the rest of the country.[53] The second opposition group was made up of the individuals who joined the G.P.R.A. during the revolution as propaganda and public relations men.

The first government formed by Ben Bella included representatives of the various political groupings. Unlike the Political Bureau, which was comprised of individuals who played a role in the revolution, the government was composed of ministers selected according to their education, as Table 5 indicates.

In a short period of time, the government got rid of two major *Assimilationistes*, F. Abbas (President of the Assembly) and A. Francis (Minister of Finance). It also crushed (with

Table 5. *Education Background of Ben Bella's*[54]
Three Cabinets

	Grade School	High School	College	No Answer
1st. Govt.	5	1	11	2
2nd Govt.	5	3	8	1
3rd Govt.	4	3	8	4

the help of the army) an insurrection instigated by Ait Ahmed (one of Ben Bella's former jail companions) and Krim Belkacem (a former leading G.P.R.A. personality).

The Second Ben Bella Government

The second government, formed on 19 September 1963, reflected the growing importance of the military and the decline of both *Assimilationistes* and *Centralistes*. The new Minister of Defense, Abdelaziz Bouteflika, the Minister of Tourism, Ahmed Kaid, and the Minister of National Orientation, Chérif Belkacem, were close friends of Colonel Boumédiène. At the same time that he parted with the old "politicos," Ben Bella came to lean on a group of leftist advisers.[55] These changes in government composition were accompanied by spectacular political measures such as the endorsement of workers' self-management and nationalization of agricultural and industrial enterprises.

With the demise of the "politicos," only two forces remained in existence: Ben Bella's and Boumédiène's. Ben Bella was open to socialist experiments, whereas Boumédiène was keen on the "specificity" of Algeria and her Islamic character. Since they both came from a similar background, they could compete for the support of the same social class, the peasantry. However, Boumédiène had secured the obedience of the army, whereas Ben Bella had not yet improved the living conditions of the peasantry who, when the coup occurred, were to remain silent.

The Party Congress held in April, 1964, provides an opportunity to specify the actual ideological differences between Ben Bella's group and Boumédiène's. Characteristically enough, the *Ulemas*, who supported Boumédiène, defended Algeria's Islamic heritage, condemned imported socialism and recommended that "the theoretical bases of their actions (the leaders') should be drawn from our Arab-Islamic doctrines, not from foreign ones."[56] This resulted in the drafting of the *Charte d'Alger*, which constitutes the most complete program of economic development. It appears that the Charter was not drawn up under Ben Bella's guidance. He is said to have seen it for the first time when it was submitted to the Congress.[57]

The composition of the new Political Bureau also reflected the contending forces of Ben Bella and Boumédiène. Indeed, this institution included nine ex-guerrilla leaders (instead of one in the first Bureau) whose hostility to Boumédiène Ben Bella hoped to exploit.[58]

In the summer of 1964, new threats to the regime appeared in Southern and Western Algeria, where armed opposition took place. At the same time, political opposition tried to regroup outside of Algiers under the leadership of Mohammed Khider, Ben Bella's former jail companion who resigned from his position of Secretary General of the first Political Bureau. The army once again intervened to crush the attemtped dissidence.

As Ben Bella became more dependent on the military, he tried to limit Boumédiène's power by reducing the jurisdictions of the latter's friends, the Ministers of the Interior and of Foreign Affairs. On 2 December 1964, a new government was formed (see Table 6). Seven new ministers were added, all of whom had no particular record of participation in the revolution. Ben Bella also took over the duties of the Ministers of the Interior, Finance and Information. By bringing in individuals not involved in the pre-independence political process, Ben Bella apparently aimed at counter-balancing the growing military influence.

Table 6. *Political Trends in Ben Bella's Three Cabinets*[59]

	1st Cabinet	2nd Cabinet	3rd Cabinet
Assimilationistes	3	2	
Centralistes	3	1	2
C.R.U.A.	3	5	4
Technocrats	5	3	9
Military	5	5	4
N:	19	16	19

The June 1965 Crisis

In the spring of 1965, preparations were being made for the Afro—Asian Conference, which, because it was to be held in Algiers, was considered to convey prestige to Ben Bella, indirectly sealing his victory over the opposition. Indeed, political prisoners were released, and the underground opposition party of the F.F.S. (*Front des Forces Socialistes*) signed an agreement with the government. At the same time, rumors spread that the Minister of Foreign Affairs might be ousted soon. On 19 June 1965, however, an army coup led by Colonel Boumédiène overthrew Ben Bella, who was accused of treason and of fostering the "cult of personality." The popular militias created under Ben Bella proved useless as their chief joined Boumédiène's forces. Among the members of the Political Bureau only two resisted the coup: the former President of the National Assembly, Hadj Ben Alla, and the Minister of Health, Ahmed Nekkache.

Students staged a demonstration in protest against the coup, but it was quickly dispersed. The workers' union (U.G.T.A.) rallied to the new regime in return for a promise that self-management would be maintained and that the union's own autonomy would be upheld. The "politicos" generally applauded the coup, while the government members who had been recruited for their skills remained in their functions.[60] The Political Bureau was suspended' as were the National Assembly and the Constitution. A "Council of the Revolution" was created, which included twenty military men and four civilians. The military members included *all* former *wilaya* leaders (the internals) and career officers, otherwise opposed forces. The ex-military men were given the task of reorganizing the Party. The Minister of the Interior was reinstated and a Council of Ministers appointed whose function was to be the organ to which ministers would report. Not all the members of this institution were members of the Council of the Revolution, which included only the Ministers of Defense, Interior, Foreign Affairs, Finance and Agriculture.

Boumédiène's cabinet has often been lauded for giving a larger participation to technically trained personnel, thereby indicating the new President's desire for efficiency. In effect, Boumédiène merely developed the trend started by Ben Bella in forming his last cabinet. It must be emphasized, however, that Boumédiène's appointment of men trained in Western universities who are, therefore, if not alien to, at least different from, his Arab-Islamic education, has a double import.

First, it testifies to the President's nationalistic feelings which led him to transcend individual differences for the sake of building a nation of Algerians by Algerians rather than unduly appealing to foreign talents.

Second, it reveals that the regime, with its avowed slogan of socialist specificity, relies heavily on individuals whose training and world views belong to the same social class as the "politicos." The latter, fired or put under house arrest by Ben Bella, exited only to leave room for a younger generation. This is all the more important in that the new government decided on a "collegial" (collective) policy according to which ministers were granted relative autonomy. Collective leadership may provide individuals with diverse class loyalties to press their interests while viewing the revolution as the ultimate goal in which all interests fuse.

The homogeneity of the new cabinet resulted in a more stable government which, however, was not devoid of conflicts. The newly reorganized Party was the arena of the conflict between Boumédiène's friend, Chérif Belkacem, and the ex-*wilaya* leader, Salah Boubnider. In addition, the Ministers of Agriculture, Reconstruction and Information defected in the summer of 1966 and joined the opposition abroad. The three of them were replaced by men having ties with the former G.P.R.A. (Provisional Government). In August 1967, the Workers' Union clashed with the Minister of Industry and Energy, who was opposed to the creation of union branches in his ministry. The latter also entered in a conflict with the Minister of Labor, Abdelaziz Zerdani, who passed for a "leftist." Rumor had it that the source of conflict had to do with workers' self-management.

The climax of the opposition to the new regime was reached when, on 14 December 1967, the Chief of Staff, Tahar Zbiri, marched on Algiers in a poorly organized attempt to overthrow Boumédiène. The coup was crushed by Boumédiène's professional officers. From then on, the new President of Algeria appeared as a strong leader.

CONCLUSION

The process of class emergence was characterized by the expression of differing conceptions of:
  1. the means to achieve political freedom
  2. the means to govern.
The first period in the Algerian colonial history saw the rise of a social category of well-off individuals of the bourgeois

type who sought either to be assimilated to the French "nation" or revive and develop the Islamic "nation." A rigid colonialism and increasing economic difficulties which accelerated the process of proletarianization of Algerian society brought into the political arena a new, more modest social category of the petty-bourgeois type. This category was more intent on achieving political rather than cultural nationalism. Being closer to the mass of Algerian society, it was able to see that political action within the colonial framework was doomed to failure. An independent Algeria, where full expression of class interests would no longer be hindered by a colonial superstructure, was the goal which this class was able to impose on the bourgeoisie.

The emergence of the bureaucratic structure of the G.P.R.A. provided the bourgeois elements with the means to play a part in the revolution, while at the same time enlarging their base by recruiting younger members with no previous political affiliation. After independence, the alliance between the petty-bourgeoisie and the military temporarily succeeded in keeping the bourgeois out of power. Although objectively belonging to the same socio-economic category, the petty-bourgeoisie and the military expressed different interests. The former were open to socialist experimentation, whereas the latter responded to the needs of the rising technocrats, keen on national development and concerned with efficiency.

The process through which the Algerian bourgeoisie and petty-bourgeoisie emerged as classes displays no similarity with the rise of the bourgeoisie in Western societies. Whereas the Western bourgeoisie secured economic power before winning political power, the Algerian bourgeoisie followed the reverse process. The colonial mode of production, based on the exploitation of the Algerian society, acted as a brake on the development of an indigenous entrepreneurial class. Furthermore, the colonial policy of formal "assimilation" of the Algerian society to the French society by subjecting the former to French law had a damaging effect on the evolution of the Algerian social structure. The Algerian bourgeoisie fought first for political rights and second for political power. Political rights were deemed a precondition of economic power (see Figure 3).

Figure 2

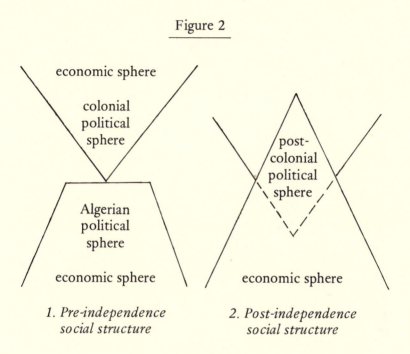

1. *Pre-independence*
   social structure

2. *Post-independence*
   social structure

Likewise, the Algerian petty-bourgeoisie struggled for a political sphere that was divorced from its own economic foundation.

This colonial determinism may account for the July 1962 crisis, where bourgeois and petty-bourgeois felt that they were equally fit to govern the country. The decisive role played by the army was made possible because the bourgeoisie had no fully developed economic base, nor could it seek the support of workers or peasants in order to defeat the petty-bourgeois' claim to power. The victory of the military fraction of the petty-bourgeoisie with its emphasis on efficiency, expertise and rapid industrialization provided the bourgeoisie with the opportunity to regroup and seek ways to articulate their interests.

5

Articulation
of
Class Interests

The political factor in Algerian history from the French colonization to the present imposes itself as crucial in understanding the changes that have affected the social structure. It will be recalled that political decisions made by the colonists radically altered the indigenous property structure in order to open the country to French immigration. At the same time, the new property relations led to aspirations the content of which was predicated upon the subsequent political moves made by the colonial administration. In this sense, the political constitutes the region in the total societal structure where interests may be deciphered. The main objection to this argument is that political decisions may be made for the sake of expediency or short-time compromises, as opposed to long-term clear-cut class interests. The issue consists precisely in analyzing the various components of a political decision and locating its place within the social totality in order to arrive at an adequate deciphering of class interests.

Class interests and their articulation will be studied through three significant political decisions taken by the first and second Algerian administrations: 1) the establishment of workers' self-management and its evolution; 2) the control exercised by the government over the Workers' Union; and 3) the creation of national corporations and the elaboration of a Code of Investments which provides guarantees to private investors.

The selection of the first indicator of class interests is based on the fact that self-management constitutes the arena where the social and the political converge. Self-management as a socio-economic organization requires that political power be wielded by society. Therefore, to study the success or failure of self-management is also to study the process through which social and political power develop.

The second indicator illustrates the contradiction between theory and practice. Indeed, on the one hand, workers are recognized as having the right to the control of the social conditions of their labor, but on the other, the government control of the Workers' Union denies them the expansion of their social power.

As to the third indicator, it is meant to uncover the interplay of the political and the economic spheres. The creation of national corporations is, in a sense, the negation of self-management. As such, it crystallizes the class interests of those who expounded it.

THE ESTABLISHMENT OF SELF-MANAGEMENT AND ITS EVOLUTION

Structure of Self-Management

When the French invaded the country and displaced the Turks, peasants were reported to have taken advantage of the confusion that resulted from the war by occupying the former government lands.[1] In similar fashion, just after the declaration of independence, rural workers moved into formerly French-owned estates, thereby "conjuring up the spirits of the past,"[2] but this time creating a *fait accompli* which the new government had to endorse.[3]

In July 1962, immediately after the declaration of independence, 1,000,000 hectares of land and 700 industrial enterprises lay abandoned by their former owners.[4] Workers, both rural and urban, had already defended farms and shops from the acts of sabotage perpetrated by departing colonists. Subsequently, workers undertook the difficult task of running industry and agriculture "under conditions of total power vacuum and dismantled economic enterprises . . . before a first Assembly, whether consituent or legislative, was installed."[5] To question the motives of the workers is inconsequential. Whether workers adopted self-management because they were conscious of their class interest or simply because they were pressed by economic difficulties is not essential. What is important is that workers did take over farms and form management committees. There is no evidence that they feared that the French colonists would come back and would keep the structure of their mode of production unchanged.

Therefore, workers may have been anxious to create a *fait accompli* by installing the groundwork for an effective participation of labor in management. There is also evidence that workers were weary of local proprietors who reportedly contemplated getting hold of abandoned equipment.[6] It must be noted that the Algerian Workers' Union took part in the early spontaneous socialization of the land holdings by providing either financial, technical or organizational support to the workers. Thus, in Algiers area, railroad workers would volunteer to repair equipment on the farms.[7] More important was the role of the A.L.N. (Armée Nationale Populaire), especially in large estates. In the Mitidja Valley, for example, the army organized "loans for the harvest and 'security stocks' of cereals on the basis of a fixed price per quintal." It also had "jobs performed by soldiers and

volunteers, the *ashur* tax paid, one soldier's widow employed
. . . for every ten workers, and bookkeeping taken care of."[8]

Whether spontaneous, sponsored or induced by the army,
self-management became a reality which the newly
constituted government endorsed through the issuance of
two decrees on 22 October 1962.[9] The first decree instituted
management committees in vacant agricultural, industrial and
mining enterprises that had more than ten workers. The
committee members were placed under the supervision of the
*Bureau National pour la Protection et Gestion des Biens
Vacants.*

The second decree regulated the transactions, sales and
rentals of vacant property.[10] However, at the same time, the
Minister of Agriculture referred to the self-managed farms
as "State farms" and advocated the assignment of "war
veterans' families, militants, ex-concentration camp inmates,
landless sharecroppers, widows and orphans to the vacant
estates."[11] This was revelatory of the contradictory nature
of the governmental decision. On the one hand, workers'
management was hailed as a revolutionary undertaking, but
on the other hand, it was implicitly admitted that it could be
no more than a stop-gap measure to compensate those who
suffered from the war.

The use of the expression "vacant property" indicates that
this wealth was still viewed as exceptional rather than as an
integral part of the national economy.[12] At no time did
the government consider the new worker-managed farms as a
permanent phenomenon. The rights of French owners
were maintained until it was made sure (through various
appeals made to them) that they were unwilling to return.
It was not until March 1963 that self-management was
claimed by the government to be the Algerian form of
economic organization. The announcement of the March
decrees coincided with the explosion of an atom bomb as
part of France's tests in the Algerian Sahara, on which

she had kept provisional rights. This gave the decrees an even greater symbolic value in that they asserted the country's desire to break out of colonialism. The decrees were devised by Ben Bella's leftist advisers. The first decree, issued on 18 March 1963, set up the criteria for declaring a property vacant. The second (22 March) specified that all mining, industrial and agricultural enterprises declared vacant would be managed by their workers through four bodies: 1) the Workers' General Assembly; 2) the Workers' Council that includes 10 to 100 members; 3) the Management Committee with three to 11 members; and 4) the Director.

The Workers' General Assembly was to be composed of all regular full-time workers. Article 4 specifically states that "seasonal workers may neither be members of the General Assembly nor have the rights and prerogatives connected with that position." The Director draws up the list of the members of the Assembly. Article 8 indicates that the Assembly "must be called once every three months. It may be convened extraordinarily on the initiative of one-third of its members." Its functions are to adopt "the development plan of the enterprise within the framework of the national plan, as well as the annual investment, production and sales programs." It is also concerned with "the organization of work, the definition and distribution of functions and responsibilities. It elects, if there is one, the Workers' Council." (Article 9).

"The Workers' Council, elected among the members of the General Assembly . . . meets at least once a month on the decision of the Management Committee." It decides on all purchases and sales of equipment, medium and long-term loans, and hiring of new permanent members. It also elects and checks on the Management Committee.

The Management Committee, one-third elected each year in rotation by the Workers' Council, "assumes the task of management of the enterprise". The Committee also elects one of its members as President.

Contrary to the President, whose role is to represent the Management Committee and countersign documents, the Director represents the State. He has the right of veto on the selection of members to the General Assembly and on the hiring of permanent personnel. He sees to it that production conforms to the norms of the national plan; he implements decisions taken by the Management Committee and the Workers' Council; he endorses financial documents and controls the available cash. The Director is a member of the Management Committee and is "nominated or dismissed by the supervisory body on the recommendation of the Communal Council for the Promotion of Self-Management."

Article 23 indicates that the latter Council is "composed of the presidents of the management committees, the respective representatives of the Party, the U.G.T.A., [Workers' Union] the A.N.P. [Army] and the communal administrative authorities."

The third decree regulates "the distribution of revenue in enterprises and concerns under self-management." Another decree taken on 26 July 1963, retroactive to 1830, declared that all property seized by or handed to collaborators of the colonial regime is state property.

It must be pointed out that the March decrees did not nationalize all European agricultural and industrial holdings. It nationalized only those whose vacancy was ascertained. The remaining property was nationalized in two stages: first on 30 April 1963 and then on 1 October 1963.

Laks suggests that there was a correlation between these nationalizations and the political context within which they occurred.[13] The more the government met with political opposition, the more accelerated the pace of nationalizations. Domestic political difficulties may partially account for the hastiness with which the March decrees were both elaborated and applied.

The logic behind the pyramidal structure of self-management was to involve the largest possible number of workers in the functioning of the enterprise. However, workers' participation was stunted by the role the texts prescribed for the General Assembly. Indeed, the latter does not have the power to make decisions; it simply endorses rather than controls decisions made within the enterprise. Besides, although the General Assembly seems to be a major body in that it actually adopts the organization and production plan of the enterprise, it does not, in effect, participate in the discussion of its minutiae. The supervisory state agency and the Director actually make the crucial choices.[14] Likewise, the role prescribed for the Director makes him more powerful than the President, under whose authority he is theoretically expected to be. At the same time, the decrees did not provide any procedure for resolving a possible conflict between the Director and the Management Committee.

Dysfunctioning of Self-Management

The theoretical vagueness and inadequacies of the decrees may be a reflection of the double purpose self-management was to serve. The 18 March decree was specifically directed against the reinforcement of the mercantile and landed bourgeoisie who had started appropriating commercial and agricultural enterprises. By the same token, it endorsed the workers' management of the means of production. In so doing, the new policy was meant to rally peasants and workers to the regime, thereby isolating the bourgeoisie. However, the March decrees were not applied faithfully, even under their imperfect form.

The nature of the difficulties encountered in their application illustrates the struggle between various antithetical political forces, which also bear the marks of the specific social environment in which they evolved. These difficulties manifested themselves on both the functional and the structural levels within the enterprise and between industry, agriculture and the Administration.

First, knowledge of the content of the decrees was weak or lacking altogether among workers. In a survey carried out in thirteen self-managed farms in the Mitidja Valley, Chaulet reports that, although almost all of the skilled workers were able to define the March decrees, more than half the permanent unskilled workers and all of the seasonal workers had no knowledge of their existence. In some cases, the word "March" evoked the cease-fire of 19 March 1962[15] just before the proclamation of independence.

Second, the general assemblies very seldom convened to adopt production programs. Thus, Chaulet also reports that "no farm had complied with the four yearly meetings or even one meeting a year. Nowhere had the Assembly played the role of sovereign organ in production, nor was it considered as such."[16] Likewise, the management committees were found to be failing to "exercise real responsibilities regarding the most important management decisions and the daily organization of the workers; they are not even informed of these problems."[17]

More significant is the pattern that this survey revealed, namely, the emergence of a "limited circle of individuals considered to be 'in charge' [of the estate]."[18] This finding agrees with an earlier study done by Laks which also underlined the emergence of a "triple cleavage within the self-managed industrial enterprise that opposes those in charge of management, closely linked to the bureaucratic petty-bourgeoisie in the enterprise, to the collectivity of workers, themselves split up into a base and a bureaucratic stratum."[19] The distinction between those in charge of management and the workers must be emphasized. Indeed, by their very functions of representatives of the state, the Directors were identified and identified themselves with the state.[20] Directors were criticized for being "sterile bureaucrats, displaying a lack of sensitivity to the internal difficulties of the enterprise by neglecting, for instance, to supervise production, and for paying themselves an inflated salary." Workers also objected to the directors because "they came to work in suit and tie," or they "use our car and our gas."21

Chaulet also suggests that the directors' attitudes toward their job and toward the workers resulted from two factors. First, the supervisory state agency bypassed the procedure of appointment of directors and deprived workers of any power over the functioning of their enterprise.22 Second, the "class values they possessed and developed" prevented the directors from being sensitive to the workers' needs.23 A third possible explanation is that directors were not appointed for their expertise, but on the basis of "appropriate connections," the sole criterion being the possession of an elementary school degree.24 They generally came from a lower petty-bourgeois background and attached great importance to social mobility. Some of them used their functions to hire their relatives as permanent workers.

Clegg argues that presidents and directors went through two stages in the development of their "class" consciousness.25 First, they concentrated on the immediate appropriation of goods for personal satisfaction, and, second, moved to the utilization of their positions for class ends. This is an attractive but unfounded proposition. Indeed, it requires an analysis over time of a sample of directors and presidents in order to ascertain that the same individuals who indulged in corrupt behavior changed to an activity governed by class norms. A distinction must be made between those who discriminated against workers by excluding them from the management of the enterprise because they felt they were not ready for it and those who discriminated against workers in order to indulge in corrupt activity. There are, for example, cases where directors are "young men often full of good will but crushed by the weight of their responsibilities. In their daily relations with the workers, their sole authority lay in their role as liaisons between the agricultural concern and the state (writing of reports, requests for credit, reading of circulars) . . . Many of them were content with this role which is less trying and less dangerous than the one that should have been theirs."26

In general, however, the directors' attitude toward the workers was one of fear and contempt. At a seminar sponsored in March 1964, workers were referred to as "illiterates one cannot do anything with. Since they haven't been lucky enough to be presidents, they give you a hard time." Some directors drew the lines even more strongly by stating that "since the workers are against the state, they are against us." They all asked for more power and rejected the idea of undergoing a training period that would also include the workers.27

The distinction that has been made by Laks between the workers' "avant garde" and the "rank and file" has a peculiar character. Although staunchly opposed to the state's interference in self-management, the "avant garde" looks down upon the workers as "too backward while our enemies are too powerful. We will educate them [the workers] when we become stronger."28 The rank and file, on the other hand, display an acute awareness of their exclusion from participation in the life of their enterprise: "They despise us; therefore, they don't tell us anything (about the enterprise);" or, after an election, "Mohand was leading by one vote; but, since he reads the paper to us and explains to us where our interest lies, they cheated in order to eliminate him."29

Self-Management and the Administration (1963-1965)

These difficulties were compounded by what appeared to be an increasingly deteriorating relationship between the self-managed enterprises and the governmental institutions. It is here that class interests become manifest because they involve an antagonistic relationship between the state bureaucracy and the workers over the crucial issue of self-management.

Clegg claimed that

> in the absence of any real theory on what the relations between
> the enterprise and the center should be, the superstructure was
> pieced together in an ad hoc fashion. Each successive stage in this
> process placed the *comité* more firmly under central control until
> the administration came to control every essential aspect of the
> economic activity of the *comité,* rendering the concept of *auto-
> gestion* derisory.[30]

Although this description of the process of containment of
self-management is accurate, the reasons given for it appear
to be inadequate. Indeed, those who drafted the March
decrees availed themselves of other similar experiments,
especially the Yugoslav one, and seem to have made their
decision wilfully rather than accidentally. Therefore, the
containment process ought to be studied through the manipulation of the theory underlying the decrees, rather than in
the assertion of a lack of theory. It must be pointed out that
the structural problems faced by self-managed enterprises and
farms did not occur in a vacuum. The intricate relationship
between a nascent form of economic organization and survi-
ving colonial capitalist structures, along with the mental
attitudes they carry with them, were perhaps most neatly
summarized by the first Algerian President, Ben Bella: "Our
economy will have to develop through the combined and
complementary interplay of two sectors: the socialist and the
private sectors, between which a semi-public sector will take
its place. The state must rest the socialist sector on sound
economic and financial foundations; and to do so, the
existing financial and commercial networks must be adapted
to the new situation created by the establishment of this
sector. But, as we have stated on several occasions, the state
also intends to encourage by all means available to it the
creation of new industrial enterprises."[31]

The contradiction between a private sector which dominated the very market that self-managed enterprises needed resulted in weakening the socialist sector. This, in turn, led to a policy of centralization which gradually deprived the workers of any effective participation and transformed them into wage labor.

A series of institutions was created for the purpose of "protecting" the socialist sector but which appear to have resulted in its containment. Thus, an *Office National de la Réforme Agraire* (O.N.R.A.)[32] was created in the spring of 1962 to supervise the management committees in agriculture and a *Bureau National d'Animation du Secteur Socialiste* was set up a few days later for the purpose of "education, stimulation, coordination and supervision of the socialist sector."[33] This institution was initiated by the group that drafted the decrees. It obviously duplicated the functions of the O.N.R.A. and consequently had to confine itself to industrial self-management. This could be taken as an indication of an antagonism between the Ministry of Agriculture and the President's Cabinet.

O.N.R.A. soon interfered with the inner workings of the management committees. Often with the help of rural branches of the F.L.N. and local administrative authorities it arranged for the election of committees that would be under its own control. This was made all the more easy in that the U.G.T.A. (Workers' Union) was unable to organize the workers. Where it did, interference by O.N.R.A. was minimal.[34] Furthermore, O.N.R.A. took over the control of the financial operations of the various committees through its subsidiary, the *Centres Coopératifs de la Réforme Agraire (C.C.R.A.)*. O.N.R.A. was known to "refuse requests by *comités* to see their accounts."[35] At the same time, it did not help the committees get the state loans they needed to repair sabotaged equipment and to obtain liquid capital. Therefore, management committees were forced to borrow from private sources at inflated interest rates. O.N.R.A.

created the conditions that made workers' self-management appear as a non-viable alternative to socio-economic development. Its role fulfilled, O.N.R.A. was dissolved in 1967 and its funds transferred to the *Caisses Régionales de Crédit.* Management committees were now placed under the direct supervision of the Ministry of Agriculture, thereby completing the process of state control.

The marketing of the self-managed farm produce also suffered from the same administrative control. The *Coopératives Régionales Agricoles* (C.O.R.A.), created to take care of domestic sales, along with the *Office National de Commercialisation des Agrumes* (O.N.A.C.O.), for example, failed to achieve their goals. It is reported that their inefficiency was such that crops were left to rot while workers were waiting for these agencies to pick them up. Some committees were even driven to sell their produce to private buyers who paid cash and better prices.

Industrial self-management met with the same problems as the agricultural sector. Here, financing was entrusted by a June 1964 decree to the *Banque Centrale d'Algérie* (B.C.A.) and the *Caisse Algérienne de Développement* (C.A.D.).[36] The former was meant to finance short-term loans, control the management of enterprises and participate in the elaboration of plans and programs. As to the latter, it was to grant long-term loans and liquid capital. It was left to the discretion of the B.C.A. to raise the interest rates in case of "bad management". In fact, neither the B.C.A. nor the C.A.D. relieved the financial problems encountered by the committees. Indeed, to grant a loan, the B.C.A. required that a committee show proof of profit for three years. This meant that a starting committee could not possibly obtain a loan.[37] It also meant that those committees with limited liquid capital could not give credit to customers who thus turned to the private sector. Besides, when the customer was a government agency, payments were practically never made.[38]

Both the C.A.D. and the B.C.A. explained their weak contribution to self-management by arguing that their role was to be performed only after certain preliminary conditions were fulfilled. This meant that, in a transition period, the C.A.D. was expected to make the necessary financial advances. The C.A.D., however, defended itself by insisting that its statutes did not enable it to do so. Even when instructed by the decree of 4 September 1964, to make direct loans, it still invoked its financial troubles and arranged advances through banks that made it a practice to delay payments.[39] In the face of increasing financial control, self-managed enterprises were unable to share in the promised production bonuses.

Thus, the Ministry of Economy declared on 6 February 1965: "We would like to hear about and publicize the names of management committees that have fulfilled their obligations; we will then fix for them the level of their participation in the various funds provided for by the March decrees, and we will for the first time give them the power to deliberate on the issue of profit-sharing—all profit-sharing."[40]

Given the conditions under which they operated, most committees were unable to "fulfill their obligations". Besides, since their budgets were in the hands of the administration, it was not clear whether their bonuses were simply cut off or merely suspended.

Apart from establishing its control over the finances of the self-managed enterprises and the marketing of their production, the administration also tended to favor the capitalized private sector. For example, when worker-managed enterprises came in direct competition with a privately owned industry, the government favored the latter.[41] In cases where difficulties were experienced in the socialist sector as a result of competition with private industry, the administration dissolved the management committee and created a *société nationale* (state-owned corporation) in its place. At the same time, there is no evidence that the state institutions favored the socialist sector as their supplier. The situation was such that in the spring of 1965 one-third of the abandoned enterprises were still not in operation. The estimated turnover of those under workers' management was about 20% of the bulk of industries in existence in Algeria.[42]

The coup d'état of 19 June 1965 initiated a double process of containment of self-management through a series of denationalizations and the creation of national companies. In this sense, the coup

> was not a counter-revolution . . . It marked a point of rationalization and acceleration of a counter-revolution that had been already under way since soon after independence . . . The coup was part of a class struggle that was already under way. In this struggle, Ben Bella represented a populist mystification; his removal clarified and sharpened its lines.[43]

Self-Management and the Administration (1965–1972)

Before analyzing the specific process through which self-management was dealt with by the new administration, it is essential to understand how Colonel Boumédiène conceived of it. In his proclamation of 19 June 1965, he blamed his predecessor for squandering the public wealth and for promoting a "haphazard and propagandist socialism". These are recurring themes in the speeches made in 1965. It is not ruled out that self-management is part of the squandered wealth. What is more interesting to note, however, is the double level on which Colonel Boumédiène consistently refers to self-management. Thus, although acknowledging the existence of "enemies"of this form of economic organization, he blames the workers for their low productivity and declares that self-management "must conform to the law and submit to control."[44] Commenting on the reorganization of the socialist sector that he initiated, he admits that "even within the revolutionary power, individuals in charge of this sector were recently acting to impede the application of self-management in order to perpetuate anarchy, neglect, squanderings and other thefts."[45]

At the same time, he insists that those workers who did not produce any profit to share "can only blame themselves for it" because "self-management means in fact participation in profits and participation in deficits, too."[46] His emphasis on productivity and profit, along with his shifting of the blame for the failure of self-management from the "saboteur" cadres to the workers, may be taken as a reflection either of his lack of information on the actual situation of the self-managed enterprises or his inability to control those in charge of the reorganization of this sector of the economy.[47] This reorganization started with a series of denationalizations of restaurants, hotels, cafés and shops. The management committee of combined hotels and restaurants (C.O.G.E.H.O.R.E.), including 55 premises and 800 workers in the Algiers area, was thus disbanded. The smaller concerns were sold and the larger ones placed under the direct control of the Ministry of Tourism.[48]

One of the most spectacular denationalizations was that of the *Coopérative Aissat Idir*, located in Blida, east of Algiers. The cooperative was managed by four committees involving 1,500 workers and was considered, despite the heterogeneous character of its component parts, "one of the most successful examples of *autogestion*."[49] The cooperative was broken up in 1966, and the concerns that comprised it were either sold or placed under the supervision of various ministries. The reasons given to justify these denationalizations were always couched in exclusively economic terms. Small enterprises were deemed too weak to be of any economic value for the state, and larger concerns were disbanded for not being profitable enough. (See Tables 7 and 8.)

Table 7

Land under Self-Management[50]

Northern Algeria	2,299,000 hectares
Southern Algeria	3,200 hectares
Total	2,302,200 hectares

The total size of privately owned land is 40,147,000 hectares.

Table 8

Employment in Self-Managed Estates[51]

Permanent Workers	173,770
Seasonal Workers	102,209
Total	275,979

The total population of rural workers not involved in self-management is 766,666, where 195,287 are permanent and 571,379 are seasonal workers. The above includes accountants and administrators.

The Creation of National Corporations

On the institutional level, the new reforms brought about the abolition of the unpopular O.N.R.A. (Supervisory Administration of Self-Management), whose functions were taken over by the Ministry of Agriculture, and the creation of the *Banque Nationale d'Algérie* to remedy the inefficiency of the former *Banque Centrale d'Algérie* and *Caisse Algérienne de Développement*. In effect, students of self-management in Algeria agree that these reforms did not improve the workers' situation, with perhaps one exception. The distinction between the permanent and seasonal workers was dropped so that all workers could benefit from social security.

The hallmark of the post-coup d'état administration is the creation of national corporations. On 19 June 1968, President Boumédiène announced that the

> self-management system is considered a deviation by certain theorists of socialism. That is why Marxists in some socialist countries, especially in the Soviet Union, have considered self-management a deviationist activity when it was applied in Yugoslavia. As for Algeria, we have decided, in spite of all the criticisms, to create national corporations because our task is to put an end to anarchy, squandering and chaos in this sector [i.e., socialist sector]. [52]

National corporations were meant to displace self-management. This was confirmed by the transformation of self-managed enterprises into national corporations such as the *Huileries Modernes d'Alger,* an oil industry, a construction and a transportation enterprise, SONATIBA and the *Société Nationale des Transports Routiers.* This new form of economic organization was apparently motivated by Colonel Boumédiène's desire to achieve economic self-reliance so that "we satisfy our needs in agriculture and industry thereby escaping dependency."[53] A series of nationalizations of natural resources (mines and oil), chemicals, banking and insurance facilities, transport, oil distribution, etc., made the creation of national corporations an even easier undertaking. At the same time, workers were deprived of the means to participate in the organization of economic life. Their role became one of consultation through the workers' committees set up in every production unit or through a central workers' council that meets once a year to provide the director general of a given corporation with some feedback.

The Agrarian Reform

Apart from the decision to create national corporations, which meant the end of self-management in industry, the agrarian reform, established by ordinance no. 71-73 of

8 November 1971, is a measure that, in effect, contains the expansion of self-management in agriculture. The preamble to this ordinance specifically states that self-management "remains, however, an advanced system of management that requires sizable units of production with an adequate technical level. Considering the complexity, diversity and fragmentation of the private sector, self-management cannot be the unique instrument of socialization in agriculture."[54]

The same preamble also indicates that "the agrarian revolution does not abolish the private ownership of the means of production, but it bans the exploitation of man by man."[55] In fact, article 65 of the ordinance points out that the area of agricultural property is limited in such a way that "the minimum income of an average family living solely off its product is equivalent to . . . three times the income of the family of a worker on a self-managed estate who labors 250 days a year."[56]

The agrarian revolution is thus intended to limit extensive private property of land and cattle.[57] It is also meant to fight land absenteeism by nationalizing absentee owners' estates and to provide small or landless peasants with adequate plots. Peasants are encouraged to change their work methods through compulsory enrollment in a service or production cooperative. Every peasant who gets a plot of land also receives a loan to enable him to buy the necessary equipment. The land distributed among peasants is derived not only from nationalizations of large estates but also from the public domain and from communal and *habus* (donated) property. The latter is expected to be worked collectively in order to respect its founders' wishes. The aims sought by the agrarian revolution are "to free the initiative of the peasants", to restore to the land its value as a condition for labor and not wealth, "to make development of land an obligation, and to upgrade individual effort."[58]

Land development is facilitated by the nationalization of all water supplies. At the same time, the continuity of "individual effort" is ensured by a provision stipulating that the land distributed to the peasants may be passed on to their descendants. This reproduces the property structure that existed in pre-colonial times.[59] However, the ordinance also announces a future readjustment of the laws of inheritance in an effort to prevent the atomization of property. Furthermore, the ordinance also stipulates that individuals who have been working *arsh* lands (inalienable property) will be considered their actual owners, provided that they give evidence of their right of usufruct within a period of ninety days. The similarity between this procedure and the *senatus consultum* of 1863 is a striking twist of history. The difference is, naturally, that where there is no proof of legitimate usufruct, the land is redistributed among landless peasants. Article 68, which emphasizes that each individual will be the "owner of his share", reveals a concern for inalienable property. In view of the fact that collective work is given preference over individual labor throughout the ordinance, it is unclear why inalienable property should be a preoccupation unless it comprises some of the largest estates. There is no indication in the ordinance to that effect.

The most significant step taken by the ordinance is perhaps the abolition of the system of sharecropping and the cancellation of the debts that the sharecropper had incurred with landlords. The sharecroppers are also given priority in the distribution of the nationalized land. The latters' owners receive a monetary compensation. The abolition of the sharecropping system is a direct indication that the agrarian revolution aims at restructuring the relations of production. However, by so doing it is, in effect, creating a new class of small proprietors which may stand in an antagonistic relationship to the workers involved in self-management.

The ordinance does not specify the relationship between the self-managed estates and the newly extended private sector. There is also no guarantee that the big landowners will not prevent peasants from taking advantage of the new laws, as was the case, for example, in Egypt.[60]

In fact, reports by Algerian students who survey the country-side every year as part of a volunteer program to help peasants acquire an adequate knowledge of the agrarian revolution reveal the existence of a "counter-revolution." Thus, it is stated that "the big landowners do not hesitate to distort the fundamental principles of the agrarian revolution to threaten and directly intimidate the poor and the landless peasants so that they do not put their names down on the lists of recipients [of distributed land]." Moreover, the proportions of landless peasants (two-thirds) and small peasants (one-third) to be listed as eligible for land attribution were not respected.

The peasants' knowledge of their rights under the ordinance has been found to be very limited. Two methods were used by the local authorities to inform the peasants of their rights. In the first, a meeting was held and the legal text read in classical Arabic, which peasants do not understand. In the second, the texts were posted, despite the fact that almost nobody is literate.[61] It is also reported that the administrative organs in charge of the implementation of the ordinance have been "infiltrated by . . . individuals whose interests might be affected by the agrarian revolution."[62] Among the many recommendations students made were those relating to the re-opening of recipients' lists, as well as the re-examination of the criteria of eligibility for more land.[63]

Meaning of Self-Management

At this point, it is necessary to assess the meaning and the implications of the acceleration of the process of containment of self-management in agriculture and its destructuring in industry. First, the economistic argument is not sufficient to explain the demise of self-management, especially if one remembers that the various management committees had from the very start been under the tight control of the administration or appointed by it. Furthermore, the administration managed both the finances of the committees and the marketing of their products. Therefore, it seems unfounded to claim that the workers were unable to manage rationally and profitably the concerns they had taken over. Rather, the interpretation of the destructuring of industrial self-manage-ment is better sought in the meaning attached to this form of organization and the implications of its expansion for the political forces in existence after the coup d'état.

Self-management implies "the suppression of all central pow-er, whether it be economic or political." "It is a social mode of production such that it is able to impel an optimum development of the total society through the development of the working class. The aim, therefore, is a socialist system of production."[64] Under socialist conditions, it is generally recognized that the state may still become the master rather than the servant of society.[65] To ensure against this occur-rence, power must be decentralized and society enabled to manage its economy. In the Algerian case, self-management appeared as an inopportune phenomenon which stood in the way of the consolidation and expansion of a newly con-stituted state with no desire to "wither away."

Whereas in Yugoslavia political power was in the hands of the working class, in Algeria workers were confronted with a class which claimed to defend their interests while at the same time promoting its own. Hence, self-management in Algeria was only tolerated rather than promoted. As soon as the class in power shifted its priorities from immediately alleviating unemployment to rapidly industrializing, self-management became a rhetorical issue.

In this sense, self-management is "a catalyst of the deep trends channeled by the various social formations and currents within these formations."[66] It had the effect of radicalizing individuals outside of the working class. Indeed, under the Ben Bella government, former members of the Pro-visional government, Ferhat Abbas and Ahmed Francis, re-signed when the March decrees were taken, as did Hocine Ait Ahmed, a prominent member of the group that initiated the revolution in 1954. At the same time, the U.G.C.A. (*Union*

Générale des Commerçants Algériens) attacked the "class struggle" as "a hideous ideological speculation which generates chaos, arbitrariness, injustice, misery, adventurism ..." and condemned "the nefarious policy of miserable collectivism."[67]

Likewise, the experience of management made the workers even more aware of the antagonism between state and society. At the Congress of the Socialist Industrial Sector, workers voiced their discontent and accused the state of impeding the functioning and the expansion of self-management.[68] One worker's comment is particularly revealing of class interests:

> To ensure its profits, the private sector is organized into chambers of commerce, industry, etc. Our one and a half year's experience in self-management shows that we only have the March decrees and for the rest we must fend for ourselves. We, too, should organize to resist the private sector, to unmask the opportunists, the profiteers who seek to utilize the state apparatus. This congress should appoint a commission to set up an organization that covers the entire self-managed sector.[69]

The workers' desire to organize was antithetical to the power-holders' goal to "build a real and efficient state apparatus, capable of enforcing discipline and revolutionary order and to shield the state and administrative agents from all forms of pressure or solicitations."[70] This state is all the more important to construct to the extent that:

> foreign political elements, Trotskyites or others, called for the collapse of the state when the latter was not even built up, since it was still lying under the rubble after the enemy destroyed it. The state, according to the propagators of this doctrine, is but an instrument of exploitation. However, the history of modern times has demonstrated that it is impossible for any society to follow the path of progress without having a state. Nothing proves this better than the socialist countries where the state apparatus is stronger than in capitalist countries.[71]

This statement clearly reveals the contradiction between self-management which, in its essence, negates the existence of an all-powerful state, and the Algerian government's desire to build just such a state. It also expresses the interest of a social class eager to consolidate itself by erecting a bureaucratic structure that will enable it to implement its decisions.

What was the role of the Workers' Union in the process of containing and destructuring self-management? It appears to be limited because of the Union's history of being controlled by the Party or the government. After independence, the first Congress of the U.G.T.A.,[72] led by cadres who had expressed their attachment to socialism, asked for participation in power and the autonomy of their central organ from the Party. While the Congress was in session, the Secretary General of the F.L.N., Mohammed Khider, had it invaded by unemployed men he had brought along with him, accused the members of syndicalism, dismissed the leadership and replaced it with a new one. From then on, the U.G.T.A. suffered from a lack of autonomy which was manifested in its inability to provide workers with an adequate platform for expressing their interests.

After the March decrees were taken, the U.G.T.A.'s role was confined to helping management committees. In fact, "state officials had not welcomed the interference of the U.G.T.A. in the socialist sector under any pretext."[73] At the same time, the Party-appointed leadership lost control over the more militant local leaders. For example, it was unable to prevent the formation of a Federation of Land Workers (F.N.T.T.), spontaneous strikes and the emergence of an independent secret leadership made up of the militant railroad and post office workers. Faced with an ever-increasing workers' militancy, Ben Bella declared on 1 December 1964 that he was satisfied to see that the "union federation . . . promotes managerial syndicalism". The second Congress sealed the victory of the militant wing of the U.G.T.A. against the party-imposed leadership. The latter was blamed for losing control of the F.N.T.T. to the National Office of Agrarian Reform (O.N.R.A.).[74] A new era of cooperation between Ben Bella and the union thus ensued. In this alliance, "the U.G.T.A. was primarily interested in self-management as an end in itself, while Ben Bella's self-management was primarily a means by which to enhance his popularity and build himself a power base."[75]

After the coup d'état, the need for an efficient union that could mobilize the workers to increase their productivity became one of the main concerns of the new regime. In October 1968, the General Secretary of the F.L.N., Ahmed Kaid, called a conference of union cadres to discuss the reorganization of the union. A document issued by the Party chastized the union leadership for being "imbued with out-of-date principles based on a narrow concern with wages, work conditions and class struggle."[76] At the Union Congress of May 1969, the leadership was thrown out, the militant union centers of Algiers and Skikda (East of Algiers) dissolved and a document outlining the new role of the U.G.T.A. adopted. The control of the latter was all the more important in that the state was now directly engaged in the process of capital accumulation for which it needed unhindered appropriation of labor power. Furthermore, "the government could by no means tolerate the fact that its extremely subtle policy toward foreign capital might be jeopardized by the 'spontaneity' of the masses."[77]

The local and international environments thus constitute two important dimensions in understanding the process of class formation in Algeria. Indeed, decolonization is the affirmation of national identity and the negation of the colonizer. But that affirmation enfolds within a world constructed by an alien entity. Colonialism imposed on Algeria a "form of consciousness as well as of management."[78] Hence, the contradictory assertions of building socialism as a means of negating the colonial capitalistic structures and at the same time appealing to foreign and national private capital to achieve a rapid industrialization. Thus, President Boumédiène could declare that "it is in the national interest, within the framework of our [politico-economic] options . . . not to exclude and especially not to discourage national private investment . . . likewise, foreign capital will be able to complete the national effort in investments, within the framework of our options."79 The contradictions between socialism and national economic independence are recognized, but rapid industrialization which required high rates of investments is given priority. In 1970, the Ministry of Commerce noted that "the state has reserved a favorable treatment to new investments that have been integrated in the country's economy, especially after the promulgation of Ordinance no. 66-204 of 15 September 1966, relating to the Code of Investments."80

THE CODE OF INVESTMENTS

The introduction to the Code of Investments reproduces the minutes of a conference held by the Minister of Finance and Planning on 30 August 1967, which explained the motivations behind the Code:

> The state, manager on behalf of the nation, will take a direct action in all that is commonly called vital sectors. It is because of the multiple obligations it has toward sectors such as National Education, Health, the maintenance and development of the infra-structure, along with sovereignty expenses, that the state cannot throughout a whole phase of development meet, with its sole resources, the expenses required by the sectors of economic construction which generate wealth and employment and which raise the gross national product. That is why the state has decided to adopt systems of mixed corporations or regulated investments in the vital sectors which are under its exclusive authority. In the important sectors, its [the state's] preference is for national investments, be they made on an individual or group basis, for the creation of personal enterprises or mixed corporations at the commune or the district level in accordance with the imperatives of Planning. It is obvious . . . that the investments to be encour-

aged are those relating to consumer goods and to the production
of means that complete the manufacture of capital goods.[81]

The preamble of the Code underscores the inadequacy of the
previous law on investments, passed on 26 July 1963, which
was too limited and too "complicated" and reiterates the
resolution of the Council of the Revolution to define "the
role, place, procedures and legitimate guarantees of private
capital within the framework of economic development."[82]
It also lists a series of advantages granted those who invest in
Algeria. These include a "ten-year total or partial exemption
from real estate tax,"[83] a reduction on duties paid on imported capital goods, "a total, partial or degressive exemption
from the tax on industrial and commercial profits." More
importantly, if an investment is higher than 500,000 Dinars
(about $2,000,000), an "exclusive" production right may be
granted in a specific geographic area. Article 2 of Title 1 of
the Ordinance announces the future publication of a decree
that would define the "sectors considered vital." This decree
has not yet appeared. It is significant that the state may
appeal to national or foreign partners in the organization and
development of the industries defined as vital.

The body of the ordinance outlines the conditions under
which permissions to invest are granted. A National Commission for Investments is created which gives its advice on investments exceeding 500,000 DA, while smaller investments
fall under the control of three regional commissions. It must
be noted that no labor representative sits on the Commissions. The effects of the Code of Investments were summed
up by the Ministry of Commerce, who remarked that "on
31 March 1968, 28 projects, 11 of which were sponsored
by foreign businessmen, had been accepted by the National
Commission on Investments and 41 (amounting to 53 million
Dinars and 7,510 jobs) by the regional commissions . . .
Since then, the National Commission has agreed to an additional 26 projects in October 1968 and 60 in February 1969.
These figures give, if need be, an indication of the importance
of the private sector in the economy of the country."[84]

The same document that reports these figures also notes "a marked regression of the self-managed enterprises since 1965,"[85] although it adds that this regression is only relative because the number of these concerns remains approximately the same since 1965 but was small compared to the expanding development of state enterprises. The following table gives an indication of the number of private enterprises in comparison with national and mixed corporations.

Table 9

Number of Enterprises in 1968[86]

National Corporations	260 or 26.4%
Other Public Enterprises	43 or 4.3%
Private Enterprises	516 or 52.4%
Self-Managed Enterprises	166 or 16.9%

More than 50% of all industrial enterprises employing more than 20 wage laborers are private. The category "other public enterprises" refers to mixed enterprises or enterprises placed under the control of a state agency.

The number of wage-laborers in these various economic sectors was distributed as indicated in Table 10.

Table 10

Employment in the Various Economic Sectors[87]

National Corporations	50,970 or 53 %
Other Public Enterprises	5,400 or 5.6%
Private Enterprises	31,604 or 32.8%
Self-Managed Enterprises	8,287 or 8.6%

More than half of the wage workers are employed by the national corporations and a little more than one-third by the private enterprises. The self-managed sector employs only 8.6% workers, in spite of a relatively large number of self-managed enterprises.

The fact that Algeria undertook to associate national and international private capital to her rapid industrialization cannot be interpreted as a deviation from some imputed socialist ideal.[88] It will be recalled that the first socialist measure was forced upon those in power by the workers. Besides, the Tripoli Program emphasized the need to prevent the bourgeoisie from developing and a desire for social justice. But it did not specifically recommend any definite socialist policy. There have also been precedents to the Algerian case. Russia's N.E.P. was a relaxation of its first phase of communist development. The difference between Algeria and the U.S.S.R., however, lies in the fact that the latter was led by working class representatives organized into a strong party, whereas the former is led by a military faction of the petty-bourgeoisie in alliance with the technocratic bourgeoisie. In this context, the guarantees offered by the Code of Investments ought to be interpreted as a further concession made to the moneyed bourgeois elements within society. The result is that the petty-bourgeoisie, the technocratic and the entrepreneurial bourgeoisies either control or own the means of production, while the rural workers retain a limited number of "socialized" estates, and the urban workers get relatively more jobs. In other words, the specific mode of production chosen, determined as it is by a post-colonial environment, has clarified the content of political opposition. Forced out of the political arena, rural and urban workers provided the petty-bourgeoisie with the opportunity to strike a compromise with the formerly stunted entrepreneurial bourgeoisie.

How long this compromise will be maintained is a function of the extent to which the latter, now relatively freed by the Code of Investments, will become strong enough to play a role in the production process of the "vital sectors" of the economy. It is not unrealistic to predict that this role will be fulfilled in the near future because of the importance of taxation for the Algerian budget. The state derives 85% of its income from tax revenues. Taxes on business turnover represent 48% of expenditure tax, as indicated in Table 11 below. The creation of new private enterprises can, therefore, only increase the national budget in the long run after the period of tax exemption (stipulated by the Code of Investments) is over.

Table 11.[89] *Evolution of Tax Revenues*

Taxes	Year							
	1967		1968		1969		1970	
	Amount (DA)	%	Amount (DA)	%	Amount (DA)	%	Amount (DA)	%
Direct Taxes	749.5	30.0	711.4	25.2	927.7	27.2	1,076.3	26.3
Taxes on Business Turnover	756.0	30.3	905.7	32.1	1,057.1	31.0	1,386.1	33.7
Indirect Taxes	708.8	28.4	759.4	26.9	833.2	24.4	895.3	21.8

This change in the balance of forces is reflected in the change in rhetoric. Whereas Ben Bella often violently referred to the "bourgeois" in his speeches, Boumédiène seldom refers to them as a class. Rather, he chastizes "senior cadres" for their lack of consciousness and their unsatisfactory relationship with the people.[90]

CONCLUSION

The establishment of self-management as a form of economic organization, the subsequent control of the Workers' Union, the creation of national corporations and the Code of Investments proved to be the areas where class interests found expression. Indeed, the official endorsement of self-management led to a crystallization of class interests. Bourgeois members of the government either resigned or entered into underground opposition. At the same time, the petty-bourgeoisie itself split between those who supported self-management and those who saw it as an impediment to the establishment of a strong state power. In command of a well organized and disciplined army, the latter assumed power as the pace of the nationalized industries to be put under self-management quickened. However, unable to run the state apparatus without experts, and imbued with a strong nationalism, the military rallied the technocratic and entrepreneurial bourgeoisies, whose development is served both by the creation of national corporations whose top positions it generally occupies and the guarantees that the Code of Investments offers. As the task of industrialization reaches its momentum and uncovers the antagonistic relationship between national development and dependence on international capital, tensions between the two may reach a breaking point.

The presence of the entrepreneurial bourgeoisie which came into existence without a struggle, the consolidation of the technocratic bourgeoisie at the command posts of the state apparatus, and the assumption of political power by the petty-bourgeoisie have theoretical implications for the concept of class. The ownership of the means of production loses its significance in the Algerian case and becomes an instrument at the service of the ideology in power. The latter defines the mode of appropriation of labor power which, in this case, takes precedence over the ownership of the means of production. Indeed, what has become important is not that classes of individuals have or do not have property but whether they are willing to manage their property under the specific conditions of state capitalistic appropriation of labor power.

6

Class Relations
and
Ideology

The transition from the political act of the coup d'état to what has been referred to as the "redressing"[1] of the political economy of Algeria has implications for the relationship between the classes in and out of power. If, as Gramsci put it, "structures and superstructures form an 'historical bloc',"[2] the links that hold the bloc together must be sought in the ideological structure of the dominant class. Since political legitimacy requires an ideological support, it is necessary to analyse the content of the Algerian ideological structure after 1962 and the process through which this ideology mediates the relations between classes.

THE CONCEPT OF IDEOLOGY

As one of the most abused concepts in the social sciences, ideology has lost the richness of the meaning imparted to it by Hegel and Marx. For Hegel, the problem of ideology or "imperfect consciousness" arose as the result of his conception of history. Hegel viewed history as a universal process with a universal Mind. To uncover the meaning and purpose

119

of history, the finite individual minds must transcend themselves. This transcendence is hampered by the embodiment
of Mind by Matter, which results in the alienation of mental
activity.[3]

Although he rebelled against Hegel's theological conception
of history, Marx retained Hegel's emphasis on the finite characteristic of the manifestations of the Mind. In other words,
Marx also stressed the fact that ideas are different at different
historical epochs. He further retained the "Hegelian convic-
tion that in the final analysis 'history makes sense!' "[4] The
historical process can be understood by men although this
understanding may be obscured. Thus, both false and true
consciousness are possible. The latter, however, may be
achieved through the use of philosophy which functions as a
critique of social reality.

Lichtheim points out that a problem arises with this formulation if it is recalled that Marx also viewed philosophy as the
"ideological reflex" of given social situations. The question
is how a true consciousness of a social reality could also be
conditioned by that reality. In this sense, Marx neglected to
"recognize the dilemma inherent in the principle that modes
of thought are to be understood as 'expressions' of changing
circumstances. He took it for granted that though consciousness is conditioned by existence it can also rise above existence and become a means of transcending the alienation
which sets the historical process in motion."[5]

What Marx took for granted, others have totally ignored.
Thus, the literature that deals with ideology in the "developing" countries is unaware of man's ability to achieve true
consciousness in that they stress the use "modernizing" or
"nationalist" elites make of economic and political ideas.[6]
Ideologies, conceived as tools of manipulation, are studied in
terms of the role they play in bringing about consensus on
economic programs and political decisions. Artificial correla-
tions are established between the degree of "underdevelop-

ment" and the need for an ideology.[7] Furthermore, these needed ideologies are often seen as being imported rather than stemming from the real social processes inherent in the societies studied.[8] Thus, it is claimed that "the principal source of ideological upsurge in the contemporary Middle East is the social dislocation caused by the breakdown of traditional social and political order."[9] It is understood that the traditional order was broken down either by the contact with or domination by Western societies.

IDEOLOGY IN ALGERIA

This chapter will not study the origins or the role of ideology but the content and evolution of the Algerian ideology viewed as the consciousness of classes contending for power. The analysis is based on the historical documents of the Tripoli Program and the Charter of Algiers. President Boumédiène's speeches made between 1965 and 1973 are used, as are additional official documents such as the preambles to the ordinances relating to the reform of self-management and the agrarian revolution. Documents of this kind usually open with statements aimed either at reiterating the prevailing ideology or redefining its content.

The Tripoli Program

It was pointed out earlier that the Program of Tripoli has been drafted by Mohammed Harbi, a Marxist, Mostefa Lacheraf, a former Sorbonne professor, and Mohammed Yazid, an ex-*Centraliste*.[10] Presented at the end of the war, it was the first ideological pronouncement of the F.L.N. meant to provide the newly independent country with a political orientation. The Program was voted without any debate taking place.[11] This unanimous vote may reflect a consensus over the basic principles the Program contained. The striking feature of this Program is its revolutionary indictment of the forces that maintained Algeria in an arrested socio-economic position and of the forces that might hinder her future growth. These are identified as colonialism, imperialism and the possible rise of a "middle class" that might consolidate itself with the help of the former colonizer. Aside from this, the Program is moderate in its recommendations for the reconstruction of the country.

The opening part of the Program condemns, among others, the Evian Accords which put an end to the war as part of a neo-colonialist strategy aimed at maintaining former colonies under the yoke of their colonizers. This condemnation of the Evian Accords reveals a conflict between bourgeois and radical petty-bourgeois over the issue of war and peace. The former were in favor of negotiating with France as early as possible, while the latter were inclined to struggle until they were able to force France to negotiate without being able to impose her own terms for peace talks.[12] This awareness of the reality of neo-colonialism and imperialism is so pervasive that the promotion of an anti-imperialist foreign policy is seen as "the indispensible corollary of the realization of our domestic objectives."[13] This anti-imperialist foreign policy finds expression in a support for "all liberation movements" and "movements fighting for unity." International cooperation, especially with Asian, Latin American, African and socialist countries, is recommended so that Algeria may contribute to curbing the arms race and nuclear tests.

When approaching matters of domestic concern, the Program often appears vague and at times contradictory. An analysis of the Algerian social structure identifies the existence of four classes, a proletariat, a peasantry, a petty-bourgeoisie and a bourgeoisie. All of these classes are described as having contributed to the revolution, although the motivations of some are questioned in reference to their genuine support of a new Algeria. It is stressed, however, that "it is in general the peasants and the workers who have been the active base of the movement and who have given it its essential popular character."[14] Hence, the rejection of the bourgeoisie as a class that can enhance or further the revolution. Indeed, the "tasks of the democratic revolution in Algeria are tremendous. They cannot be accomplished by a social class, the bourgeoisie, however enlightened it may be. Only the people are prepared to carry them out, that is, the peasantry, the workers in general, the youth and the revolutionary intellectuals. [Thus, the] Peoples' Democratic Revolution is the deliberate construction of the nation within the framework of socialist principles and of power in the hands of the people."[15] In order to be fully integrated within the nation, the bourgeoisie must "lend its support to the revolutionary cause and renounce its desire to direct the destinies of the country."[16] To combat bourgeois aspirations, there is need for developing an ideology also referred to as "political and social philosophy."

In an effort to answer the criticism that the F.L.N. did not have an ideology, it emphasizes that there is "no ready-made ideology; *there is a constant creative ideological effort.*"[17] The Program also recalled that "during the war of liberation the mere military struggle was enough to induce the revolutionary hopes of the people and profit by them. Today . . . it is essential to rekindle without delay the spirit of the masses on the ideological level."[18] The new philosophy should be rid of "subjectivism" and "moralism" which is "an idealistic and infantile tendency that wishes to change society and resolve its problems through the aid of moral values alone." Further, "a national revolutionary and scientific culture" must be worked out. The stress placed on the scientific aspect of culture constitutes a direct attack on "petty-bourgeois moralism," namely, "the practice of using Islam for demagogic purposes in order to avoid real problems . . . For us, Islam, freed of all the excrescences and superstitions that have stifled or tainted it, should be manifest not only in religion as such but also in these two vital areas: culture and character."[19] In fact, apart from the remnants of "administrative feudalism," those engaged in "clericalism" are condemned as the colonialists' "henchmen."

Regarding the social and economic reconstruction of Algeria, the Program upholds "a social policy benefiting the masses in order to raise the living standards of labor, eliminate illiteracy, improve housing, health, emancipate women and create a national economy. The implementation of the social welfare policy is entrusted to mass organizations and to the army. The guidelines for the creation of a national economy include:

1. The principle that *"the land belongs to those who work it."*[20] This promotes a limitation on large holdings, the setting up of "state farms on part of the expropriated land, the participation of the workers in the management and in the profits of such farms, the cancellation of the debts incurred by peasants, *khammes* [sharecroppers] to landowners, money lenders and public services," and the free distribution of land to landless peasants.[21]

2. *The nationalization of credit and foreign trade, mineral and energy resources*

3. *The industrialization of the country through the creation of heavy industry under state control.* This last point is not specified except in warning against the fact that "the state should not contribute as it has done in some countries to the creation of an industrial base by which the local middle-class can profit. It is the state's duty to limit the development of this class by appropriate measures." At the same time, private initiative is to be encouraged within the bounds of a planned economy. Likewise, foreign capital is welcomed but "within certain limits."[22]

Planning is upheld as an ultimate value, even though it "will face serious obstacles such as the lack of capital, qualified personnel and the cultural lag." It is affirmed that "between stagnation in a liberal system and progress through economic planning, our Party chooses planning."[23] The Party, according to the Program, was to be physically distinct from the state. Its role was to "draw the guidelines of policy for the Nation."

In conclusion, the Tripoli Program stressed an ideology that did not, in effect, transcend the various statements made by the F.L.N. throughout the war.[24] Thus, the rejection of imperialism and economic liberalism, the assertion of nationalism in cultural and economic affairs along with the affirmation of the sovereignty of the people were in keeping with the experience of the war and the desire to overthrow a colonial regime. Socialism is rarely mentioned as the political and economic orientation of the future Algerian state. Emphasis is placed on raising the standard of living of the people rather than on achieving socio-economic equality. Similarly, planning is adopted not as part of a commitment to a world view but because it prevents stagnation. This moderate approach is also illustrated by the treatment that the bourgeoisie receives. The latter is discarded from the task of leading the revolution not necessarily because it may distort it but because the task itself is too big to be carried out by one class alone. The Tripoli Program is sometimes interpreted as revolutionary because it upheld the principle of "the land to those who work it," thereby advocating an equitable land reform.[25] Considering that the Army of National Liberation was recruited mostly among the peasantry, the adoption of this principle was practically inevitable, no matter what group led the country after independence.

The first government (1962—1965) upheld the value of nationalism in both culture and economics. Arabic was restored as a first language in schools, although, at the same time, French was maintained and even developed as part of a program of cultural exchange provided for by the Evian Accords On the economic level, nationalizations of land and industrial enterprises were the most spectacular measures taken, as was indicated in the previous chapter.

In 1964, a new document was issued by the Party Congress under the name of the Charter of Algiers. This Charter essentially specifies and, at times, redefines the pronouncements of the Tripoli Program. A first draft apparently met with the opposition of a respected F.L.N. member who presented a counter-draft.[26] It is not clear what were the exact differences between the two drafts which were combined to form the final text of the Charter.

The Charter of Algiers

The Charter of Algiers differs from the Tripoli Program in that it was based on two years of experience in government. This also accounts for its more detailed treatment of issues that were merely touched upon in the Tripoli Program and its introduction of new themes relating to the socio-economic development of the country. It retains the anti-imperialist ideology expounded by the Program and stresses its deleterious effects on the task of independent socio-economic reconstruction. The politico-economic orientation of Algeria is defined as socialist. Socialism is construed as being made possible by the "global dynamics of the social struggle as it manifested itself just after the liberation of the country."[27] This hints at the class struggle as a cause of the July 1962 crisis. The main foundation of socialism is said to be constituted by self-management in both agriculture and industry. "In this process, the role of the urban and rural workers involved in self-management will become more and more decisive because the social foundation of the revolutionary power can only be the masses of workers allied to the poor peasants of the traditional sector and to the revolutionary intellectuals."[28] The struggle against "exploitative private property both in the countryside and in the city"[29] must be carried out in order to improve the process of socialization of the economy. However, the small "non-exploitative property" must be respected. This is evidently a concession made to the small peasants who do not use hired labor to work their plots. Enemies of socialism are denounced and their attitudes accounted for in historical terms. Thus, colonialism is seen as having "developed among Algerians habits of consumption incommensurate with the real capabilities of the country. Aggravated by the war, these habits constitute an extraordinary factor of corruption. The Party cannot accept the existing income disparities without cutting itself off from the masses. It must vigorously combat the parasitic conceptions born under conditions of forced exploitation of the mass of laborers. The successful completion of this struggle is linked to the elimination of the privileged strata from prominence and to the exercise of the political and managerial responsibilities of the laboring masses themselves."[30] The social structure is analyzed along the same lines as in the Tripoli Program. However, to the bourgeoisie which was estimated at 50,000 (or 1/40 of the total population) and the petty-bourgeoisie, "a potential source of individuals with an anti-socialist ideology," is added "a new social stratum being rapidly formed" in the "administrative apparatus, the state and the economy."[31] "By its position in the state machinery and the economy, this force may become considerably more dangerous for the socialist and democratic evolution of the revolution than any other existing social force in the country."[32] It is not made clear whether this "force" is, in effect, the outgrowth of the petty-bourgeois stratum which General de Gaulle was eager to promote as an intermediate entity (a "third force") between the revolutionary fraction of the F.L.N. and its more moderate but also unpopular fraction. De Gaulle was hoping to achieve his goal through a program of socio-economic development known under the *"Plan de Constantine,"* which was meant, among other things, to give Algerians access to public functions. The Charter of Algiers does point out, in this respect, that "the F.L.N. leadership has failed in not having understood soon enough that the third force was a social phenomenon linked to the leading organs of the revolution and that it aspired to organize Algeria in favor of the exploitative strata and to hitch the country up to the trailer of imperialism."[33] This statement provides a further interpretation of the July crisis in class terms.

A third theme in the ideological foundations laid out by the Charter is self-management as the principle of economic organization guiding the transition period. The latter is described as being particularly problematic. Indeed, it is characterized by the contradiction between "methods and structures that belong to a capitalist development" and socialist goals.[34] At the same time, the scarcity of qualified personnel and the necessity of offering them high rewards in order to attract them may lead to the creation of a "caste" whose technical privileges may be transformed into political ones. As to the task of industrial development, it is based on the principle of planning as indicated in the Tripoli Program, but it is described in more detail. Thus, "mixed and national corporations" should be created in order to strengthen the socialist sector and fight private enterprises. However, it is significant that the Charter recognizes that "one should not forget that cooperatives as well as mixed and national corporations or state capitalism can take on a very different significance depending on whether the state is itself dominated by the socialist or reactionary forces."[35] "If the state represents the interests of the national bourgeoisie, the mixed corporations will serve as the articulation between the interests of the latter and those of the imperialists. If, on the other hand, the state represents the interests of the people of whom it is in charge, the association with foreign private groups could, under certain conditions, be beneficial."[36]

This increased importance given to the state constitutes the main contradiction of the Charter, especially if it is recalled that it praises self-management as the principle of socialist Algeria that brings about "the beginning of the reign of freedom."[37] This contradiction is further illustrated by a warning against the "forced" search for a maximum rate of capital accumulation which can be "transformed into its opposite" and may lead to a "bureaucratism which is the very negation of socialism."[38] Indeed, it is not specifically indicated how the state would create national and mixed corporations while avoiding bureaucratization when it has already been pointed out that a new class was in formation in the very administrative and economic state apparatus. A general solution is proposed in the section of the Charter dealing with the state. It is recommended that "key positions of all the branches of the state apparatus be assigned to militants whose political training and strong and vigilant consciousness of the interests of the revolution constitute indispensable guarantees for the Party and the masses of workers. It is imperative that the appointment of the cadres to all the branches of the state be subordinated to the Party's approval."[39] However, given the scarcity of cadres among "militants", the solution offered appears to have been academic.

The fourth ideological theme contained in the Charter is democracy. The arena where democracy will be tested is stipulated as the Party. The latter is meant to create a "new conception of democracy." "This is a democracy whereby the workers' collective will express itself fully. . . . The synthesis between a direct democracy wherever it is materially possible and a strictly controlled centralization will enable the organization to renew itself continuously, adapt to new situations and display an extreme flexibility."[40] This new democracy will thus prevent a cleavage between the concrete, day-to-day economic and political problems and more general societal problems; it will also prevent depoliticization which is a result of isolation from the decision-making centers.[41]

Social equality is the last ideological theme. This equality is to be achieved through mass education, the protection of veterans, orphans and war widows and the "emancipation" of women.[42]

In conclusion, the Charter of Algiers promotes an ideology based on anti-imperialism, nationalism, socialism, democracy and social equality. Its repeated emphasis on socialism marks its major difference from the Tripoli Program. It also points up the predominance of the political over the economic, thereby admitting that its economic recommendations and ideals may be implemented within a political perspective alien to socialism. In other words, it is clearly admitted that unless the leadership is committed to socialism, all the economic solutions offered in the Charter may be used to serve a social system alien to socialism. It specifically states that "the technical formulas of organization can never be considered as solutions that bring with them the socialist ideal."[43]

Class Relations

How does this ideology mediate the relations between classes? It was pointed out earlier that the Tripoli Program was the product of the collaboration of a group of men representing different political orientations. The Charter of Algiers was first drafted by a group of Marxists and later edited to overcome objections made by non-Marxists. It appears that two years of government had radicalized the individuals in power, thereby producing cleavages that may reflect "irreconcilable internal contradictions."[44] However, the solution to these contradictions did not result in a change in the prevailing ideology. From 1962 to 1965, the Ben Bella regime attempted (regardless of what its real motivations were) to build a socialist society. The endorsement of self-management, nationalizations of land and industrial enterprises, along with the organization of a series of national campaigns for, among others, tree planting, fund raising and literacy, gave some substance to the pronouncements of both the Tripoli Program and the Charter of Algiers. At the same time, the government's inability to implement its program in absolute terms revealed an increasing gap between ideology and reality.

The structure of self-management was undermined through the misapplication of the March decrees. The Workers' Union was prevented from functioning democratically and from organizing the rural workers effectively. On the level of class relations, ideology appears to have promoted dissension between the urban working class and the fraction of the petty-bourgeoisie in power on the one hand, and between the latter and the national bourgeoisie on the other hand. Those segments of the peasantry involved in self-management remained content with the status quo although critical of it, as was demonstrated at the Congress of the Industrial Sector.

With the 1965 coup d'état, a new use of the same ideology took place. A selective process of both reification and interpretation was started. Thus, the rationale for the containment of self-management, the creation of national and private corporations, along with the specific use of Islam in politics, provide partial illustrations of this process. Before analyzing each of these factors, it must be pointed out that, in his proclamation of 19 June 1965, President Boumédiène declared that "it is obvious that the fundamental choices [made] are irreversible and the achievements of the revolution inalienable. Nevertheless, only rigorous corrective steps and a firm and clear policy can lead us out of the general morass which is exhibited in low productivity, decreasing economic profits and disquieting dis-investments."[45] This was a prelude to a more direct speech where the President attacked "demagogic socialism" and reiterated that the "fundamental choices contained in the Tripoli Program and the Charter of Algiers recapture the spirit of November 1st . . . In this sense, socialism is part of our historic heritage."[46]

These statements evoke the notion of a deviation from the revolutionary orientation of the country as outlined in the Tripoli Program and the Charter of Algiers. New decisions were announced, therefore, to redress the situation that existed on 1 November 1954. This announcement meant that the political forces then in existence should be brought back in order to contribute to the revival of a specific socialism implicit in the Algerian culture since 1 November 1954. This strategy provides an example of the cooptation, by one fraction of a class, of the ideology expounded by another fraction. At the same time that this ideology is coopted, it is also undermined by being reinterpreted in terms that are familiar on a conceptual level and yet have ceased to be part of daily practices. In this context, Islam as a philosophy emphasizing a solidarity among men that transcends race, class or nationality is reaffirmed because it conforms to the socialist ideal of a classless society. However, no attention is given to the fact that the original Islamic philosophy has been undermined by the French colonial domination.[47]

The French colonists' policy of "assimilation" in effect meant both the erosion of the economic foundation of the Muslim community and the replacement of Islamic law by French law. Independent Algeria carried this process of erosion even further. While upholding Islam as the distinguishing feature of Algeria, the government is nevertheless led to use and perpetuate a legal system modelled after the French. Yet, on the ideological level, these changes that affected Islamic practice are ignored, and socialism is claimed to be already contained in this practice.

The containment of self-management follows the same pattern of reification and interpretation. Thus, after reiterating that self-management is one of the many achievements of the Algerian Revolution, President Boumédiène remarks that it will be supported by the state if "this system turns out to be profitable."[48] In none of his speeches does he refer to the expansion of self-management to newly created industries. In the preamble of the ordinance establishing the Agrarian Revolution, it is stated that self-management is an ideal and not a unique road to socialism. It is further explained that it cannot be achieved at present because Algeria lacks the necessary material conditions and the required personnel.[49] Likewise, the creation of national and mixed corporations is actually an implementation of the prescriptions contained in the Charter of Algiers. At the same time, the structure and functions of these corporations are a departure from the Charter. Indeed, up to 1971, national corporations were governed by French law, ill-adapted to the socialist goals of the country. Some operated as both "anonymous" and "public corporations."[50] A committee sponsored by the Ministry of Commerce was formed to reorganize the legal framework within which the corporations should operate. However, although the formal legislation of these corporations has become more "national," their structure is still patterned after capitalist corporations.[51] But, because they are state-owned, the capitalist structure of the national corporations is not expected to have any significant effect on the socialist goals of the country.

Indeed, what is at stake is less a specific mode of economic development than the pursuit of productivity and profit (*rentabilité*).

A third example of ideological manipulation is the interpretation of the role of Islam in the social and economic development of Algeria. It was mentioned earlier that the Tripoli Program denounced the distortions that Islam was subjected to during the colonial era. Superstitions, the cult of the saints, the obscurantism of semi-literate clerics were contrasted with pure, original Islam that emphasized the search for knowledge and science. It is incorrect, in this respect, to maintain that the "Charter of Algiers represents a retreat from the secularism of the Tripoli Program."[52] In fact, both documents stress the importance of a "national, revolutionary and scientific culture."[53] The passage in the Tripoli Program dealing with culture was reproduced word for word in the Charter of Algiers. Therefore, the alleged disagreement between the members of the military and the Marxist members of Ben Bella's Cabinet on religious matters that apparently accounted for the difference between the two documents is also inadequate. Islam is often advanced as the second main reason, besides the political role of the army, for the 1965 coup. This type of explanation overlooks the fact that Ben Bella was as much an advocate of an Islamic Algerian culture as is Boumédiène. Under Ben Bella's government, Muslim precepts such as fasting and abstinence from alcohol were enforced, whereas under the present regime they are less so.

Islam as an explanatory device for socio-political phenomena fits in the sociological perspective that focuses on the study of elites and their conflicts at the expense of the dynamics of the relationship between elites and larger social groups. In the words of a student of Islamic societies, "the emphasis on the role of the Muslim religion, added or substituted to the role of the will to an ethno-nationalist identity, cannot dispense with the study of internal dynamics. The role of Islam is real, but it cannot be understood without seeking its relation to the external or internal dynamic, that is, to the larger external social projects (autonomy, power) and the internal ones. . . . No internal or external social project is purely religious."[54]

Indeed, both Ben Bella and Boumédiène used religion as a tool for maintaining unity over economic development. They differ in the specific Islamic tenets to which they appealed. Ben Bella appealed to the more universalistic principles contained in Islam that transcend social, ethnic and national differences. Hence the presence in Ben Bella's entourage of non-Algerian counsels whom Boumédiène derided in his 1965 speeches. The Islamic components emphasized by the latter are those relating to the *Umma*, or Islamic community, as opposed to the non-Islamic world. This stress on a non-adulterated Islamic identity is reflected on the economic level as a socialism adapted to the Algerian reality. Socialism and Islam are thus seen as complementary by Ben Bella, whereas Boumédiène never explicitly made the connection between the two. Boumédiène's use of Islam appears to be a tool against communism rather than one for the construction of a socialist society. Thus, it may be claimed that the "antinomy was not between Islam and Socialism but between Islam and Communism."[55]

It must be pointed out that in this context, Islam as an ideology has been compared to Communism and the relationship between the two described as antagonistic, cooperative or neutral, depending on whether doctrinal differences or international strategy prevail.[56] In this sense, the *Ulemas'* (Islamic theologians') alliance with the army in 1965 may be interpreted as a protest against the foreign, "communist," entourage of the former President Ben Bella. Interestingly enough, after the coup, a Ministry of "Original Affairs" in charge of matters related to religion was created. But at the same time, fundamental Islamic tenets were no longer enforced with the same intransigence as under Ben Bella's government.

CONCLUSION

The ideology of the faction of class in power underwent two evolutions. First, the pronouncements of the Tripoli Program concerning land reform became radicalized in that self-management was accepted as the Algerian form of economic organization. This appears to have had the effect of splitting up the very social forces that voted in favor of the Program in 1962. After the 1965 coup, the ideological foundations of both the Tripoli Program and the Charter of Algiers were proclaimed "irreversible choices", and an attempt at detaching ideas from their social base was made in order to effect shifts in the ideological content of these documents. Hence President Boumédiène's repeated remark that "socialism is an ideology, and any ideology that tends to be personalized is doomed to failure."[57] This was meant to both explain the coup and charge his predecessor with "deviationism." Thus, the ideology of socialism is retained, but its actual content and the method to go about it are subject to change. Paradoxically enough, this made it possible to say that the Tripoli Program and the Charter of Algiers were part of "paper work . . . destined for foreign consumption."[58]

The role that ideology played in the emergence of a petty-bourgeoisie as a dominant class was twofold. First, it enabled one faction of this class to seek support from the peasantry while denouncing their common enemy, the bourgeoisie. Second, it permitted the more conservative faction of this class to appeal to the all-encompassing aim of national reconstruction that transcends class differences, while at the same time denouncing the "enemies of socialism and the revolution". The latter are referred to as cadres who do not fulfill their functions conscientiously enough, rather than as a class hostile to a system of economic organization intended to improve the material conditions of workers and peasants.

The roles thus played by ideology in class emergence and crystallization have theoretical implications. In the Algerian case, ideology did not "amount to a distorted interpretation of this [man's] history or a complete abstraction from it."[59] Rather, it started out as a program of action that legitimized specific socio-economic and political orientations. However, the characteristic feature of ideology as being "directly inter-woven with the material activity and the material relation-ships of men shows that changes at the ideological level re-flect changes in the social structure."[60] In Algeria, ideology shifted from a reference to the concrete to a reference to the abstract. Indeed, as mentioned above, efforts were made after the coup to detach ideology from its social foundations so that it acquires a life of its own, independent of the reality of which it is expected to provide an interpretation.

The significance of the Algerian experience lies in its revela-tion of the genetic process through which the ideology ex-pounded by one faction of a class is used to promote the antithetical interests of another faction. The process of rein-terpreting the ideological principles contained in the Tripoli Program and the Charter of Algiers led to their reification. The result is that concepts such as socialism, self-manage-ment, anti-imperialism and democracy either become abstract ideals to achieve in the remote future or are claimed to be alien to the specifically Algerian reality and therefore require adjustment. Either way, the urgency of action inherent in ideology conceived of as a program of action is no longer a concern. In this sense, the process of abstraction that the Al-gerian ideology has undergone has enabled the politically dominant class to achieve the unity it requires to promote its interests while making concessions to the social forces that support it. Hence the policy of encouraging and protecting Algerian private capital. It is not clear at this point whether ideological elaboration and political power are in the same hands. However, there is evidence that economic power is flowing to the entrepreneurial faction of the bourgeoisie, whereas the technocratic faction has increasing administra-tive control over the means of production.

7

Class
and
Party

What is the role of the Party in the formation of classes in
Algeria? An answer to this question revolves around the
determination of the process through which the F.L.N.
evolved from a war organization to a political party. It
must also be sought in the formal structure of the Party and
the functions it fulfills within Algerian society.

THE CONCEPT AND ROLE OF THE SINGLE PARTY

Algeria shares with a number of African and Asian societies
a single-party system of government.[1] In most cases, the
single-party state is "an outgrowth of the mobilization of per-
sons and groups in the pre-independence period."[2] At first
studied by political scientists in terms of their "totalitarian"
characteristics, single parties in the newly independent countries were later seen as tools for "building national unity"

and "promoting economic development."[3] In reality, economic development has proven to be the concern of the state rather than the Party. In this respect, what is most important is not the rise of the single party but "its rapid loss of meaning."[4] In the Algerian case, rather than declining, the F.L.N., in effect, has lived out its purpose. Before independence, it provided a framework in which all classes might unite against the colonial regime. After independence, it could not evolve into the Party of one class without antagonizing the other classes. It could only serve as the symbol of a bygone era where the unity of all Algerians had to be preserved.

The socialist claims of Algeria, however, required that an organized party be set up to fulfill the revolution. But Algeria's post-colonial chaotic situation made the building of a state apparatus an even more urgent necessity. It will be shown that a peculiar conception and use of the Party resulted from these circumstances. Both Ben Bella and Boumédiène viewed the Party in isolation from classes. At the same time, this conception is implicitly denied by the theory set forth in the Charter of Algiers which emphasizes the role of a vanguard Party that serves as the political guide of the government and the mobilizer of the masses against the counter-revolutionary bourgeoisie.   Attempts made by Government and Party to conform to this theory led to inconsistencies that make the F.L.N. appear as more of a symbolic than a real entity.

A comparison of the F.L.N. with the Chinese Communist Party which faced similar problems as the F.L.N. will underscore the particular characteristics of the F.L.N.'s role in Algerian society. This comparison is relevant to the extent that among the individuals who drafted the Charter of Algiers some were familiar with Marx's writings. Besides, like China, the Algerian revolution was based predominantly on the peasantry and later met with analogous problems of how to integrate non-revolutionary groups in revolutionary institutions.

THE F.L.N. BEFORE INDEPENDENCE

Structure

Like the Soviet and Chinese Communist Parties, the Algerian F.L.N. arose in a revolutionary situation. Its aim was the seizure of state power through the liberation of the country from colonial domination. Like the Chinese and Cuban Communist Parties, the F.L.N. was supported by peasants and led mostly by urban cadres. It is, however, the peculiar characteristic of the F.L.N. that it could not "be identified with either a union of parties or with a single party. . . . The F.L.N. is not a purely ideological party of the liberal Western type, nor a class party in Marxist terms, nor an aristocratic and conservative party of the Fascist type, but a revolutionary equalitarian and democratic party."[5] Indeed, the Party was open to "every Algerian man or woman who is engaged in fighting for the objectives of the organization to which he belongs, in accordance with the rules currently enforced therein, and who fulfills all his obligations to that organization."[6]

This party encourages "constructive criticism," and the "leaders whatever their place in the hierarchy enjoy the same rights and are subject to the same duties as the rank and file."[7] The Party is claimed to be a "union party"[8] that includes all members of the various organizations, such as the students' Union Générale des Etudiants Musulmans Algériens, the workers' U.G.T.A. and the Algerian National Liberation Army (A.L.N.). Despite allegations to the contrary, this characteristic of the F.L.N. is not unique. In fact, it is similar to the Soviet Union's Communist Party, which is claimed to be the "expression of the interests of the entire nation," as distinguished from the Chinese Communist Party, which "represents the interests of the people."[9] The only difference is that the F.L.N. anticipated the formation of the nation, whereas the Soviets had already achieved it. What is unique about the pre-independence F.L.N. is its sophisticated organization within Algeria, an organization set up to supersede

the existing French bureaucratic structure. Indeed, the first
Congress held in the Soummam Valley in August 1956 decided to create "Peoples' Assemblies" (*Djemaas*) throughout
the Algerian territory, "conclusively replacing French administration and French courts of law and giving the Algerian
people the opportunity to manage their own affairs." These
assemblies controlled "supplies, the collection of taxes, the
administration of justice, the recruiting of *mudjahidine*,[10]
security services and intelligence."[11] Algeria was divided into
six *wilayas* (districts) each *wilaya* into *mintaqas* (zones), and
the latter into *nahias* (regions), *qism* (sectors), *duars* (small
villages) and *mechtas* (hamlets).

The Soummam Congress also resulted in the creation of a
provisional legislative body, the Conseil National de la Révolution Algérienne, whose members were nominated rather
than elected because the war had made it impossible to hold
national elections. The C.N.R.A., which had not only legislative powers but also control over the government of the
country until its political liberation, was responsible to the
National Congress, thereby ensuring the primacy of the Party
over the parliament. The C.N.R.A., in turn, appointed a
Coordinating and Executive Committee (C.C.E.), which
"foreshadowed the institution of government."[12] Indeed, by
1958 it was divided into several specialized departments
which resulted in the creation of a Provisional Government
(Gouvernement Provisoire de la République Algérienne) appointed by the National Council, to which it is accountable,"
thereby still maintaining the control of the Party over the
government.

Dysfunctions

The F.L.N., an organization of all Algerians, rich and poor,
politically moderate and revolutionary, underwent both a
structural and a functional change with the proclamation of
independence. The Tripoli meeting of the C.N.R.A. in the
summer of 1962 debated the creation of a Political Bureau
that would supersede the C.N.R.A. and, under the leadership

of its general secretaries, create a Party according to the principles enunciated in the Tripoli Program. It is important to point out that the latter chastised the F.L.N. on five points:

1. The F.L.N. misunderstood the "deep revolutionary potentialities of the people of the countryside. It neglected the fact that a colonial war cannot be won according to a simplistic predetermined schema. It did not allow for the emergence on the individual level of a total questioning of the social order that must find expression in new structures." What this means essentially is that the F.L.N. was not sensitive to the changes that occurred amidst the rural population as a result of their involvement in a protracted war. Indeed, it is explicitly stated that the F.L.N. cadres "are often likely to underestimate or overestimate certain new facts, to refer to other revolutionary movements, to practice ideological mimetism, all of which often give their conceptions eclectic and unrealistic characteristics."[13] This criticism bears some resemblance to Mao's attack on "commandism," which results from "overstepping the level of political consciousness of the masses and violating the principles of voluntary mass action," and "tailism," which comes from "falling below the level of political consciousness of the masses and violating the principle of leading the masses forward."[14] The following criticism of the F.L.N. makes this comparison even more relevant.

2. The F.L.N. allegedly allowed a lag to occur between "on the one hand, the collective consciousness which had for a long time matured through its contact with realities and, on the other hand, the practice of F.L.N. authority at all levels."

3. The F.L.N. was unable to prevent the abuse of authority, which resulted in a "feudal turn of mind" and a subsequent "formalism."

4. The F.L.N.'s lack of ideological firmness provided the proper conditions for the flourishing of a "petty-bourgeois

spirit," especially among "cadres and youth. This spirit
which is readily suffused with a pseudo-intellectualism carries, without knowing it, the most frivolous and wicked concepts produced by the Western mind." This condition may
confine the "future Algerian State to a mediocre bureaucracy
that will be unpopular if not in fact, at least in principle."[15]

5. The F.L.N. was responsible for a "lag" (*décalage*) between
the leadership and the mass of the people. This was made
possible after the Coordinating and Executive Committee had
to leave Algeria to hide abroad. The most significant result of
this lag was the progressive depoliticization of the structures
that remained in Algeria and of those that were transferred to
or were created abroad."[16]

The Tripoli Program also points out that, in practice, there
was no distinction between the F.L.N. and the G.P.R.A.
"The amalgamation of the state institutions and the F.L.N.'s
has reduced the latter to a mere managerial administrative apparatus. In the interior [of Algeria] this amalgamation resulted in stripping the F.L.N. of its responsibilities in favor of
the A.L.N.; and, with the war, it practically annihilated
it."[17] In short, on the eve of independence, the Party existed
only in name.

THE F.L.N. AFTER INDEPENDENCE

After independence, the first political debate focused on the
elaboration of a constitution rather than the organization of
the Party. During the debate that took place in August, 1963,
it was pointed out that "before voting a constitution, a Congress should be held to draft a doctrine, a program, to seek
new elites that take their responsibilities in total awareness
of the situation. Strong power threatens to become arbitrary
in the face of a non-organized Party and an Assembly that is
reduced to playing a minor role."[18] A response to this statement reveals the vicious circle in which defenders and opponents of an immediate restructuring of the Party were

locked: "The Party is not sufficiently structured, that is true; but it is precisely because of this that it is not in a position to hold a Congress before the adoption of the Constitution."[19] The latter describes the functions of the Party as follows: "It defines the policy of the nation and inspires the action of the state, controls the work of the National Assembly and the government, reflects the deep aspirations of the masses which it educates and leads."[20] But the installation of government institutions prior to the consolidation of the Party foreclosed the implementation of these functions.

Structure

The Party's inability to play any significant role after independence has been traced to two competing conceptions of its structure held by Mohammed Khider, Secretary General of the Political Bureau, and Rabah Bitat, a Party cadre, on the one hand, and Ben Bella on the other. The former favored a mass party, whereas the latter advocated the idea of a vanguard party, a "party of militants" and not a "political gang, a political oligarchy."[21] The first Congress of the F.L.N. that convened after independence defined and laid out the new structure of the Party. Article Two of the Annex to the Charter of Algiers specifies that "the F.L.N. must be neither a mass Party, a formula that presents the danger of diluting responsibility, of negative action from representatives of the petty-bourgeoisie against the population, nor an elite Party comprising intellectuals and professional politicians cut off from the people and reality."[22] The F.L.N. is further defined as "the vanguard of the Algerian people. It derives its strength from the masses of peasants and workers and the revolutionary intellectuals: it is the guide of the people in their struggle for complete independence, socialism, democracy and peace linked to peoples' demands for liberation."[23] In comparison, the Chinese Party rules state that "the Chinese Communist Party is the vanguard of the Chinese working class. Its goals are to realize socialism and communism in China."[24] There appears to be more awareness on the part of the Chinese of cleavages and contradictions among the people. The Algerians' desire to project an image of unity of the people necessarily drives them to the assumption of class-lessness, which, in turn, is contradicted by the enumeration of a limited number of social groups from which the Party "derives its strength."

Membership in the Party is open to any Algerian aged at least eighteen who has taken part in the war of national liberation and who pledges "actively [to] militate and regularly pay his dues, to conform to the socialist orientation of the Party and to display moral qualities."[25] A Party militant cannot belong to another political organization. Membership is divided into militants and *adhérents* (auxiliaries). The latter must be sponsored by two Party members and receive political training for at least one year before being recommended for membership in militants' cells. Auxiliaries cannot vote or run for office within the Party. All militants have the same rights and duties and are encouraged to "practice criticism and self-criticism as a method for continuously improving the work of the Party."[26]

These membership rules are more restrictive than those of the Chinese. The latter do not list participation in the revolution as a criterion. Rather, membership is open to every Chinese citizen "who works, who does not exploit the labor of others, who recognizes the Party Program and rules."[27]

The F.L.N. was to be governed by the rules of democratic centralism, which "combine genuine democracy for each one of its members, a leadership that is necessarily centralized, and discipline."[28]

The organic structure of the Party is made up of the "cell," which includes 20 to 50 members at the neighborhood or village level, the *kasma*, or Party council at the communal level, and the "federation," a council at the regional level. Each level has a committee. The leaders of cells are organized into *kasma* councils and the latter into federation councils.

The cells fulfill the function of disseminating and explaining the Party's decisions, training Party members and workers, "mobiliz[ing] the masses" to implement "the objectives of the socialist revolution." The *kasma* councils discuss all problems posed by the Party. They also review reports from the *kasma* committees and choose the members and leader of the latter.

The supreme organ of the F.L.N. is the national Congress. This Congress ordinarily meets every other year. Between meetings, the highest institution is the " Central Committee," whose task is the implementation of decisions taken by the Congress, the control of the Party's finances and the creation of new structures. On the recommendation of the Political Bureau, it also appoints members to government, parliament and state positions. The Political Bureau "executes and applies the decisions taken by the Central Committee, before which it is responsible." Its activity is directed, coordinated and controlled by a secretary general. The Political Bureau also controls "the politicization of the army."[29]

Although it was endowed for the first time with a precise structure, the Party does not appear to have fulfilled its functions, as was demonstrated by the political unrest of the summer of 1964, riots and labor strikes, along with the growing dysfunctioning of self-management. The Party's inefficiency would be due to the heterogeneous composition of the Central Committee. Indeed, the latter included opposition leaders and relatively unknown men from the various national organizations. This has been interpreted as Ben Bella's desire to "balance off the influence of the army by reintegrating previously hostile elements into the F.L.N. leadership, while at the same time searching out virtual sub-elites to bolster his own unstable position as head of the Party."[30]

Role of the Party in National Crises

In the summer of 1964, armed opposition to the government started in Kabylia and in Southern and Western Algeria. As a result, the Central Committee expelled five of its members and formed popular militias, while at the same time the army, under Boumédiène's leadership, successfully destroyed all armed dissidents. In all this, the Party did not intervene in any significant fashion. It was also unable to prevent or mitigate the instability of local government; prefects, for example, were changed over two hundred times.[31] Furthermore, a series of demonstrations occurred between May 1963 and February 1964 involving war veterans, war widows and unemployed individuals. The largest of these demonstrations took place in Oran, where the prefect's offices were invaded.[32] This is all the more significant in that the Party staged a counter-demonstration, thereby appearing as a force that competes with rather than organizes the masses.[33]

As pointed out in Chapter Three, the Party had already entered in conflict with the Workers' Union (U.G.T.A.), whose leadership it dismissed and replaced. This, however, did not prevent the former Union leaders from agitating amongst the rank-and-file. The Party's control over the Union resulted in the same situation that existed between the Party and the people, namely, a gap between the Party-appointed Union leadership and the workers. Thus, spontaneous strikes occurred that called for the nationalization of enterprises still under French control or, ironically, of socialized firms. The latter demands were made in an effort to remedy the administrative problems that were posed to the worker-managed enterprises.

Attempts at Rebuilding the Party

In June 1964, the Central Committee decided to "take concrete steps for the reorganization and democratization of the Party . . . within two months." The purpose was to establish "a more direct contact between the base and the leadership."[34] However, by the spring of 1965, the projected reorganization was not yet accomplished.

The coup d'état of 19 June 1965 resulted in the dismantling of the Central Committee, which was replaced by a five-man Executive Secretariat. The former Secretary General was replaced by a Coordinator. In September 1967, the Council of the Revolution issued a statement indicating that "the Party apparatus will be reorganized on a new basis."[35] On 5 February 1968, President Boumédiène announced that the Party had priority over the many issues the government had decided to tackle in 1968. "Return to the base" was the motto in accordance with which the Party was to "rely on militants who are *engagés* and convinced of the righteousness of the political line drawn by the Revolutionary Power, and discard all non-*engagés* individuals because the problem of *engagement* is primordial."[36] Criteria for membership in the Party were changed: "The door is open to all those who accept our politics and who are willing to work toward its application. Others may leave the Party and pursue any action of their choosing."[37] At the same time, criticism within the Party appears to be less tolerated. The Party is blamed for "having become a vast arena for rumors, insults and tendentious criticism of the cadres that do not befit the character of a militant."[38]

Through their emphasis on the involvement of Party members in the specific politics of the regime, these statements point to a new use of the Party. In an interview accorded the daily paper *El Moudjahid* on 26 November 1968, President Boumédiène was asked how he planned to remedy the fact that the new Party organization had had little impact on the cadres in the state apparatus. He pointed out that the "intellectual elite is disinterested in the Party and tends to be content with the work it performs within the framework of its functions. It appears that this elite aspires to certain privileges and to progressively drift away from militantism. Besides, by not engaging in militant activity, this elite is driven to deviate and could in the long run become a distinct class with interests contradictory to those of the poor classes."[39]

What is interesting to note is the "elite's" reaction to this charge. A number of cadres (especially president-directors general of state corporations) were interviewed by *El Moud-jahid* on 5 December 1968. The arguments given for these cadres' lack of participation in the reorganization of the Party were: (a) the Party's lack of a doctrine; (b) the Party being reorganized by careerists; (c) the problems debated within the Party being trivial; and, (d) reluctance to being indoctrinated by the Party. Thus, the President of the National Steel Corporation (S.N.S.) declared: "What use is a membership card to a manager? Is it good for participating at the base level, for discussing problems which 99% of the time are problems of information and sometimes neighborhood problems? I was a militant for one year. That's all I learned." The President of the Algerian Textiles (T.A.L.) made a response which was even more revealing of management's attitudes toward the Party: "I think that to work in a corporation, to be in charge, to manage, means that we are *engagés*. We are asked why we have not contributed to the recruitment campaign and to the renewal of membership. Well, I, personally, believe that I was a member once and that's enough. I am not going to renew my membership." Thus, the situation is one in which managers consider themselves militants without joining the Party. To underscore this contradiction, the paper concluded that this was all "a mad story" and, ironically enough, called for "all managers of the country [to] unite!" [40]

President Boumédiène also remarked that the most important problem was to overcome the prevailing conception of the Party which defines it as a political institution, when in effect it is also " a philosophy." Considering that the "elite" is not interested in the Party since it is not active in its ranks, it is, therefore, not part of the obstacles that made Party reorganization difficult. Indeed, President Boumédiène emphasized that "the principal difficulty encountered by the Party has been the criticism that some countrymen, who have lagged behind the people, propagate in order to justify their not fulfilling the most elementary obligations required of a militant."[41] Given the fact that Boumédiène's regime has been from the beginning ostensibly open to the old and the new technocratic bourgeoisies, the "countrymen" referred to here could be the old veterans or those Party members who supported Ben Bella's policies.

This hypothesis seems to be more likely in view of two events that occurred in 1968, the "year of the Party." Posters covered walls of cities and villages, asking for a "Stop to Foreign Interference," and explaining that "because of its [political] stances, its *engagement* and its will to be independent, the F.L.N. has become a danger for some in the world. . . . All appropriate means are used to weaken it. Anti-Party men, paid agents . . . some adventurers, along with all sorts of hoodlums are being used. Any Algerian who consciously provokes, encourages or facilitates interference is a traitor who must be punished; if he does it unconsciously, he is dangerously naive and must be educated. Whether you are in the office, in the shop, on the farm or at home, dignified citizen, control your speech! Militant, be vigilant! Stop interference!"[42] A second poster entitled "War to the anti-Parties" specifies that all revolutions "necessarily generate counter-revolutions" and warns that the "anti-Parties will be unmasked and denounced wherever they are and whoever they are. Militant, watch the anti-Parties' action at your work place, in your neighborhood."[43]

What is curious about these exhortations is that the actual anti-Party men are already in the open and have voiced their opinions, as the *El Moudjahid* interviews indicated. One possible interpretation of this inconsistency is that, unable to fight the technocratic bourgeoisie's opposition to it, the government deflected its action on the opposition operating from abroad. What must be noted at this point is that the government appears more eager to draw administrative cadres to the Party than peasants and workers. At the same time, the Party's role seems to shift from mobilizing the masses to

controlling militants. In this respect, an F.L.N. leader explained to an audience of 3,000 militants that "experience
has made it necessary to impose sanctions as an essential at-
tribute of the functioning of the structures. If we know how
. . . to control and sanction, the Party will make a gigantic
contribution to the construction of the country." A "tightly
screened corps of controllers [will] be in charge of the failings and comportment of the militant." These controllers will
"bring their contribution to the awakening of the populations. In this way, the people will adopt the Party."[44]

Through its authoritarian formulation, this statement in effect indicates that the people have no trust in the Party. This
lack of trust is related to the disenchantment of the local
Party cells with the leadership. Interviews carried out in late
1967 revealed that the prestige of the Party was in decline
and that the base was often by-passed by the leadership on
decisions concerning "the organization of the Party or the
future of the country. Quite often, the ministers are the first
to make decisions. We wonder whether it's really useful for
us to exhaust our energy in tasks often rewarded with disappointment."[45]

This lack of communication between the Party's leadership
and the middle levels and the base is not new. The Chinese
Communist Party, for example, experienced similar shortcomings. Indeed, Mao pointed out that "in some (of course
not all) leading bodies it is the habitual practice for one individual to monopolize the conduct of the affairs and decide
important problems."[46] However, the solution he advocated
was not sanctions but "persuasion" first and in the last re-
source "struggle" if guidance is not accepted. Mao also recommended acceptance of criticism and differences: "Pay attention to uniting and working with comrades who differ
with you."[47] "All work done for the masses must start from
their needs and not from the desire of any individual, however well-intentioned he may be."[48] The Party's control consists in seeing that "no comrade at any post is divorced from

the masses."[49] Furthermore, the line that determines the Party's success or failure is clearly stated to be Marxism-Leninism. Thus, "to be good at translating the Party's policy into action of the masses, to be good at getting not only the leading cadres but also the broad masses to understand and master every movement and every struggle we launch—this is the art of Marxist-Leninist leadership."[50] Compared to the Chinese Party, the F.L.N. has no specific doctrine except the repeated assertion of a "socialism" that clashes with the realities of daily existence for both peasants and workers and is in accordance with the managerial technocratic bourgeoisie in that it derives material advantages from this particular form of socio-economic organization.

The practical problems of Party cadres are also somewhat similar to those faced by the Chinese. In 1938, Mao stated that use must be made of "the great amount of talent that exists outside of the Party," just as Boumédiène tried to involve administrative cadres in the reorganization of the F.L.N.[51] When, after 1949, it became necessary to recruit cadres from outside of the Party, recruitment was made among the working class and not the bourgeois intellectuals, who, however, were allowed to take up managerial positions. The training of large numbers of cadres was started in "regular schools." But at the same time, "peoples' universities" were set up as institutions of political training. What is happening in Algeria seems to be the reverse of the Party changes that occurred in China. Indeed, instead of managerial positions being open to non-Party members, it is the Party that is being opened to managerial cadres. While in the Chinese case those who have "ability" are checked by those who have "virtue," in Algeria technical ability is expected to engineer political virtue. On the functional level, it appears that the F.L.N. differed from the Chinese Communist Party in that the former hardly operated at the communal level and within the various state organizations, whereas the latter "stands as an alter-ego alongside every unit of political, social, economic and cultural organization in the country."[52]

A survey carried out among communal secretaries in the Constantine area to determine the role of the *kasma* (Party cell) in local affairs found out (although responses were very low) that the *kasma* was perceived as an active agent in the political life of the commune. This efficiency was mitigated, however, by the fact that the commune exercised a legal function that overshadowed Party members' roles in communal affairs. Indeed, eligibility to the Party cells was predicated upon the commune's approval. Besides, whenever the Party cells developed a community of interests with the people in the face of government agencies, especially those dealing with the agrarian revolution, they were usually too weak to make their interests prevail.[53] Otherwise, cells generally act as a "brake" on the communities' interests, thereby justifying the Party's characterization as "a Party of false cadres and genuine notables."[54]

The relationship between the F.L.N. and the administration has been described as assuming a variety of forms, the most significant being characterized as "cold war" and "peaceful coexistence" relations.[55] A "cold war" exists between the Party and the administration when each body wants to assert its authority on the other. This is manifested by boycotts of meetings and character assassinations. When they coexist peacefully, Party and administration manage to transcend their differences.

In general, the Party is not able to fulfill its prescribed functions of "guidance, mobilization and control of the Administrative apparatus."[56] The Party is often considered by the Administration as a consultative rather than controlling institution. Thus, "the Party is invited to administrative functions just as any other institution would be and with a power equal to other participants."[57]

CONCLUSION

The study of the role of the Party in Algerian society along with the relationship between Party and administration sheds some light on the actual relationship between Party and class. Algeria's colonial background was the determining factor in the creation of a Party that included all classes. With independence, the F.L.N. could not promote the interests of one class over the others, since it "represented" all of them. It was left to the politically dominant class to initiate a reconversion of the Party. The Ben Bella faction of the petty-bourgeoisie devised a theory of the Party it felt was consistent with its socialist goals. Ben Bella wanted a vanguard Party whose membership would be composed of all war veterans. The assumption was that the revolution had levelled out the militants' class differences. Boumédiène's use of the Party is more in tune with the pre-independence conception of the F.L.N. as a "nation-Party." He opened the F.L.N. to all Algerians who accept his policies, just as the 1954 F.L.N. accepted in its ranks any Algerian who shared the goal of freedom.

Ben Bella's and Boumédiène desire to reconcile opposing class interests prevented their setting forth a precise doctrine that would serve as a reference point to the incoming members. This resulted in alienating peasants and workers from a structure theoretically organized to promote their interests insofar as it was claimed to be "the avant garde organization of the Algerian people."[58] Contrary to the Chinese Communist Party, the F.L.N. did not rely on the "masses," nor did it mobilize them. It turned into an arena where the radical and conservative factions of the petty-bourgeoisie fought each other out until the 1965 military coup helped the latter prevail.

Boumédiène's appeal to the technocratic cadres to restructure the Party heightens the contradiction between theory and practice and reveals the confusion between economics and politics, expertise and revolution. The state administrative cadres are indeed equated with the avant garde of the Party's political positions which "require a lot of conscience and culture."[59] The antagonism between this high "culture" of a bourgeois nature and a politics that claims to be socialist

is overlooked. The appeal to cadres who are explicitly recognized as forming a privileged "elite" further denotes a
basic mistrust in the ability of the masses to achieve both
"conscience and culture." It also focuses the debate over
the restructuring of the Party at the leadership level, thereby
excluding the base. This attitude is in sharp contrast with
Mao's remark that the "masses have boundless creative power. They can organize themselves and concentrate on places
and branches of work where they can give full play to their
energy."[60]

Like the Chinese Communist Party, the F.L.N. theoretically
controls the government and the military. Unlike the C.C.P.,
it has been created by the government and it is controlled by
the military. Although both China and Algeria encountered
similar problems in terms of scarcity of qualified administrative and party cadres, poor communication between the leadership and the base, they differ in the ways they handled
them because they looked for support in different classes.
China leaned first on the peasants and later extended its base
to the workers, whereas Algeria relies on the petty-bougeoi-
sie. While China created "peoples' universities" to train Party
cadres and put pressure on the bourgeois administrative "experts" to supplement "ability" with "virtue," Algeria's Party
cadres have no formal training, nor do they maintain any
close contact with the masses. It has been said that "politics
for them remains a privilege of closed circles."[61] As happens
in many areas of Algerian political life, the F.L.N. fulfills a
formal commitment to the Algerian ideal of socialism. Being
in contradiction with the peasants and workers whom it theoretically represents, it is also in contradiction with itself in
the sense that the theory that created it denies the practice to
which it has been put.

On a theoretical level, the Algerian experience has relevance
for a greater understanding of the relationship between Party
and class. Lenin's conception of the Party as a vanguard of
the working class implicitly indicates that the party is not to

be identified with the class as a whole.[62] In fact, the difference between the Social-Democratic view of the Party and Lenin's was precisely that the former maintains that the Party embodies the class, so that when the capitalist state falls, it is the Party rather than the working class that appropriates state power. Lenin was aware of the importance of a "really iron-strong" organization of "all those who are out to fight."[63] The Algerian case shows that the absence of a distinction between Party, class and government resulted in the dilution of the revolutionary ideology through the opening of the Party to all classes.

8

Class
and
Bureaucracy

The existence of a bureaucratic apparatus which Algeria inherited from the colonial government and expanded, along with the creation of a bureaucratic structure to administer part of the state economy, raise the question as to whether the dominant class is identical with the bureaucracy. To determine the nature of the dominant class and its relation to the state apparatus, it is essential to understand the class origins of the social category of the bureaucracy and its relationships with the class in power.

THEORETICAL BACKGROUND

Non-Marxist theorists usually view bureaucracy as a tool of administration which may, under conditions of weak parliamentary representation, play a political role. Thus, Weber expressed both the inevitability of the increasing bureaucratization of the "modern state" and the need to control the bureaucracy's propensity to seek power.[1] At the same time, Weber also argued that the structure and the ethos of the bureaucracy are such that bureaucrats are unable to wield power successfully. Weber's description of bureaucracy as a "precision instrument which can put itself at the disposal of quite varied, purely political as well as purely economic or any other sort of interests in domination"[2] has led to two trends of thought. First, Dahrendorf's view that bureaucracy is a "reserve army of authority . . . a mercenary army of class conflict." As such, "it is always in battle, but it is forced to place its strength in the service of changing masters and goals." This means that "although they always belong to the ruling class, because bureaucratic roles are roles of dominance, bureaucracies as such never *are* the ruling class."[3] This view agrees with R. Bendix's assertion that "bureaucracy is . . . all powerful and at the same time incapable of determining how its power should be used."[4] This apparent paradox is due to the fact that the administrative skills that bureaucrats possess provide them with an autonomy which is undermined by their professional code of independent and impersonal performance. Indeed, the latter requires that they fulfill their duties regardless of their disagreements with the policies they are expected to implement.

The second trend of thought derived from Weber's conception of bureaucracy is to be found in the political science studies on bureaucracy and "development."[5] These studies typically focus on the role of the bureaucracy in the political and economic development of the Third World. While it is recognized that the Western model of bureaucracy does not necessarily apply to the new nation-states, the preoccupation with the possible political dominance of the bureaucracy remains prevalent.

Although stemming from different premises, the Marxist evaluation of the bureaucratic phenomenon as discussed by Lenin appears to be somewhat parallel to Weber's. Lenin agrees with Weber that when representative institutions are weak, the center of power shifts to the bureaucracy. That this is a feature of a capitalist society is an opinion they also share.[6] Lenin's suggestion that the vanguard party is a suitable organism for the control of the bureaucracy bears some similarity with Weber's working parliament. Lenin and Weber disagree on the use of the bureaucratic structure of the state and its future. Weber views the state as a "compulsory political association with continuous organization . . . insofar as its administrative staff successfully upholds a claim to the monopoly of the legitimate use of physical force in the enforcement of its order."[7] Implicit is the notion that a leader or an elite wields organizational power.

Lenin, on the other hand, views the capitalist state as an institution designed to suppress the class struggle while promoting the interests of the ruling class. By contrast, the socialist state is one in which bureaucracy is used to serve the people rather than control them. Thus, Lenin recommends "smash[ing] the bureaucratic machine of the modern state—and you will have a mechanism of the highest technical equipment, free from the 'parasite,' capable of being wielded by the united workers themselves."[8]

However, he did not give this use of the concept of the bureaucracy a comprehensive treatment, and it still remains a debatable issue.[9]

Recently, Marxist thought has focused more specifically on a theory of the state, although it does not appear to have fully developed the embryo of a systematic conception of the state found in Marx. Thus, Poulantzas views the capitalist state as both "the factor of cohesion of a social formation and the factor of reproduction of the conditions of production of a system"[10] by maintaining class domination. This formulation is based on a critical evaluation of the pluralistic theories of the state which typically aim at "masking the class base of the institutionalized political power,"[11] by ignoring the specificity of the political sphere and dissolving it into a series of counter-powers and decision centers.[12]

Poulantzas argues that these conceptions are inadequate mostly because they do not provide an understanding of "the relative autonomy"of political power which is "preyed upon by the plurality of the carriers of these fragmented powers."[13] His conception of the relative autonomy of the state is meant to transcend the seemingly contradictory views expressed by Marx with respect to the state's being on the one hand the locus of society's general interest and on the other, the alienated form of civil society. According to Poulantzas, the key to this inconsistency is provided by Marx's analysis of "Bonapartism." Indeed, Marx pointed out that "only under the second Bonaparte does the state seem to have made itself *completely independent* (emphasis mine)."[14] However, Marx did not take Bonapartism to be *the* type of capitalist state.[15] Therefore, Poulantzas treated the particular characteristics of a concrete case as constituting the fundamental features of a general type.[16]

This procedure was possible only because Poulantzas' structuralist reading of Marx focused on deciphering the hidden meaning of words, somewhat irrespective of their concrete reality. Hence, he interprets Engels' remark that the relative autonomy of the Bonapartist state is "the true religion of the modern bourgeoisie" as showing that "Bonapartism is 'thought' by Marx and Engels . . . as being a constitutive theoretical feature of the very type of the capitalist state."[17] This conception of the relative autonomy of the state in effect describes what individual members of capitalist society perceive the state to be, but it does not provide an explanation of the fact. Besides, Poulantzas' theory displays a hiatus: it is not made clear how and why the state obeys the commands of the bourgeoisie, despite its autonomy. This is an important question because Poulantzas specifically indicates that the capitalist state uses the dominated classes against the dominant ones in order to preserve its own autonomy.[18] In Poulantzas' formulation, the state is somehow predetermined to be autonomous.[19] Poulantzas' emphasis on the relative autonomy of the state bureaucracy is also predicated upon the "concrete functioning of the state apparatus."[20] In other words, the bureaucracy as a social category depends on the continued existence of the state apparatus and "not on its own state power."[21]

The role that a state apparatus plays within a specific society determines the extent to which a bureaucratic social category affects class antagonisms. Thus, in societies such as Algeria where the state has been constituted relatively recently, the political sphere overshadows all others; consequently, the state apparatus, locus of the political power, acquires greater importance. As a result, the class to which the bureaucracy belongs has a significant although not a decisive influence on its political behavior. Two situations may be envisioned:

First, the bureaucratic social category may not belong to the class or fraction of class that possesses state power. In this case, bureaucracy serves the political interest of the dominant class. On the other hand, it cannot exercise the power of the class it belongs to because of the very fact that it is constricted by the structure of the state apparatus.

Second, the bureaucratic social category may belong to the class that holds state power. Even in this case, "the relationship between bureaucracy and its political power is still not directly determined by its class origin: it is mediated by the state. This is precisely what permits its relatively autonomous political functioning vis-à-vis the class or hegemonic fraction whose power it exercises."[22] Therefore, the specificity of bureaucracy lies in its being relatively autonomous on the political level, although it does not have its own political power. This does not mean, however, that it is neutral in its relationship with the class it belongs to and the class that holds state power. It may be the means for preparing the rule of a non-dominant class. This is expressed in "limitations" and "barriers" that bureaucracy may set up for the dominant class.[23]

In sum it appears that the Weberian approach to bureaucracy and its potential for acquiring political power has not been transcended by the marxist theory of the state. While the former denounces the political potential of the bureaucracy and proposes ways to deal with it, the latter asserts the autonomy of the bureaucracy while falling short of conceiving it as constituting a class in its own right.[24] One element common to these two perspectives may be retained for studying the relationship between the Algerian bureaucracy and the dominant class. The focus will be on the structural constraints that the bureaucracy suffers in its quest for power. Although the role played by the bureaucracy in Third World societies is more extensive than in other societies, this does not constitute sufficient grounds for concluding that Third World bureaucracies have evolved into classes.

In the Algerian case, the state bureaucracy is used as an instrument of both class production and reproduction. The Algerian state apparatus reproduces the conditions of production because of its colonial foundation. The Algerian state was juxtaposed to an already existing structure suited to capitalist norms of government. The ideology of socialism and the drive toward economic self-sufficiency made it imperative that the colonial bureaucratic structure be converted to serve the new socio-economic goals. The nationalization of natural resources required an expansion of the existing bureaucratic structure and the training of qualified personnel who, in fact, perpetuated that structure. Conversely, the need for national private capital has led the state apparatus to lay the groundwork for the emergence of a class of capitalist entrepreneurs.

Within this theoretical perspective, the relationship between the Algerian dominant class and the bureaucracy must be sought in the nature and role assumed by the state apparatus. It will be recalled that, at the Tripoli Congress held in July 1962, the divisive issue was the form and organization of the future Algerian state. Indeed, the debate centered around the preservation of the Provisional Government (G.P.R.A.) or its replacement by a Political Bureau which would prepare for elections and a new government. The related issue of the control of the state apparatus was resolved through a military confrontation between those pro- or anti-G.P.R.A.

NATURE OF THE ALGERIAN BUREAUCRATIC STRUCTURE

The first Ben Bella Cabinet retained the bureaucratic structure left by the French colonists. The adoption of this structure required the proper personnel to run it. This was found among members of the petty-bourgeoisie who had been employed in the colonial bureaucracy and among the "Lacoste Promotion." The latter refers to a group of 23,182 Algerians especially trained in administrative functions within the framework of the "Constantine Plan," a plan set up in the late fifties as a corrective socio-economic program in an effort to bring an end to guerilla warfare.[25] The following table provides an indication of the composition of the post-war bureaucracy.

Table 12

Composition of the Bureaucracy[26] in 1963

	percentage of individuals in colonial administration
A—Prefects, Secretary Generals, Cabinet Directors, etc.	43%
B—Office supervisors, skilled personnel	77%
C—clerical	12%
D—messengers	3%

Level A refers to senior members. Half of this category was made up of individuals who had not been employed by the colonial administration. They came from the F.L.N. or the G.P.R.A. Level A has been broken up into two categories, A1 and A2, by decree No.62-503 of 19 July 1962. This decision was meant to make the recruitment of civil servants easier by modifying the educational requirements. Thus, level A1 includes individuals with a baccalaureate degree who spent at least two years in graduate studies. Level A2 refers to those who possess a baccalaureate only and level B to those who have completed only half of the baccalaureate.[27]

Level B includes individuals responsible for execution and was "almost entirely composed of members of the colonial administration."[28] They used to be employed at a lower level and therefore had been promoted after the war to fill positions left vacant by the departing Frenchmen. Categories C and D were filled by clerks and messengers. These were mostly individuals with no specific skills who had contributed to the revolution and were given the jobs as a compensation.

Added to these categories was a corps of French functionaries who served as technical aides within the assistance program laid out by the Evian Accords. The latter specifically mentioned that "the French presence will also be maintained through qualified cadres by technical cooperation, missions for study, scientific information, and the functionaries that France will continue to provide to Algeria."[29] The number of Algerian civil servants reached 186,738 in 1969, up from 36,518 in 1959.[30] Excluded from this figure are the administrative personnel of the military and the public industrial and commercial enterprises. Parallel to this increase in the number of Algerian civil servants, the French functionaries decreased by 6,539. However, the process of "decolonization" of the Algerian bureaucratic structure has only been partial. It has been pointed out that the "current regulations constitute a juxtaposition of pre-independence texts and measures that tend to adapt the organization of public function to the realities of the country (namely, its insufficient number of cadres) and its political options (Algerianization and socialism)."[31] In effect, the new Statute of Public Function published in 1967 was confined to abolishing the grossest colonial arrangements such as the recruitment of personnel on a contractual basis, which made for instability, and redefining the various job categories and procedures of recruitment.[32]

COMMUNAL AND WILAYA REFORMS

Communes

On the same organizational level, four codes were issued in 1965-66 dealing respectively with civil and penal procedures, penal law and investments. On the structural level, the codes of the Commune (1967) and the *Wilaya* (1969) aimed at redefining the administrative units of Algeria and their socioeconomic functions. While the first five codes were measures of centralization, the last two appear to allow for more decentralization. Under the new "communal charter" issued in October 1966, the commune is "the basic territorial, economic, social and cultural collectivity."[33] The difference between the new commune and its colonial counterpart is that the latter operated within a restricted legal framework which did not enable it to participate in economic life. On the contrary, the Algerian commune is endowed with legal, financial and economic autonomy. Its main objective is to "increase the participation of the local community to the general economic development which, at present, does not meet the job and consumption needs of the Algerian people."[34] It may even become a partner in a mixed or national corporation. In fact, this apparent autonomy is predicated upon a "period of transition" during which it is strictly controlled by the appropriate authority, depending on the size of the commune. The administration of the commune is carried out by a people's assembly elected every four years, which, in turn, elects a president and two or more vice-presidents. It must be noted that the number of communes increased to 676 in 1973 from 632 in 1963.35

Four years of experience with this communal reform revealed that the legal texts concerning the actual definition of the functions of the peoples' assemblies have not yet been issued. At the same time, communes encounter financial difficulties which prevent their achieving their goals. Besides, "clashes with the controlling authority and bureaucratic slowness constitute . . . many obstacles that can be overcome only by a revision of the legislation which should now permit the reconversion of the structure of the *wilaya*." Furthermore, "the lack of qualified personnel, underemployment and demographic explosion undermine the efforts made by some communes, especially on the social level."36

Wilayas

The reform of the *wilaya* (or district) is a development parallel to that of the commune. The *"wilaya* charter" issued in May 1969 describes the role of the *wilaya* as the link between the commune and the state. The *wilaya* is a "decentralized institution." However, this decentralization cannot be made to "express some autonomy of the *wilaya* because our state is a unitary state. It [decentralization] is only a technique for increasing the active participation of the *wilaya* and the masses of people in the revolutionary power."37 Like the commune, the *wilaya* is composed of an assembly elected by universal suffrage from a slate of candidates presented by the Party. It is directed by an executive council whose head, the *wali*, is the representative of the state. The deconcentration of power does not affect areas such as justice, national defense, education and the financial control of taxation.

Compared to the decentralization policy implemented by China in the late fifties, the Algerian effort at decentralizing the bureaucratic structure appears more formal than real. In the Chinese case, the aim was to "cut down the power of the ministries" so that the party could engage in "a social mobilization that could guarantee a rapid increase in farm output."[38] Thus, in China, decentralization benefited the regional party committees which were then able to start ambitious development programs. In effect, the Chinese decentralization scheme kept a balance between the ministries which maintained their control over heavy industry, the party committees who counteracted the influence of the ministries by concentrating on light industry and agriculture, and the managers of the production units who strove for independence from both.

By contrast, the Algerian decentralization program lacks a balanced structure. The weakness of the Party at both the national and regional levels makes it difficult to mobilize the people around a specific program of action. Besides, the vagueness of the job descriptions of those in charge of the communes, along with the lack of sufficient human and material resources, invite and perpetuate the control exercised by the ministries. Thus, the intended effect of bureaucratic decentralization has been limited. In fact, the aspect of the communal reform most exploited by the press has been the democratization of the governmental process as expressed by the elections to the People's Assemblies. In this sense, there is a parallel between the government endorsement of self-management and the communal reform. In the same manner that "the crises and contradictions which took place in the F.L.N. have led Algeria to opt to socialism,"[39] the resentment and criticism of the 1965 coup d'état as signaling military rule may have led to reforms whose theoretical import overshadows their practicability.

Functions and Dysfunctions of the Bureaucratic Apparatus

The Algerian bureaucratic structure has been described as showing a lag between conception and execution, the former being ahead of the latter. Indeed, "the legislation which the revolution is in the process of setting up, as well as the ordinances it has initiated for several years, is perhaps at present beyond the reach of the human potential of this country. The communal charter, the communal law, the *wilaya* charter, the law on self-management, the charter and the laws concerning the socialists' enterprises are indeed stronger in their essence and their concepts. . . . But we have wanted these laws to be of the future instead of being limited [in our aim] by the existing insufficiency of cadres. . . . Everything is a function of the future and the efforts that will be made to create a new man in Algeria."[40]

This optimistic assessment of the Algerian bureaucracy couched in terms reminiscent of the Fanonian phraseology leaves room for further interpretation. It is legitimate to wonder about the reasons that led to positing concepts before facts, theory before practice. Does this precipitation mean that these laws had to be passed when they were, or they would not have been passed otherwise? Is this a sign of the radicalization of the power holders as they face increasing resistance from their allies? Whatever the answers to these questions, Boumédiène himself had to explain the dysfunctioning of the reformed communes and the *wilayas* in terms other than a lag between conception and execution:

On the human level the commune has not reached its goal and has not yielded altogether good results. This is due first to the general circumstances under which our country lives (insufficient number of competent cadres) and second to the lack of experience and practice. This is perhaps also due to *certain individuals in charge of the commune* [emphasis mine] . . . The presidents and members of the communal People's Assemblies who were elected by the people have failed to fulfill their duties and neglected the people's affairs to take care of their own . . . It is essential that these negligences cease because if they were to continue, the responsibility for them will fall on the People's Assemblies and on those in charge of their control at the *wilaya* level since the *walis* share in this responsibility . . . It is necessary, brother Presidents of the communal People's Assemblies, that you along with the *walis*, heed these remarks.[41]

This statement explicitly recognizes the inadequacy of an explanation of the dysfunctioning of communes and *wilayas* in terms of a lack of qualified personnel alone. It points to a resistance to decentralization by specific groups of people. If it is recalled that the latter were elected from a list of candidates drawn up by the Party, the inescapable conclusion is that the Party chose its own opponents.[42] Indeed, candidates are not necessarily Party members. Many belong to prominent local families whose elected office provides them an opportunity to counteract government policy. Thus, some presidents of communal People's Assemblies have deliberately distorted the content of the agrarian revolution for the peasants. As a temporary solution by the central government to overcome this resistance, students are sent every summer to explain the principles of the agrarian revolution and investigate socio-economic situations of the peasants by holding informal meetings with them. Reports forwarded by students to the Ministry of Agriculture are often radical in their tone and pinpoint the weaknesses of the People's Assemblies. The students' action has aroused the anger of the presidents of People's Assemblies, who complained about the students' overstepping their roles and posing as self-styled investigators. What is significant here is the appeal to students to fulfill the functions that would have normally been carried out by the Party.

Given these conditions, the Four-Year Plan launched in 1969 was meant to "prepare the administration not only for the exigencies of the present but also for the future progress of planning which requires more technicity, work, consultations and involvement in the long and difficult path of a programmed construction of an economy that meets the high needs of a population in rapid expansion."[43] The Plan especially calls for the "simplifying of procedures, a sense of responsibility, an awareness of national interest, a rejection of formalism and quarrels over the distribution of functions."[44] These objectives are all the more difficult to achieve in that "the administration presents itself as a juxtaposition of institutions (structures, legislation, regulation, procedures) erected at different times and within different contexts without any total reconversion being effected to avoid duplication of functions or institutional 'holes' and permit its adaptation to both the realities of the country . . . and national options . . . The state apparatus is out of kilter in relation to our national realities because of: a) the cost of its maintenance, and b) the excessive specialization that in spite of a dramatic shortage of cadres results in about 100 departments and 200 divisions at the central level of administration; about 100 decentralized public organisms at the level of technical collectives; about 30 to 40 external services."[45] Besides, there exists a misuse of qualified personnel coupled with an excessive number of employees of "C" and "D" categories. Furthermore, the foreign (especially) French personnel have also been ill-used in that they have not been efficient enough to train indigenous personnel and they thus risk by their prolonged presence in Algeria "having an influence that goes counter to the political and economic orientations of the country (especially with regard to the diversification of our foreign trade)."[46]

Appeals made for a restructuring of the bureaucratic apparatus have pointed out that contradictions between the preservation of a colonial structure which was meant to serve a capitalist economy and the socialist goals set up by the Algerian government have led, among other things, to an increase in the distance between the rulers and the ruled, in a country where over 85% of the population is illiterate. Under these circumstances, the Algerian state apparatus does provide an adequate structure for groups with divergent interests to operate. The post-independence legal apparatus based on the French institutional model is conducive to the perpetuation of pre-independence attitudes, especially among those trained under the Constantine Plan.

The elaboration of a socialist economy requires a personnel qualitatively different from the one already in place. The post-independence schools turn out too limited a number of executive cadres to redress the existing structure in the hypothetical case that they wanted to do so. The top positions of the state administration are filled with educated individuals who usually received their training abroad. The level of education is evidently an indication of one's social background in spite of the fact that scholarships are often granted to students by the Algerian government or by foreign countries. The higher levels of the administration are thus staffed with members of the technocratic bourgeoisie. The middle and lower echelons are recruited among the petty-bourgeoisie.

The problem at hand is to determine the ways in which the class loyalties of these groups affect their performance as civil servants entrusted with the implementation of policies taken by the central government. The bureaucracy's resistance to policies that are deemed to limit the scope of its activity appears in the form of open opposition to the passage of laws, selective interpretations of the latter, delays of decisions and/or misimplementation of socio-economic projects. Since data on the first strategy are not readily available, the focus will be on the remaining three strategies.

In agriculture, as early as 1964 a legal draft was drawn for the purpose of restructuring the rural conditions of production. The draft was delayed in 1965 for "further preparation." In 1966, it was passed but it was to take effect in the fall of 1967.[47] The opponents of the agrarian reform were (besides the landowners) Algerian cadres who argued that the reform would entail the fragmentation of large property which would result in the weakening of the rationalization of production. They also argued that the agrarian reform had already taken place since the former colonists' lands were under workers' self-management. Delays also marked the history of self-management. The most striking examples are perhaps the delays in the payments of workers who had performed jobs for governmental institutions, as pointed out in Chapter Four.

The strategy of selective interpretation of government decisions may be studied through the evaluation of the success or failure of specific policies. Thus, the containment of self-management was made clear by the creation of national and mixed corporations. But when it became evident to the government that the industrial bureaucracy was growing too powerful, it was decided that room should be made for workers' assemblies under the guidance of U.G.T.A. (Workers' Union). Elections held during the same year resulted in the creation of 256 assemblies.[48] However, it appears that the National Federation of Workers in Petroleum, Gas and Similar Products (F.N.T.P.G.A.), a U.G.T.A. organization, includes executive employees of these industrial enterprises among its leaders.[49] In fact, the third Congress of the Federation was held on the premises of the largest national oil and gas corporation, SONATRACH, which also provided room and board for the delegates.

The increasing scope of the bureaucracy's activity does not appear to be accompanied by a similar increase in political power to the point where the bureaucracy would establish its hegemony over all classes or factions. Rather, the process is one of compromise. For every measure benefiting the peasantry or the workers, a countermeasure is taken in favor of the bourgeoisie. Thus, the agrarian reform which purports to fight the exploitation of man by man also upholds the rights of the large landowners to property and a high income even though the latter is determined by the Administration. Similarly, the Code of Investments provides the legal guarantees which create the necessary conditions for the strengthening and expansion of the commercial and entrepreneurial fraction of the bourgeoisie. A satirical comic strip, *Krikeche II*, that appeared in the daily paper, *El Moudjahid*, summed up the peculiar role of the bureaucracy in these terms: "I have heard of a grave epidemic called bureaucratization that threatens the administrations of all countries. Not knowing what it was, I asked a friend, an expert in administrative organization, to explain it to me. He told me it was 'the power of offices.' Armed with this scientific definition, I tried to find out whether we had a bureaucracy at home. Well, I am in a position to state that Algeria is fortunately almost free of this disease. Our offices are not powerful, not in the least. The proof for this is that no office can deliver a document if it does not have another document delivered to it by another office and so forth and so on . . . I think my friend is wrong. He must confuse power and powerlessness."[50]

BUREAUCRACY AND POLITICAL POWER

The issue of whether the Algerian bureaucracy wields political power is difficult to ascertain, not only because of a lack of adequate information, but also because of the role that the military has played in Algerian politics since 1965. As was remarked earlier, there are two ways in which bureaucracy as a social category may exercise power. One possibility consists in becoming autonomous as Marx pointed out; the other is to be a "means to prepare the class rule of the bourgeoisie."[51] In the Algerian case, access to power is blocked by two elements: first, the relative weakness of the class to which the higher reaches of the bureaucracy belongs. This may lead the latter to seek power within the bureaucratic structure which it is eager to strengthen, thereby practicing "bureaucratic politics." This is characterized by particular departmental interests, as opposed to the national interests of implementing policies aimed at combatting economic dependence. This may account for the desire expressed in the 1969 Four-Year Plan to do away with "bureaucratic quarrels." Second, the military support of political leaders constitutes an obstacle for the bureaucracy toward achieving political power, while, conversely, it may increase its bureaucratic power in that it values expertise, efficiency and discipline. Consequently, the Algerian bureaucracy appears to be engaged in the dual process of preserving its class interests while at the same time serving the politically ascendant faction of the petty-bourgeoisie.

The necessity of industrializing the country at a rapid pace, the increasing rate of demographic expansion, the existence of a subdued opposition have made the need for a strong state imperative. The focus of governmental action since 1965 has been the consolidation of the state. A content analysis of President Boumédiène's speeches showed that the frequency of his references to the state was the highest, compared to those relating to the Workers' Union. There were 404 references to the state, as opposed to one reference to the Workers' Union.[52] The nature of this state is meant to be decentralized and democratic, while at the same time the communal People's Assembly is claimed to be "a unit integrated in the state which it is obliged to serve."[53] The state is also expected to be run by a personnel that is not only competent but also "politically *engagé.*"[54] Given the weakness of the Party which would normally be responsible for the political training of all bureaucratic cadres, this last provision denotes a formalistic approach to reality. The consolidation of the state as an entity over and against civil society has had the effect of increasing the role and importance of the middle levels of the bureaucracy which comprise mostly members of the petty-bourgeoisie. If it is true that "the petty-bourgeois hope to climb, to swindle their way into the bourgeoisie" for fear of being "thrown down into the proletariat,"[55] then the state apparatus may be seen as the tool of such eager mobility. Thus, it has been suggested that "a portion of the petty-bourgeoisie plays on the bureaucratic level the role of the traditional bourgeoisie," while holding down the proletariat through the "combined effects of a certain political ambiguity in which populism is the most salient feature."[56]

CONCLUSION

The peculiar nature of the Algerian state apparatus as a combination of capitalist structures and socialist goals has consequences for the relationship between the politically dominant class and the bureaucracy.

First, the bureaucracy labors under competing ideologies. Those among the high level bureaucrats who were trained by the French colonial regime may contribute to the inertia which characterizes the Algerian bureaucratic apparatus. Indeed, delays in policy implementation may be due to the fact that French trained bureaucrats find it difficult to adjust to new socio-economic norms which require more expedience than commitment to formal rules of bureaucratic procedure. But the fact that these bureaucrats belong to the bourgeoisie and, therefore, are ideologically opposed to policies which appear to them as strengthening the working class or the peasantry may also account for their negative role within the state apparatus. The fact that elements of the petty-bourgeoisie occupy positions in the state apparatus is significant although these positions are not among the highest. The interests of the petty-bourgeois bureaucrats are confined to keeping their positions rather than seeking to promote a new form of socio-economic organization. Hence the contradictory situation in which they find themselves: their strategies coincide with the bourgeoisie while their goals are far more limited.

The second consequence of the particular nature of the Algerian bureaucratic structure bears upon the dedication of the bureaucrats to socialist goals. The program of economic reconstruction which the dominant class is anxious to implement requires a dedicated bureaucracy that transcends its social background. Hence, President Boumédiène's emphasis on building a strong and autonomous state apparatus that would realize the Weberian ideal of a "precision instrument." A balance appears to have been struck between a skilled bourgeoisie and a nationalistic petty-bourgeoisie. The former cooperates with the latter within certain understood boundaries. Thus, measures taken in favor of the peasantry are counterbalanced with decisions in favor of the bourgeoisie.

A third consequence of the grafting of the Algerian State

onto an alien foundation consists of the heavier structural constraints on Algerian bureaucrats. French laws had to be maintained while applied to different social, political and economic situations. Tensions arise out of the efforts to meet the demands stemming from a new social order and the pressure to bend a foreign structure to highly specific needs. These constraints, combined with the role played by the military as the ultimate arbiter, do not permit one to conclude that the Algerian bureaucracy is identical with the dominant class. Rather, the state apparatus appears to be the arena in which different classes and fractions of classes meet. It is used by the technocratic and the administrative bourgeoisies, along with the petty-bourgeoisie, as a means to reproduce their conditions of existence. By the same token, the state apparatus is also used to produce a new class of industrialists, as was pointed out earlier. The emergence of a class of industrial capitalists is one of the outcomes of the structural constraints placed on class interests within the state apparatus. Indeed, the rise of these industrialists may be interpreted as a way for the technocratic bourgeoisie to build a social support outside of the bureaucratic apparatus. Likewise, the fact that these entrepreneurs' activity is ultimately controlled by the state enables the petty-bourgeoisie to perceive itself as being in command of socio-economic developments.

9

Summary
and
Conclusions

SUMMARY

The study of the impact of colonial domination on the Algerian social structure has yielded certain insights regarding the process of class emergence. The Algerian pre-capitalist economic formation was characterized by three types of property, *melk* (or equivalent of freehold), *arsh* (non-alienable property), and *habus* (property in trust), which combined private and communal features. The basic characteristic of this property system was that the private appropriation of the land was a result of the individual's involvement in the working of that land.

The Turkish domination of Algeria added two elements to the existing property structure, the *beylik* and *azel* appropriation of the land. The *beylik* was the Turkish public domain which the *deys* (or Turkish governors) used for their own needs and for compensating officials for their services. *Azel* lands were initially tribal lands appropriated by the *deys* and rented back to the tribes. The Turkish superstructure gave the Algerian society a feudal character. However, as a whole, the Algerian pre-capitalist socio-economic formation was not reducible to the feudal type.

During the Turkish era, three types of aristocracy existed: the Turkish, the *Makhzen* (tribal leaders allied to the Turks), and the religious. Conflicts between the *Makhzen* and religious aristocracies on the one hand and the religious and the Turkish aristocracies on the other were not uncommon. In these conflicts, the peasants who worked as *khammes* (or sharecroppers) played a large part. A mercantile bourgeoisie which also held landed property existed, but the Turkish government did not allow it to grow.

The invasion of Algeria in 1830 by the French army for the purpose of creating new markets and placating the political opposition to King Charles X led to the creation of a settlement colony which had far-reaching consequences for Algerian society. The ordinances and laws taken by the French government between 1844 and 1873 expropriated the local tribes and destroyed the existing property system. French law was upheld over Islamic law. This "land grab" policy resulted in the breaking up of the tribal structure and the resettlement of the Algerian population in the least fertile lands. At the same time, the introduction of the French legal system meant for the Algerians the payment of exaggerated fees, which they could meet only by selling the very land they were trying to defend. A process of pauperization of all social groups ensued. It was precipitated by various tribal rebellions which brought about land sequestrations as a French retaliatory measure. Real estate speculation and frenzied usury combined to complete the destruction of the indigenous forms of property.

The destruction of the Algerian property system began a process whereby small Algerian owners slowly turned into wage laborers. Those among the Algerians who escaped expropriation started producing for the new intensive export economy. The land expropriations, the dissolution of the social structure of the tribes and the subsequent creation of a large rural proletariat constituted so many necessary conditions for the primitive accumulation of capital. In this sense, the French colonization of Algeria bore no similarity with the previous Turkish occupation. The colonial mode of production, based on the ruins of the Algerian mode, did not and could not integrate the Algerian forces of production. The colonial political structure which was created by and for the colonists systematically excluded Algerians from any genuine participation in the political process. This feature of the colonial system stunted the development of an Algerian bourgeoisie which remained confined to the interstices of the colonial export economy. And a policy of pseudo-"assimilation" did not give the French trained Algerians and the self-employed professionals the chance to acquire a political identity.

By the same token, political oppression by the colonial regime brought about a new solidarity among Algerians which transcended family, tribe and class. The contradiction of producing for a colonial economy and being deprived of a meaningful political participation had fateful consequences for the social structure as a whole. It diverted to the colonists the struggle which landless peasants and urban workers might have waged against the indigenous landowners and bourgeoisie who survived the colonial expropriation or benefited from it. At the same time, the initial demands that Algerians made for political rights reflected a lack of awareness of the dynamics of colonialism whose essence is the exclusion of the colonized society from political and economic equality with the colonists. In this sense, the claims made by the *Assimilationnistes* and the *Centralistes* denote that class consciousness preceded national consciousness.

National consciousness which was precipitated by both an adamant colonial policy of segregation and deteriorating material conditions in Algerian society absorbed the class differences within the latter, making it a community of faith and fate temporarily united against a common enemy. The tactical alliance between the bourgeoisie, the petty-bourgeoisie and some working class elements after the annihilation of the Messali-led Nationalist Movement (M.N.A.) resulted in the creation of the Front of National Liberation. As its name indicates, the F.L.N. was a party that united groups having a practical goal in common, rather than an ideological orientation, as was the case with the Soviet and the Chinese Communist Parties. In the course of a protracted war, ideological differences among members of the F.L.N. crystallized. The ex-*Assimilationistes* of the Union Démocratique des Musulmans Algériens and the ex-*Centralistes* of the Mouvement pour le Triomphe des Libertés Démocratiques remained faithful to a moderate approach to solving the problem of decolonization. This moderate attitude was strengthened by a fear of the military and the rising masses of unemployed. Hence, the maintenance of cultural and economic ties with France as prescribed by the Evian Accords of 1962 that put an end to the war.

The members of the Comité Révolutionnaire d'Unité et d'Action who started the armed struggle could not control the disputes within the F.L.N., since they were divided in their political orientations and themselves were either jailed by the French police or isolated from the center of decision-making (Provisional Government). This enabled the ex-*Assimilationistes* and *Centralistes* to lead the Provisional Government, while at the same time recruiting new members who looked up to them for participation in the expanding structure of this institution.

The fact that the Tripoli Program specifically recognized that "the Evian Accords constitute an irreversible political victory" only "on the level of principles," since they "provide for political cooperation between Algeria and France as a compensation for independence," is revelatory of the struggle between the bourgeoisie, identified with the Evian Accords, and the petty-bourgeoisie.[1] This is further explained in terms of the French government's desire to "promote the 'moderate' trend within the F.L.N. over the actual revolutionary forces, which would make possible a French-F.L.N. experiment within a neo-colonialist framework. France will exploit our weaknesses and our errors to upset the course of the revolution in order to organize a counter-revolution."[2]

The class struggle within the F.L.N. was also evoked in the Charter of Algiers, which indicated that "the crisis between the leadership [of the Provisional Government] and the A.L.N. [Army of National Liberation] occurred the moment the latter became an organized, homogeneous force. By contesting the leadership, it [the A.L.N.] objectively contested the Provisional Government's alliances, its social implications, and even the forces on which its leadership planned to rest."[3]

After independence was achieved, the contradictions within the F.L.N. which had already reached a high point of tension exploded over the issue of who would form the new government. Supported by the army, the radical faction of the petty-bourgeoisie was able to seize political power. The parliamentary government which was subsequently formed resulted from an effort to reconcile differences among groups with opposed interests. Ex-*Assimilationistes* and *Centralistes* objected to the nationalizations that also affected Algerian landowners and industrialists. At the same time, a few C.R.U.A. members opted out of the Ben Bella government, arguing that his regime was not democratic enough and his socialism was unscientific. The fact is that their withdrawal coincided with that of the older generation of bourgeois and was motivated by the same issues. In this sense, they may have acted according to their class interests or their class-bound values.

The first three years of the Ben Bella government were marked by a push and pull strategy meant to consolidate the

power of the radical faction of the petty-bourgeoisie and reduce the growing strength of the populist and military faction, while at the same time securing the allegiance of the
rising technocratic bourgeoisie so essential to a country in
desperate need of qualified personnel. These three years of
governmental experience had the effect of further radicalizing the Ben Bella-led faction of the petty-bourgeoisie which,
in turn, made the populist faction more rigid in its opposition
to the regime. Meanwhile, the importance of the technocratic
bourgeoisie increased as the need for rapid industrialization
was strongly felt. A faster pace of immigration to France, the
relocation of war refugees, and endemic unemployment were
problems the ascending class felt inadequate to solve alone.
The theoretically revolutionary entourage of Ben Bella was
unable to transcend this colonial legacy. Indeed, the legaliza-
tion of workers' self-management, which was meant to rally
the rural and urban workers, failed in its purpose.

The upper and middle levels of the bureaucracy, the majority
of whom were trained by the departing colonial government,
turned every measure taken in favor of the workers into an
administrative problem. Self-management thus became the
arena where the interests of workers, technocratic bourgeoisie and bureaucratic petty-bourgeoisie found expression. To
the technocratic bourgeoisie, a successful system of workers'
self-management meant the extension of this form of socio-
economic organization to an ever-increasing number of enterprises which they would not be able to manage. To the
bureaucratic petty-bourgeoisie, it meant a loss of power to
control and administer and, therefore, job insecurity.

What is most significant in this development is that Boumédiène's regime has laid the groundwork for the emergence of
an entrepreneurial bourgeoisie legally restricted to light industry or industry that has not been defined as "vital" to
the economy. However, the possibility for this bourgeoisie to
enter into partnership with the state hints at its potential for
growth. The revised Code of Investments, which provides this

social entity with legal and financial privileges, conformed to a specific rationale. It was understood by the dominant class that a strong power can control the economic dynamism of any social group or class. Again, private ownership of the means of production is here seen as secondary. What is important to the dominant class is not that entrepreneurs own some means of production but that they respect the rules of the game, namely, that they invest capital in *specified* sectors of the economy.

However, subordination to the national interests as expressed in the regime's desire to industrialize Algeria as fast as possible is secured only if the politically ascending class is hegemonic. Chapters Six and Seven have indicated that it is not. This lack of hegemony is expressed in the multiple obstacles which the functioning of self-management (even in its restricted form) and the implementation of agrarian reform have encountered. It is also expressed in the little support which the government has received from the technocratic bourgeoisie in the restructuring of the Party. The process of what has been here referred to as ideological abstraction contributes to the weakening of the hegemonic aspirations of the dominant class. The move made by the Algerian dominant class to make possible the emergence of an entrepreneurial fraction of the bourgeoisie raises the issue of its own class consciousness.

The inquiry into the social structural consequences of the colonization and decolonization of Algeria has revealed that a specific type of colonial economic development laid down the necessary conditions for class interests to emerge and crystallize in a way that cannot be adequately explained with the traditional Marxist class categories. Marx's class analysis does not take into account colonial formations with their ethnic and national characteristics. The dynamics of a colonial mode of production may override what has been taken to be the "normal" pattern of class evolution. In the following, the Marxist categories of labor power, class consciousness and political organization will be reviewed and specified in the light of the Algerian colonial experience.

SPECIFICATION OF THE MARXIST THEORY OF CLASS

Appropriation of Labor Power

Pre-capitalist Algeria was characterized by a specific property structure in which communal work was given precedence over the private appropriation of the land. However, the legal distinction between the *melk* (freehold) and the *arsh* (non-alienable) forms of property foreshadowed a situation where direct private ownership of the land might prevail. Indeed, this was precipitated and realized when the colonial "land grab" laws destroyed the individual's right to the usufruct of the land and forcefully established private ownership as *the* mode of property. Thus, the right to work which the Algerian community guaranteed its members was replaced by the abstract right to individual ownership.

During the pre-French era, classes existed as potentialities in that the guarantee of work deflected the consciousness of disparities of wealth onto ideo-political rather than material circumstances. The various uneven taxes that the Turks levied selectively, along with the occasional expropriations they ordered, were so many factors that interfered with an adequate assessment of one's position within that particular social structure. However, in spite of this, the very property relations prevalent at the time stressed the social aspect of land appropriation, so that *melk* (or freehold) and *arsh* (private and non-alienable) property appeared as a special case of tribal collective land. It was only necessary to work a plot of land to be recognized as its legitimate owner. Under these circumstances, the notion of potential classes is intelligible only if the concept of class is specified.

Given that the ownership of the means of production was considered secondary to and dependent on the actual labor invested in it, social relations between individuals were not based on their positions in the production process. Rather, they appear to be predicated upon the individual's direct self-activity in nature. Indeed, to be a *khammes* (sharecropper), to work for someone else, was undignified as a full-time occupation. Direct unmediated productive labor (which implies the idea of the control of labor power by the laborer) was, thus, the most important criterion in the definition of the individual's position in the social structure. The significance of the role played by labor in pre-colonial Algeria was all the more enhanced after the French took over and started their systematic policy of expropriation. Then, labor lost its character as productive activity for the development and appropriation of the land and soon became divorced from the ownership or possession of that land. The subsequent institution of wage-labor, which upset the former relations of production, was interpreted in the folk culture as another aberration just like the sharecropping system. Indeed, to be a wage laborer had for a long time been considered by the Algerian population during the early phase of colonialism as a sign of social regression.

The specific type of colonial organization which prevailed in Algeria from 1830 to 1962 had, therefore, forcefully created an economic, legal and political framework meant to replace the indigenous one. At this stage, any class analysis of the Algerian social structure will have to take into account the fact that two antithetical societies were in existence. The point of contact between the two societies, the French and the Algerian, was the class of Algerians who retained control over the means of production and maintained relations with the colonial structure. This "rural bourgeoisie," with sons gradually involved in professions that took them to the city, was nevertheless unable to shake the restrictions which the colonial government imposed upon it. Its presence was merely tolerated in the interstices of the colonial capitalist society, so that it could not, in and of itself, develop sufficiently to explode the contradictions inherent in the lag between the forces of production and the social relations of production.

At the same time, the rise of a mercantile bourgeoisie which took advantage of the new capitalist approach to production was stunted in its growth. The systematic production of wheat and raw materials for export to France and the new import possibilities were the monopoly of French traders, who, here and there, tolerated the existence of a few Algerians. Thus, urban merchants and rural bourgeoisie held a position in the production process without playing the socio-political role that this position would normally bring to it. In other words, they had the ownership but not the control of their means of production.

This situation has theoretical implications. It points to a de-emphasis of the role that ownership of the means of production plays under certain specific historical circumstances. Although economics cannot possibly be overlooked in the process of class formation, ownership as such, in this particular case, may not impose itself as the most important factor "in the last instance." It is only if the individual ownership of the means of production is taken as a secondary rather than as a crucial defining criterion of class that certain politico-economic moves made by the Algerian ascendant class after independence can become intelligible. Indeed, the government's containment of self-management, the creation of national corporations and the drive toward encouraging the investment of private capital become logical developments within this perspective, rather than merely the contradictions of a country trapped in the throes of rapid change.

In Chapter Three it was explained how the spontaneously evolved movement of workers' management of large estates and industrial enterprises was endorsed by the first Algerian government and, at the same time, progressively prevented from spreading further. What mattered for the ascending class (especially its military faction) was not the fact that the private property of the estates taken over by the workers was abolished, but that productive labor was under the laborers' control. Likewise, the creation of national corporations was an assertion of the ascendant class' will to control labor. This same concern with the control of labor rather than ownership of the means of production, irrespective of whether this control is carried out through private or public ownership, may also account for the Algerian government's appeal to national private investors to whom privileges were accorded. In this particular instance, the dominant class appears to identify the control of who owns what with the control of that very ownership. In a sense, the new entrepreneurs are considered as privileged laborers who produce for the national good.

It is not possible to maintain that because ownership of the means of production is not a crucial characteristic of a society, therefore that society does not display classes but social strata or social categories. Indeed, French colonialism imposed a capitalist mode of production onto a pre-capitalist society without integrating the latter into the former. Under these circumstances, the particular pre-colonial social structure based on productive labor was gradually undermined, and the new capitalist order created the material conditions for the formation of classes of the European type. Thus, pre-colonial inequality in the means of production, which was overshadowed by the recognition of the individual's right to produce, emerged as a significant factor of social differentiation under the colonial regime. But, because of the very existence of an alien French population which held the quasi-monopoly of the ownership of the means of production, the significance of this factor for the Algerian social structure was not crucial.

This explains why the first Algerian political movement demanded equal rights with the French colonists so that they could join the French *Cité*. This move is particularly revealing of the class affinities which the "Young Algerians" and later the *Assimilationistes* felt with the colonial bourgeoisie. The

consistency with which they adhered to their demands points
up their political shortsightedness. It was not until it became
clear that the colonial power structure was steadfastly opposed to a complete integration of the Algerian bourgeoisie
that the latter shifted its demands from assimilation to political autonomy.

Class Consciousness

The Marxist conception of class consciousness as consciousness of kind, which impels members of the same class to defend the interests of the entire class as their own, is both too
restrictive and not amenable to accurate determination. It is
restrictive in that it confines active behavior to a complex
series of definitions and locations of self and others which
may not always be clear and readily graspable. Indeed, to be
class conscious, a class member must not only know that he
belongs to an objective class but also know exactly what the
interests of that class are and then act accordingly. This assumes a transparency of the springs and aims of action which,
when interfered with, results in false consciousness.

Is, then, the Algerian petty-bourgeoisie a falsely conscious
class, since it is in effect paving the way for the emergence of
a capitalist industrial class? Or, should the concept of false
consciousness not be applied to it since in the Marxist literature it is mostly used in reference to the working class?

If a strict Marxist approach is adhered to, it appears that the
Algerian dominant class has both class consciousness and
false consciousness, depending on which class it is faced with.
The concept of class consciousness, in this case, loses its importance as a crucial criterion of class definition. Indeed, in
the present instance, one ends up asserting that the Algerian
petty-bourgeoisie is both a real and virtual class since it is
characterized by true consciousness of its interests when
dealing with the working class and false consciousness when
relating to the bourgeoisie.

An alternative approach to this problem is to consider consciousness as contained in the action a class member undertakes. If "life is not determined by consciousness but consciousness by life,"[4] then it is legitimate to recognize that the individual's action is determined by the class context within which he acts. When, for example, Algerian workers took over abandoned estates and decided to manage them collectively, they acted as conscious individuals. The type of action they took is meaningful within the framework of their class. Without being necessarily perceived by each worker as the correct class action, this takeover in effect expressed the actual aspiration of the collectivity of workers who happened to be without work and who feared that the colonists might return and exclude them from the management of their labor.

It may be objected that a distinction between class consciousness and organized interests must be made. This argument overlooks the fact that consciousness of class is also consciousness of the interests of that class. Whether these interests are promoted economically in the sense that workers fight for wages, rather than politically, is an issue that does not detract from the existence of consciousness as such. In other words, in the case under study, the Algerian workers performed an act that can only be understood as one inspired by their class position. Whether the ultimate aim of that act was narrow economic interest or an assertion of the working class desire to achieve political power is immaterial under the conditions described in this study.

Indeed, to be able to ascertain which of these aims was the motivating one requires a determination of the coincidence between psychological and ideological consciousness. But psychological consciousness is not a reliable indicator of class consciousness, and ideological consciousness requires a conception of the historical role of the working class, which a worker may not have. It is not possible to deny, therefore, the existence of a consciousness that is influenced by class position, as Poulantzas does. It is also difficult to abide by Marx's view of class consciousness as a criterion of class definition without running the risk of asserting that classes do not exist when they do.

The various statements made by Algerian workers at the 1964 Congress of the Socialist Industrial Sector, cited in Chapter Four, indicate that workers' consciousness of their position in the production process exists. These statements also reveal that workers were aware of forces that prevented them from exercising an effective management of their estates and were searching for ways to overcome them. How representative these workers are of the totality of laborers involved in self-management cannot be answered here. What is significant is the fact that the experience of self-management, instigated by workers, crystallized among some of them the consciousness of belonging to an entity alien to the state administration and the private corporations.

Political Organization

The issue of class consciousness is also linked to the no less problematic Marxist criterion of political organization as a condition of class existence. Under circumstances where political association must be sponsored by the Party and where the ascending class is backed by the military, the use of this criterion cannot possibly be taken into consideration. Indeed, it inhibits the analysis of real, objective classes which exist without necessarily being able to promote an organization that would express their political interests. Even in 19th century France, as analyzed by Marx, the peasantry, a class-in-itself, *existed* at the political level through the measures (even though symbolic) taken by Napoleon III.

Likewise, in the Algerian case, the existence of the peasantry as a class has been acknowledged and dealt with by the Boumédiène regime, in that it launched an agrarian reform. The empirical reality under study does not bear out, therefore, the Marxist view that a class exists as such only if it is politically organized. Political organization may be a crucial element in a bourgeois democracy where possibilities of organization exist and are not utilized. But under conditions where such opportunities do not exist, classes must be studied differently. In the Algerian case, if the criterion of political organization were to be adhered to, it would be difficult to understand the dynamics of the various social forces that account for the seizure of state power by some groups rather than others.

To the criteria of appropriation of labor-power, class consciousness and political organization that have been reviewed so far must be added the extraneous factor of economic dependency. Indeed, the fact that Algeria is still dependent on foreign regimes for her own industrialization interferes with the direction of the evolution of her social structure. Although the Algerian economic policy is nationalistic in that it attempts to secure Algerian control over natural resources and minimize the dependency effects of foreign investments, it is still unable to reach self-sufficiency. This has implications for the type of class that ascends to power.

The fact that Algeria needs capital investment and outlets for her oil and natural gas does not necessarily impinge on the shape and evolution of her social structure. The Russian revolution also used foreign capital in the early phase of its development. The specificity of Algeria lies in her having been a colony whose economic structure was built around needs alien to her indigenous population. The result is that, after independence, the reconversion of this structure required the maintenance of ties and cooperation with France. This determined the content of the Algerian political economy, despite several instances of Algerian resistance to French and other foreign economic domination.[5]

The relevance of this extraneous factor for the Algerian social structure is that factions of the petty-boureoisie display differing degrees of openness to foreign capital. Thus, although the dominant class is aware of the imperialist aims of its capitalist partners, it nevertheless maintains that industrialization can be brought about with the help of foreign capital and in spite of its political side effects. It has been said in this respect that "between a brusque rupture which is practically unrealizable and the pure and simple submission which is politically unthinkable, Algeria has chosen a third route: cooperation. The problem is not for underdeveloped countries radically to destroy foreign capital, at least in the short term, nor to cancel its profits, but to make sure that a part of those profits, the largest part possible, is used for growth."[6] However, in this combination of struggle against and collaboration with foreign capital, it is recognized that "the real conditions of success are ultimately the socio-political factors, in particular, the effective participation of the producers in the management and control of the national economy."[7] This raises the issue of whether the Algerian dominant class is willing to involve the workers in the fight against foreign capital.

Chapter Four indicated how the dominant class has neutralized the militant leadership of the Workers' Union (U.G.T.A.) and confined self-management to the least profitable branches of industry. It is true that subsequently it has established the principle of workers' councils in the various corporations. However, evidence has been provided that the national economy is managed by a technocratic bourgeoisie which also preempted positions on the workers' councils. The point is that, while making theoretical concessions to the workers, the politically ascendant class is engaged in a bargaining game with foreign capital which enables it to improve its material situation and at the same time induces it to see foreign investors as partners rather than adversaries. This means that the Algerian dominant class must project the image of a stable and powerful class in order to reassure its foreign business partners and maintain a continuing cooperation. The implication is that the cleavages between the working class on the one hand and the technocratic and petty-bourgeoisies on the other will increase.

The external factor of economic dependency is not specifically taken into account in Marx's definition of class. Although the detailed analysis of the component parts and the process of the economic dependency of Algeria are beyond the scope of this study, it is nevertheless well to bear in mind the social structural effects of a close "cooperation" with foreign capital despite the legal safeguards that the Algerian dominant class has taken in this regard.[8]

Use of Specified Theoretical Terms

This review of the inadequacies of the traditional Marxist categories of class analysis explains why in this study an effort was made to: 1) present an understanding of the historical reality of the Algerian mode of production as it evolved from the pre-colonial to the post-colonial era; 2) identify the connections between Algerian political groupings and the specific changes that occurred in the mode of production and the relations thereof; 3) examine the elements contained in a number of major political decisions in order to decipher class interests.

Consequently, it was found that under the specific historical circumstances of the Algerian colonial heritage classes could be analyzed in terms of the mode of appropriation of labor power *and* the mode of appropriation of the means of production. In the Algerian case, the mode of appropriation of labor power is constant, whereas the mode of appropriation of the means of production is variable. This means that the coexistence, in Algeria, of three modes of production (pre-capitalist, socialist and capitalist) does not necessarily indicate a social structure, where some classes are still incipient, others emerging and still others in the process of disappearing. Rather, these modes of production specify the conditions under which the appropriation of labor power (namely, wage-labor) is realized.

This accounts for the view sustained in this study, that the Algerian dominant class, namely, the petty-bourgeoisie, is one that has control over some means of production and over the organization of all modes of production. It also plays a dominant role in the distribution of surplus value, ideological elaboration, and political decision-making. That the political decisions taken by the dominant class are not necessarily implemented (as was pointed out in Chapter Four) does not detract from the fact that this class is the only one to make such decisions. It merely indicates that the class struggle occurs at the level of execution rather than conception.

The conception of class used in this study makes allowance for the existence or emergence of non-dominant classes which fulfill only part of the criteria outlined. The Algerian entrepreneurial bourgeoisie, for example, controls some means of production through ownership, but it does not play a predominant role in the determination of the existing modes of production. Besides, although it may have some input in the political process of decision-making, it does not yet control it.

At the same time, this conception of class clarifies the role and stresses the importance of class fractions. Thus, the Algerian technocratic bourgeoisie is here viewed as a competing entity with both the dominant class and the rising entrepreneurial fraction of its own class. Indeed, depending on the historical period considered, its interests may lie in the perpetuation of a state economic apparatus which guarantees its material privileges, rather than in the expansion of a private entrepreneurial sector which may outgrow the restrictions put onto it and demand more freedom to develop. On the other hand, short-term measures taken by the dominant class in favor of the peasantry and the workers may throw the technocratic bourgeoisie into an alliance with its entrepreneurial counterparts.

Post-Colonial Societies in Perspective

The fact that this study has dealt with a post-colonial society and, therefore, has emphasized the peculiarities inherent in this type of social structure makes it possible to generalize to similar cases. Indeed, Algerian society may be taken as the prototype of a society whose class formation has been determined by the particular mode of French colonial domination. Given that the latter extended to East and West Africa, although the specific colonial method used differed from one country to the other, comparisons of the relationships between colonialism and class formation are in order between Algeria and other post-colonial societies. Such comparisons of process more than substance might determine whether the dynamics of colonization have resulted in the emergence of a new pattern of social structural evolution.

This pattern may not be new in the sense that it has never been observed before. It may be new insofar as its complexity is unique in its composition. Different and often clashing philosophies, ideologies and values have been the hallmark of post-colonial societies. Antagonisms have coexisted in unique configurations and have affected post-colonial societies in some unique ways we must uncover.

Regardless of whether colonial governments adopted a direct or indirect method of domination, "they all shared the same presumptions concerning the supremacy of Western values and the moral obligations of imposing on Africa at least part of these values."9 Comparative studies with not only African but also Asian and Latin American societies may very well shed more light on the process of class evolution. The identification of the specific determinism that colonial government imposes on different socio-political and economic structures, along with the processual development of that determinism under various historical epochs, is perhaps a major element in an understanding of class relations in post-colonial societies.

Postscript

Since this book was written in 1974, a number of events of varying importance have occurred in Algeria. Of these, the most significant were the commemoration of the tenth anniversary of the 1965 coup d'état, the active involvement of Algeria in the restructuring of the world economic order and the clash with Morocco over the Western Sahara issue (ex-Spanish Sahara). In what follows, a few remarks will be made on each one of these occurrences as they relate to the substance of this study.

The significance of the commemoration of the tenth anniversary of the 1965 coup lies in the content of the policy statements made by the President on that occasion. In a televised speech, President Boumédiène reviewed the reasons that led him to "assume his responsibilities on 19 June 1965."[1] One of the reasons given is instructive insofar as it concerns the President's conception of the state. He indicated that the previous government had attempted to "destroy the state" through the destruction of the people's Army "which was then the only organized force, capable of saving what needed to be salvaged and [alone able to] guarantee the continuity of the normal revolutionary process."[2] There is no explanation of what is meant by a "normal revolutionary process." However, it is essential to note that the Army is identified with the state as a whole. Although in a later passage of the same speech, the President specifies that "the state essentially rests on political, economic, social and cultural structures,"

197

he nevertheless adds that "the establishment of a state further implies the organization of a national army."[3] This importance given to the army has relevance for the class analysis presented in this study. Although the Algerian state is staffed mostly with civilians, the military is the ultimate overseer. The antagonistic relationships between the technocratic bourgeoisie, the administrators and the new entrepreneurs may reach the breaking point, yet their resolution will be determined by the extent to which the military will intervene.

However, this situation is different from the moderator pattern of military intervention that characterizes the political history of Latin American societies, especially Brazil, up to 1964.[4] The specificity of Algeria lies in the fact that the military, under the control of the petty-bourgeoisie, competes for social support with the other classes and fractions thereof which are anxious to capture state power. Hence President Boumediene's move towards "returning the Revolution to the Algerian peasantry"[5] from which it originated. This is implemented through the Agrarian Reform and the construction of "socialist villages," which provide peasants with houses equipped with all the necessary utilities, health services, schools for their children, and the opportunity of collectively working the land.

One of the most far-reaching announcements made during the commemoration of 19 June 1965, was the forthcoming elaboration of a National Charter to be freely discussed and voted upon in a referendum to take place within a year. This Charter in effect will serve as a constitution. It envisages the election of a National Assembly along with a President by 19 June 1976. All these measures are aimed at securing popular legitimation for a government maintained in power over ten years without direct popular ratification. It appears as though the process of responding to peasants' needs and seeking greater legitimation has been all the more accelerated as opposition from the social forces intent on economic laissez-faire has become more and more manifest. In this sense, Boumédiène's position bears similarities with Ben Bella's

at the time that he endorsed workers' self-management and
accelerated nationalizations of Algerian private estates and
businesses.

The issue of Western Sahara has acted as a catalyst for the
balance of power in Algeria. Within the framework of the
analysis provided in Chapters Five and Eight of this study,
the recent internal opposition to the Algerian government's
rejection of the annexing of the former "Spanish" Sahara by
Morocco and Mauritania is a measure of the strength of the
Algerian bourgeoisie. When Spain decided to withdraw from
the portion of the Sahara stretching between Morocco and
Mauritania and turn it over to Moroccan control, Algeria expressed her opposition to this arrangement. The Algerian government upheld the principle of self-determination for the indigenous people of the Sahara. However, it was not able to
secure enough support for its position at the United Nations
and was outmaneuvered by Morocco. The end result was a
diplomatic defeat for Algeria with one alternative left: military intervention either directly or through active support to
the guerillas of the POLISARIO Front.[6] A series of skir-
mishes between Algerian troops allegedly delivering medical
supplies and Moroccan army units led to an unexpected development within Algeria. On 9 March 1976, Mr. Benyoucef
Benkhedda, the second President of the defunct Provisional
Government (G.P.R.A.) passed out a petition to the press appealing to the Algerian people to "stop the war" against Morocco and "put an end to personal rule."[7] The petition,
which also called for a "bourgeois" democracy, was further
signed by the first President of the Provisional Government,
Ferhat Abbas, now seventy-seven years old. Two other names
also appeared on the document: Mohammed Khereddine, an
ex-member of the National Council of the Algerian Revolution (C.N.R.A.) and Hocine Lahouel, a one-time Secretary-
general of the pre-independence Movement for the Triumph
of Democratic Liberties (M.T.L.D.). Although the exact identity of the groups that may have instigated the petition is not
yet known, it is possible to conjecture that they are linked to

the new entrepreneurs and/or the landed bourgeoisie. One of the sponsors of the petition, Mohammed Khereddine, is a landlord and has affinities with the Muslim Brotherhood.[8] Hocine Lahouel was at the head of a state-owned business enterprise. The socio-economic positions of these men may not be sufficient to draw conclusions as to their political affiliations. However, it is important to understand why these particular men chose to speak up.

There has been considerable speculation as to the reasons leading Ferhat Abbas and Benkhedda, "men from the past," to venture an indictment against the established government. Some Algerians argue that the forthcoming elections and the debate over the National Charter were simply too threatening to the bourgeoisie operating within and outside the state apparatus. The elections and the ratification of a Charter would mean the consolidation of Boumédiène's power. The two famous figures of the Algerian revolution could have been induced to voice their discontent by a threatened bourgeoisie hoping to exploit this time of crisis to overthrow Boumédiène. Others claim that the economic situation of Algeria has deteriorated and that the state bureaucracy is inefficient and far from being neutral and impartial. Therefore, the sponsors of the petition may have acted out of a genuine concern for the nation. All of these speculations could be seen as plausible but they are limited. They do not ask a crucial question, viz., how was it possible at all to make such a strong public indictment of the policies of Boumédiène's government? How is it that after ten years of socialist experience the government could be threatened by the same forces that in July 1962 opposed the dismantling of the Provisional Government (G.P.R.A.)? What has happened over the past decade is that Boumédiène and the technocratic bourgeoisie have struck an alliance to eliminate the radical faction of the petty-bourgeoisie. Once in power, Boumédiène relied heavily on the expertise of the technocrats (the "cadres") who were able to bring about changes in the socio-economic conditions of the entrepreneurs. This was done through the liberalization of investments and through incentives to do business. But the economic forces he unleashed could no longer tolerate the legal restrictions placed upon their full development. At the same time, the very forces he protects, the peasantry and the conservative fraction of the petty-bourgeoisie, have become increasingly discontented in the face of what they see as gross inequities in the distribution of wealth.

The Western Sahara issue brought all these contradictions to light. Boumédiène appears to be in a position similar to Nasser after the war of June 1967. The war exposed Nasser's isolation and inability to control the social forces he helped create and/or consolidate, namely the technocratic bourgeoisie and urban petty-bourgeoisie. This is not to say that the Western Saharan episode is comparable to the June war, but only that, as in Egypt after 1967, the class alliances made in 1965 are no longer functional.[9] It also means that Boumédiène may have to move to the Left and build a genuine socialist culture that up to now has been severely lacking.

It is sometimes argued that the Algerian government is not a class government because it is deeply concerned with a better distribution of the world's economic resources. This concern has made Algeria a leader in Third World politics. The radicalism of Algerian foreign policy and the desire to achieve economic independence have historical roots that overshadow rather than cancel class antagonisms. It was skillful diplomacy, combined with the waging of successful guerilla warfare, that won Algeria its independence in 1962. Since then, regardless of the nature and direction of domestic policy, Algerian foreign policy has retained its revolutionary values. The latter have nevertheless suffered an erosion as the Western Sahara issue demonstrated. Indeed, it suddenly became clear that Morocco, a monarchical regime, could strengthen itself without any fear of a "socialist" neighbor, and even prevail over it diplomatically and militarily. The gap between domestic and foreign policy was thus narrowed, and the weakness of Algerian socialism revealed. The dominant petty-bourgeoisie's internal policy of *entente cordiale* between divergent class interests has proved damaging to the social integration and mobilization of the Algerian people.

Notes
to
Chapter 1

[1] This is a notion found in the Charter of Algiers, a document which constituted the first ideological program of the newly formed Algerian republic.

[2] Jacques Berque, "L'Idée de Classe," *Cahiers Internationaux de Sociologie* 38(1965): 169-184.

[3] The figures are 0.3% for agriculture and 3% for industry. The last figure reflects the proportion of self-managed industries over all industrial enterprises except oil, gas and construction works. See Secrétariat d'Etat au Plan, Direction des Statistiques, *Tableaux de l'Economie Algérienne* (1971), pp. 115, 117, 146.

[4] In this respect, an economic advisor of the Algerian government pointed out that underdeveloped countries ought to use the latest technology in order to "catch up with the industrialized countries." See Gérard Destanne de Bernis, "L'Industrialisation en Algérie" in *Problèmes de l'Algérie Indépendante*, ed. François Perroux (Paris: Presses Universitaires de France, 1963), p. 134.

[5] Kalman H. Silvert, *Expectant Peoples: Nationalism and Development* (New York: Vintage Books, 1967), p. 28.

[6] Isaac Balbus, "Ruling Elite Theory vs. Marxist Class Analysis," *Monthly Review*, May 1971.

7 René Galissot, "Classification Sociale en Système Précapitaliste: l'Exemple Algérien," *Cahiers du Centre d'Etudes et de Recherches Marxistes*, No. 60 (1968).

8 For a discussion of the need for a class analysis of Islamic societies, see Maxime Rodinson, *Marxisme et Monde Musulman* (Paris: Editions du Seuil, 1972), p. 286.

9 Immanuel Wallerstein, "Class and Class Conflict in Africa," *Canadian Journal of African Studies* 7, no. 3 (1973), 375-380.

10 Ibid., p. 380.

11 Karl Marx, *Grundrisse* (London: Penguin Books, 1973), p. 96.

12 Karl Marx, *The 18th Brumaire of Louis Bonaparte* (New York: International Publishers, 1969), p. 124.

13 Nicos Poulantazs, *Pouvoir Politique et Classes Sociales*. 2 vols. (Paris: Maspéro, 1971), 1:76. [Translation mine.]

14 Ibid., p. 62.

15 Ibid., p. 64.

16 Ibid., p. 66.

17 Frederic Jameson, *The Prison House of Language* (Princeton: Princeton University Press, 1972), Part I.

18 Ibid., p. 105.

19 Poulantzas, *Pouvoir Politique*, p. 66.

20 Ibid., p. 67.

21 Ibid., p. 76.

22 Ibid., p. 77.

23 Ibid.

24 Ibid.

25 Ibid., pp. 69-72.

26 Marx, *Grundrisse*, pp. 101-102.

27 Roger Dumoulin, *La Structure Asymétrique de l'Economie Algérienne* (Paris: Editions M.T. Guenin, 1959).

28 Claudine Chaulet, *La Mitidja Autogérée* (Alger: SNED, 1971), pp. 79-80 and p. 114.

29 Milovan Djilas, "The New Class," *Structured Social Inequality*, ed. Celia Heller (London: The Macmillan Company, 1969), p. 156. Djilas makes a logical "leap" from a capitalist ownership to socialist control. His "new class" is in this sense the replica of the capitalist "ruling class." The only difference is that the former controls rather than owns

the means of production. This is a mechanistic definition, implicitly admitting that "control" is owned by a group of individuals and identifying positions in the State apparatus with class position.

30 Charles Benoist, *Enquête Algérienne* (Paris: Lecène, Oudin and Cie., 1892), pp. 11-20.

31 At the rural workers' congress held in May 1965, workers generally made a critical assessment of the conditions under which they functioned. One worker, for example, declared that "workers are able to apply the March decrees themselves, but some functionaries prevent them from doing so." "Brothers, you are aware of all the Administration's pressures and oppression. We will struggle against despotism no matter who uses it." "As to those who give orders with their hands in their pockets, they are not our people. Those who want to control the workers are above the workers." See Daniel Guérin, *L'Algérie Caporalisée* (December 1965), p. 64.

32 Vladimir I. Lenin, "What Is to Be Done?", *Essential Works* (New York: Bantam Books, 1971), p. 74.

33 It has been noticed that "Algerian private capital . . . has demonstrated its dynamism, which can eventually transform itself into expansionism." See Khalfa Maameri, *Orientations Politiques de l'Algérie* (Alger: SNED, 1973), p. 131. It has also been remarked that there is evidence of a "beginning of a collaboration between national private capital and foreign capital." See Ahmed Akkache, *Capitaux Etrangers et Libération Economique: l'Expérience Algérienne* (Paris: Maspéro, 1971), p. 132. When the Agrarian Revolution started in the spring of 1972, members of the government donated some of the land they owned. The daily paper, *El Moudjahid*, wrote in this respect: "the cadres at the highest level . . . have demonstrated their militancy. . . . A real wave of donations has been noted." See Tariq Maschino and Fadéla M'rabet, *L'Algérie des Illusions* (Paris: Editions R. Laffont, 1972), p. 218.

34 The concept of control of the means of production is different here from the way it was used by James Burnham in *The Managerial Revolution*. The property that the Algerian managers control does not belong to private individuals but to the State, which is assumed to represent the people.

35 Jean Claude Douence, *La Mise en Place des Institutions Algériennes* (Paris: Centre d'Etudes des Relations Internationales, Etudes Maghrébines, 1964), No. 2, p. 55.

36 Quandt, *Revolution and Political Leadership in Algeria*, 1954-1968 (Cambridge: The Massachusetts Institute of Technology Press, 1969).

37 Clegg, *Workers' Self-Management in Algeria* (New York: Monthly Review Press, 1971).

38 This is because conflict is seen within the framework of general consensus.

39 Quandt, *Revolution*, Chap. I.

40 Djilas, "The New Class," p. 156.

41 Weber, "Bureaucracy," in *From Max Weber: Essays in Sociology*, ed. C. Wright Mills, and Herbert H. Gerth (New York: Oxford University Press, 1968), p. 232. The "normal conditions" mentioned by Weber seem to apply more to the Prussian State than to all forms of states, although, as Bottomore remarked, Weber's thesis "has gained support from the events of recent European history, in particular . . . the socialist revolution in Russia." See Thomas B. Bottomore, *Elite and Society* (Baltimore: Penguin Books, 1964), p. 83.

42 Weber, "Bureaucracy," p. 232.

43 The concept of control here refers to the ability to oversee the ownership of some means of production and the ability to administer some others.

44 The concept of dominance refers to the ultimately binding decisions made by a class about the choice of a mode of production, ideological elaboration and general policy.

45 For example, state corporations are often described as being "state companies with regard to the ownership (of the means of production) and capitalist in their functioning." See Akkache, *Capitaux Etrangers*, p. 100.

46 Poulantzas, *Pouvoir Politique*, 2:10.

47 Quandt, *Revolution*.

48 Pierre Bourdieu and A. Sayad, *Le Déracinement* (Paris: Les Editions de Minuit, 1964).

49 Pierre Bourdieu et al, *Travail et Travailleurs en Algérie* (Paris: Mouton et Cie., 1963), pp. 382-389.

50 Frantz Fanon, *The Wretched of the Earth* (New York: Grove Press, 1966), pp. 148-205.

51 Gérard Chaliand and Juliette Minces, *L'Algérie Indépendante* (Paris: Petite Collection Maspéro, 1972).

52 Ian Clegg, *Workers' Self-Management*. Chap. 6.

53 Ibid., p. 182.

54 There were several reasons for the Algerian workers' reluctance to stand up to the state, as for instance, faith in the leaders of the Revolution and their numerical weakness.

55 Kader Ammour, Christian Leucate and Jean-Jacques Moulin, *La Voie Algérienne* (Paris: Maspéro, 1974).

Notes
to
Chapter 2

1 For a description of Berber social life in Algeria before the Arab invasion, see Yves Lacoste and André Prenant, *L'Algérie, Passé et Présent* (Paris: Editions Sociales, 1960).

2 The history of the *Maghreb* has yet to be written. Most history books were written by colonial historians who often failed to grasp historical meanings objectively. For a critique of the handling of the history of the Maghreb, see Abdallah Laroui, *L'Histoire du Maghreb* (Paris: Maspéro, 1970). 2 vols., especially, Vol. 1, Introduction and Vol. 2, pp. 66-69.

3 Charles André Julien, *Histoire de l'Afrique du Nord*, Vol. 2: *De la Conquête Arabe à 1830* (Paris: Payot, 1964), pp. 250-302.

4 Julien, *Histoire*, p. 254.

5 The janissaries were Turkish soldiers, whereas the corsairs were professional pirates.

6 Dubois-Thainville's letter, dated 18 November 1809, published in *Collection de Documents Inédits sur l'Histoire de l'Algérie Après 1830* (Paris: Librairie Ancienne Honoré Champion, 1927).

7 In 1558, the *Taifa* owned 35 galleys, 25 ships and a large number of small armed boats. See Julien, Histoire, p. 26.

8 The corsairs referred to here were the leaders (the *Raïs*) of the corporation. The members were mostly Christian navigators from Calabria, Sicily and Genoa who would become "professional turks" in what was a highly profitable trade. Some of the non-Turkish members rose to prominence, as for example the Corsican Hassan and the Sardinian Ramdan, who became *pashas*. See Lacoste and Prenant, *L'Algérie*, p. 142.

9 René Galissot, "Classification Sociale en Système Précapitaliste: l'Exemple Algérien," *Cahiers du Centres d'Etudes et de Recherches Marxistes*, 60 (1968): 30.

10 In fact, interpretations of this point of Islamic law vary from one writer to the other. See Charles Robert Ageron, *Les Algériens Musulmans et la France, 1871-1919* (Paris: Presses Universitaires de France, 1968), 1:68-72; Benoist, *Enquête Algérienne*; and Joost Van Vollenhoven, *Essai sur le Fellah Algérien* (Paris: Arthur Rousseau, 1903).

11 Julien, *Histoire*, p. 264.

12 Galissot, "Classification Sociale," p. 27. The permanence of the towns in Algeria and their links with the country were enhanced by the Turks, who made it a condition for the Arab tribesmen who received a land benefice to keep their crops and a house in the nearest town. See Marcel Emerit, "L'Algérie à l'Epoque d'Abd-El-Kader," *Collections de Documents Inédits sur l'Histoire de l'Algérie* (Paris: Editions La Rose, 1951), Vol. IV, p. 236.

13 Warnier, a French administrator, declared: "We shall substitute the generic word 'property' to the different forms of Algerian land ownership." Quoted in André Nouschi, *Enquête sur le Niveau de Vie des Populations Rurales Constantinoises de la Conquête jusqu'en 1919* (Paris: Presses Universitaires de France, 1961).

14 Robert Ageron, *Les Algériens Musulmans et la France* (Paris: Presses Universitaires de France, 1966). 1: 73.

15 Ibid., p. 393.

16 Galissot, "Classification Sociale," p. 2.

17 Nouschi, *Enquête*, pp. 85-89.

18 The exclusion of females from inheritance of *arsh* property has been suggested to reveal the importance that the ability to work the land holds for this type of ownership.

19 Nouschi, *Enquête*, pp. 89-94.

20 Ibid., p. 90.

21 Hildebert Isnard, *La Réorganisation de la Proprieté Rurale dans la Mitidja* (Alger: Imprimerie Joyeux, 1947), Chap. I.

22 I. Halabi, quoted in John Ruedy, *Land Policy in Colonial Algeria* (Los Angeles: University of California Press, 1967), p. 6.

23 Ibid., p. 7.

24 Ibid.

25 Karl Marx, *Pre-capitalist Economic Formations* (New York: International Publishers, 1969), p. 83.

26 Ibid., p. 10.

27 Ibid., p. 82.

28 Ibid., p. 79.

29 Ibid., p. 28.

30 Ibid., p. 78.

31 Galissot, "Classification Sociale," p. 16. Although Galissot's study constitutes perhaps one of the most serious attempts at understanding the mode of production and the forms of property of pre-colonial Algeria, his analysis, nevertheless, is inaccurate because it is based on the identification of *arsh* property with "collective property." In fact, the generalized complaints made by the various tribes when the French army undertook to classify the tribal land as "collective" point to the inappropriateness of this assimilation. Besides, reports made by the censors in 1863 made it clear that tribesmen did not attach the same meaning to *arsh* as the French did.

32 Galissot, "Classification Sociale,' pp. 25-30. Galissot denounces the "Europocentric" model of feudalism which he claims is inadequate and historically limited because it refers to the weakest and shortest phase of feudalism that coincides with increased royal powers over the nobility immediately before the rise of capitalism. "Command feudalism" refers to the form of socio-economic organization prevalent in Europe before the eighteenth century. This type of feudalism was characterized by a concentration of property rights, military and legal powers in the hands of the feudal lords.

33 Walsin-Esterhazy, *De la Domination Turque dans la Régence d'Alger* (Paris: Librairie Charles Gosselin, 1840). Esterhazy describes the firmness with which the Turks maintained their hold over Algeria.

34 There were some exceptions. For example, the Bey of Constantine maintained social ties with some of the strongest tribes who were particularly powerful and therefore much needed in keeping order. In situations of this kind, marriages were not infrequent.

[35] Marx, *Pre-capitalist Economic Formations*, p. 73.

[36] An indication of this divergence of interests may be found in the uprisings that occasionally erupted and in the tax reforms that were made in Western Algeria by Emir Abd-El-Kader as soon as the Turks were toppled by the French.

[37] The religious aristocracy created religious confederations (*zawias*) which were often opposed to one another. Some *zawias* did ally themselves to the Turkish government; but, in general, religious confederations were at odds with the Turks.

[38] Hamdane Ben Othmane Khodja points out in *Le Miroir* (Paris: Goetschy Fils et Cie., 1833), Book One, that Algerian products (wheat, wool, leather, olive oil, silk, etc.) were exported to Europe and Asia.

[39] The lack of prestige of this bourgeoisie was demonstrated in 1836 when, in the city of Tlemcen (Western Algeria), the bourgeoisie attempted to get rid of Turkish rule and appointed a bourgeois as governor of the city. The neighboring tribes took to arms and unseated the new governor. See Emerit, "L'Algérie à l'Epoque d'Abd-El-Kader," Chapter I.

[40] Galissot, "Classification Sociale," p. 13.

Notes
to
Chapter 3

[1] The invasion was advertised in Marseille's newspapers with invitation to "ladies" to watch the show.

[2] *Collection de Documents Inédits sur l'Histoire de l'Algérie Après 1830*, 2ème serie (Alger: J. Carbonel, 1924), p. 22.

[3] Kenya and the Union of South Africa were similar settlement colonies.

[4] Charles H. Benoist, *Enquête Algérienne* (Paris: Lecène, Oudin et Cie, 1892), p. 11.

[5] Robert Ageron, *Les Algériens Musulmans et la France, 1871-1919*, 2 vols., (Paris: Presses Universitaires de France, 1968), 1:67.

[6] Maréchal de Bourmont quoted by Hamdane Ben Othmane Khodja, *Le Miroir* (Paris: Goetschy Fils et Cie., 1833), Book One.

[7] Daumas, the head of the Bureau of Arab Affairs (1841-47), promoted the idea of "indirect rule," whereby the local aristocracy would administer Algeria in behalf of the French government. However, this policy, which is similar to that of the British in Egypt, Northern Nigeria, Tanganyika (Tanzania), Sierra Leone, Gambia and Zanzibar, was not pursued for long because of the opposition from the civilian colonists.

[8] Ageron, *Les Algériens Musulmans*, pp. 139-144.

[9] By "assimilation" was meant the application of French law to the Algerian population. But the colonists themselves were not initially subjected to all French laws. For example, they did not at first pay income tax, and until 1875 were exempted from the draft. One aberrant outcome of the policy of assimilation was the *Code de l'Indigénat*, or Natives' Code, which until the Second World War was used to condemn Algerians for offenses such as "not moving when called upon to fight a forest fire . . . and delay in the payment of taxes." Vincent Confer, *France and Algeria, The Problem of Civil and Political Reform, 1870-1920* (Syracuse: Syracuse University Press, 1966), p. 24.

[10] From 1870 to 1900, the problem of the political rights of the Algerrians was debated by the colonists' representatives and the French legislators. The decrees of 27 December 1866, which gave Algerians the right to elect one-third of the municipal councillors, was superseded by the decree of 7 April 1884, which placed a limit on the number of Algerian representatives (two for the first 1,000 people and one for each additional 1,000 people; the total was not to exceed six, or one-fourth of the entire Council). To elect a mayor, Algerian representatives had to be naturalized French, which meant renouncing their Muslim status, according to the naturalization law. See Ageron, *Les Algériens Musulmans*, p. 360. At first confined to a restricted category of individuals, the Algerian electorate was later organized into a "second *college*." Algerian candidates were separately elected by Algerians but did not have the same power as their colonist counterparts. See "Les Institutions Algériennes," in *Documents Algériens*, Jan. 1, 1948—Dec. 31, 1948, pp. 9-57. Up to 1962, there was no effective local representation for Algerians, nor was there a machinery for expressing grievances.

[11] Immanuel Wallerstein noted in this respect that "Algeria was the most (legally) 'assimilated' of all the French colonies, Tunisia and Morocco being the least." See Immanuel Wallerstein, *L'Afrique et l'Indépendance*, trans. Arnelle de Lesquen (Paris: Présence Africaine, 1966), p. 90.

[12] Ageron, *Les Algériens Musulmans*, pp. 68-70.

[13] Isnard, *La Réorganisation de la Propriété Rurale dans la Mitidja* (Alger: Imprimerie Joyeux, 1947), p. 30.

[14] John Ruedy sees two reasons for the seizure of *habus* property: financial and political. "From a political viewpoint, the existence of a power center disposing of considerable funds and wide influence constituted what appeared at the time a threat to the consolidation of the new power." See *Land Policy in Colonial Algeria* (Los Angeles: University of California Press, 1967), p. 68.

[15] Ibid., pp. 25-26.

[16] Ibid., p. 44.

[17] Ibid., p. 42.

[18] Ibid., p. 103.

[19] Ibid., p. 111.

[20] Ibid., p. 112.

[21] Ageron, *Les Algériens Musulmans*, p. 74.

[22] Ibid., p. 75.

[23] Ibid., p. 77. Up to 1870, the administration of Algeria was divided up between the military and civilian authorities.

[24] Ibid., p. 77.

[25] The use of French law was meant to "crush Arab property with legal fees it will not be able to pay for." See Ageron, *Les Algériens Musulmans*, p. 79. Legal fees under Islamic law are nominal.

[26] Xavier Yacono, *La Colonisation des Plaines du Chéliff*, 2 vols. (Alger: Imprimerie Imbert, 1955), 1:303.

[27] Ibid., p. 306. Yacono also reports that one notice of expropriation delimiting the domain and listing its owners was spread over six posters one meter by sixty-four centimeters.

[28] Ibid., p. 325. Licitation is the legal term for the auction sale of land held in indivisium.

[29] Isnard, *Réorganisation*, p. 112.

[30] Ibid.

31 Ibid., p. 114.

32 Ibid., p. 115.

33 Ageron, *Les Algériens Musulmans*, p. 372.

34 Ibid., p. 384.

35 In 1865-67, there was a drought; in 1864-66 and 1867, a cricket invasion; in 1865-67, an epidemic of cholera, and in 1872, an epidemic of smallpox.

36 Ibid., p. 375.

37 Yacono, *Colonisation*, 1:329.

38 Ageron, *Les Algériens Musulmans*, p. 369.

39 Ibid., p. 285. A *duar* is the smallest tribal unit, made up of a limited number of families. The French administration aimed at substituting the French type of commune to the *duar*.

40 Ibid., p. 294.

41 There were at least three main rebellions that took place in 1845, 1864 and 1871.

42 Quoted in Ageron, *Les Algériens Musulmans*, 1:393.

43 Yacono, *Colonisation*, 2:304-5. Yacono makes the point that "there was no disappearance of one social category, but only the substitution of some large landowners by other equally large landholders" who enriched themselves by buying up the poorer *fellah's* plots. However, the table of property changes which he provides indicates there was a small number of large landowners. There were five families holding between 100 and 500 hectares and only one owning 1,000 hectares. As he, himself, notes, the very conditions that made it possible for some to concentrate wealth also accounted for the undoing of these new owners in a very short period of time. Indeed, the colonists were opposed to the existence of indigenous proprietors.

44 The French administration maintained all the taxes that were levied by the Turkish government. In 1874, these taxes were rendered more uniform and new ones were added, as for example, a tax on trees! See Ageron, *Les Algériens Musulmans*, pp. 252-263.

45 Ibid., p. 631.

46 Ibid.

47 The historian Rinn reproduced a letter in which a member of the declining aristocracy expressed his feelings about the French administration: "You sacrifice us *djuads* (i.e., warrior aristocracy) who have helped you and are still helping you . . . so, despite all our efforts,

despite the blood we shed for you, we will not leave our children the dignity our forefathers left us." Ageron, *Les Algériens Musulmans,* p. 390.

48 Yacono, *Colonisation,* 2:237.

49 The word "middle class" is somewhat inappropriate because, in this case, it refers to small proprietors who were making do without hiring themselves out as *khammes* (sharecroppers). According to Ageron, one out of five peasants had less than ten hectares, and one out of 100 owned more than 100 hectares. Yacono: *Colonisation,* 2:829. Statistics on the actual number of these small proprietors are inaccurate. The best regional statistic was provided by Nouschi in *Enquête sur le Niveau.* It shows that for the region of Constantine, which had the highest concentration of small proprietors, out of 191, 297 fellahs, 55.3% had less than 10 hectares, 19.5% had 11 to 20 hectares, 12.4% had 21 to 30 hectares, 7.7% had 31 to 40 hectares, 4% had 41 to 100 hectares, and 0.85% had over 100 hectares. Therefore, small property was the norm and the so-called rural middle class was but a "plebe of minuscule proprietors." See Ageron, *Les Algériens Musulmans,* p. 829.

50 Ageron, *Les Algériens Musulmans,* p. 824.

51 Yacono, *Colonisation,* 1:312, indicates that until 1902 individuals who lived on wages alone were extremely rare. Wage labor developed as a result of the economic crises of the late 19th century which made expropriations easier. The argument was that the colonists needed more land to keep the economy going.

52 Ageron, *Les Algériens Musulmans,* 2:837.

53 The point made was that "colonization returned in wages more than the confiscated Arab lands produced." Ibid., p. 841.

54 Ibid., p. 842.

55 Ibid., p. 847.

56 Ibid., p. 846.

57 Ibid., p. 852.

58 Ibid., p. 853.

59 Karl Marx, *Capital* (New York: International Publishers, 1972), Vol. III, p. 723.

60 Ibid., p. 724.

61 Ibid., pp. 728-730.

62 More often than not, sequestrations led to the deportation of entire tribes, such as, for example, the *Hachem* tribe in the province of Constantine, who because of its participation in the 1871 insurrection lost

40,000 hectares of land and was condemned to displacement. To stop those tribesmen who kept returning to their territory, a General proposed that their houses be burnt down. See Nouschi, *Enquête sur le Niveau de Vie des Populations Rurales Constantinoises de la Conquête jusqu'en 1919* (Paris: Presses Universitaires de France, 1961), pp. 443-444.

63 Marx, *Capital*, pp. 732-733.

64 Nouschi, *Enquête*, p. 313.

65 Money existed in Algeria before 1830. However, the introduction of French currency gave rise to an active speculation so that the peasant incurred heavy losses because he had to use French currency for his payments and yet accept the other local monies when he sold his goods. Ibid., pp. 165-167.

66 For the size of this group, see Table 1.

67 Yacono, *Colonisation*, 1:314-321, presents two case studies of large landowners. In each case they were considered a threat by the colonists who managed to build colonial villages on their estates.

68 This category numbered 226 individuals in 1911. See Ageron, *Les Algériens Musulmans*, p. 824.

69 Ibid., p. 848.

70 About Turkish rule in Algeria, the colonist writer Walsin-Esterhazy said: "Theoretically weaker than us, the Turks . . . were much stronger in practice; and although they made no claim to be philanthropists, they were ultimately more so in the results they achieved. It would not be difficult to prove that seven years of our sentimental administration cost more blood to the Regency than twenty years of their bloody government. They were feared and we are not; they were respected and we are despised . . . masters, they wanted by all means possible the submission of their slaves so that they could exploit them; victorious France could have demanded the same submission not to exploit the vanquished but to regenerate them, to free them after enlightening them." Walsin-Esterhazy, *De la Domination Turque dans la Régence d'Alger* (Paris: Librairie Charles Gosselin, 1840), Preface.

71 Ageron, *Les Algériens Musulmans*. See also Confer, *France and Algeria*.

72 Ageron, quoted by Confer, Ibid., p. 117.

Notes
to
Chapter 4

[1] Charles-Robert Ageron, *Les Algériens Musulmans et la France 1871-1919*, 2 vols. (Paris: Presses Universitaires de France, 1968), 1:343. Also André Nouschi, *La Naissance du Nationalisme Algérien, 1914-1954* (Paris: Editions de Minuit, 1962).

[2] Ageron, *Les Algériens Musulmans*, 1:344.

[3] Ibid., 2:1049.

[4] Ibid., 2:1054.

[5] Ibid., 2:1053.

[6] Ibid., 2:1055.

[7] His organization was abolished in 1929. It appeared in 1932 under the name of P.P.A. (Algerian People's Party). After being abolished a second time in 1939, it came out again in 1946 as the M.T.L.D. (Movement for the Triumph of Democratic Liberties).

[8] Quoted in Nouschi, *La Naissance*, pp. 63-64. The *Assimilationistes'* demands were, among others, "proportional representation in parliament for Algerians, abolition of exceptional laws, obligatory education, free press, freedom to go to France. See Ferhat Abbas, *Guerre et Révolution d'Algérie*, Vol. I, La Nuit Coloniale (Paris: Julliard, 1962).

[9] Lhachemi Berradi et al., *La Formation des Elites Politiques Maghrébines* (Aix-en-Provence: Centre de Recherches et d'Etudes sur les Sociétés Méditerranéennes, 1973).

[10] Michael Clark, *Algeria in Turmoil* (New York: Grosset and Dunlap, 1960), p. 18.

[11] Ibid.

12 Quandt, *Revolution and Political Leadership in Algeria, 1954-1968* (Cambridge: the Massachusetts Institute of Technology Press, 1969), p. 38.

13 *Métayer* is a farmer who pays his rent in kind.

14 Source: Nouschi, *Naissance*, pp. 97-124. Grand total as in the original text.

15 Ibid., p. 121.

16 Abbas, quoted in Clark, *Algeria in Turmoil*, p. 21.

17 Nouschi, *Naissance*, p. 138.

18 Quandt, *Revolution*, p. 52.

19 Nouschi quotes the colonist Henri Benazet as stating that the repression was "fierce, ruthless, indeed inhumane in its lack of discrimination." Abbas reports, in *Nuit Coloniale*, that Senegalese troups, fighter bombers and ad hoc bands of colonists were used in the massacre of men, women and children.

20 In fact, 398 arrests were made throughout the country, according to a French official. See Quandt, *Revolution*, p. 59.

21 Ibid., p. 60.

22 Alf A. Heggoy, *Insurgency and Counterinsurgency in Algeria* (Bloomington: Indiana University Press, 1972), p. 47. It has also been suggested that Messali and the *Centralistes* disagreed on the actual procedure for moving from the political to the armed struggle. See Abbas, *Nuit Coloniale*, p. 124.

23 Mohammed Bedjaoui, *Law and the Algerian Revolution* (Brussels: International Association of Democratic Lawyers, 1961), p. 84.

24 Quandt, *Revolution*, p. 46.

25 Ahmed Ben Bella, in *Ahmed Ben Bella*, ed. Robert Merle (Paris: Gallimard, 1965), p. 97.

26 The first F.L.N. charter pointed out that the Front's goal was "national independence through the restoration of the Algerian State, sovereign, democratic and social, within the framework of Islamic principles." See André Mandouze, *La Révolution Algérienne par les Textes* (Paris: Maspéro, 1961), p. 159.

27 Fanon, *The Wretched of the Earth* (New York: Grove Press, 1966).

28 Quandt, *Revolution*, p. 13.

29 Ibid., p. 97.

30 Clark, *Algeria in Turmoil*, pp. 186-198. In fact, the sixty-one members of the U.D.M.A. and Algerian elected officials had decided before

the meeting was convened to abide by the majority vote over the issue of whether to accept the new French policy of integration. Twenty-five members voted for the motion repudiating integration; seventeen voted against it, while nine were absent.

31 Abane Ramdane was later killed by a member of the Algerian provisional government (G.P.R.A.) for his outspoken criticism of the lack of revolutionary spirit among its leadership. For a detailed account of this event, see Mohammed Lebjaoui, *Verités sur la Révolution Algérienne* (Paris: Editions Gallimard, 1970), pp. 152-162.

32 Thomas Opperman, *Le Problème Algérien* (Paris: Maspéro, 1961), p. 116.

33 Ben Bella, along with four F.L.N. members, was hijacked by the French on 22 October 1956, while on a Rabat-Tunis flight.

34 Ben Bella, in *Amed Ben Bella*, pp. 113-114.

35 Mohammedi Said, quoted in Quandt, *Revolution*, p. 101.

36 Ibid., p. 103.

37 Ben Bella, in *Ahmed Ben Bella*.

38 Ibid., pp. 115-116.

39 Lebjaoui, *Vérités*, pp. 167-169.

40 Quandt, *Revolution*, p. 112.

41 Quandt refers to this group as the "Intellectuals." *Revolution*, pp. 115-124.

42 Lebjaoui, *Vérités*, p. 170. Also Ben Bella, *Ahmed Ben Bella*, pp. 135-136.

43 Among other sources, see appendix to Joachim Joesten, *The New Algeria* (Chicago: Follett Publishing Co., 1964), pp. 202-228.

44 Ibid., pp. 206-207.

45 Ibid.

46 Lebjaoui,*Vérités*, p. 170.

47 B. Mezhoudi, quoted in Quandt, *Revolution*, p. 173. In his biography, Ben Bella, too, accuses the G.P.R.A. for wanting to "twist the neck of the Revolution." *Ahmed Ben Bella*, p. 141.

48 Quandt, p. 15.

49 Adapted from Berradi et al, *Formation des Elites*, p. 118.

50 Ibid., p. 116. These tables do not reflect the total distribution of the G.P.R.A. (Provisional Government) members.

51 *Annuaire de l'Afrique du Nord* (Aix-en-Provence and Paris: Editions du Centre National de la Recherche Scientifique, 1962), Vol. I, p. 118. (Rounded percentages.)

52 Quandt, *Revolution*, p. 183.

53 Ibid., p. 198.

54 Adapted from Berradi et al, *Formation des Elites*, p. 116.

55 These were the Trotskyist Greek, M. Raptis, the Egyptian, Lotfallah, and the Algerian Marxist, M. Harbi.

56 B. Ibrahim, quoted in Arslan Humbaraci, *Algeria: A Revolution That Failed* (New York: Frederick A. Praeger, 1966), p. 237.

57 Ibid., p. 95.

58 The ex-*wilaya* leaders blamed Boumédiène for neglecting them as he restructured his army with old professionals (men who made a career in the French army).

59 Quandt, *Revolution*, p. 232.

60 These will be referred to in this study as the technocrats.

Notes
to
Chapter 5

1 Isnard, *La Réorganisation de la Propriété Rurale dans la Mitidja* (Alger: Imprimerie Joyeux, 1947), p. 23.

2 Marx, *The 18th Brumaire of Louis Bonaparte*, (New York: International Publishers, 1969), p. 15.

3 It is generally agreed that self-management started out as a spontaneous phenomenon. See Douglas E. Ashford, "Political Aspects of Rural Developments," in Leon C. Brown, *State and Society in Independent North Africa* (Washington, D.C.: The Middle East Institute, 1966), pp. 220-222. Also Gérard Chaliand, *L'Algérie Est-Elle Socialiste?* (Paris: Maspéro, 1964); François d'Arcy et al, *Essais sur l'Economie de l'Algérie* (Paris: 1964); Daniel Guérin, *L'Algérie Qui Se Cherche* (Paris: 1964). It has been argued that instead of being spontaneous, self-management had, in effect, been induced by the army. See Chaulet, *La*

Mitidja Autogérée (Alger: S.N.E.D., 1971). In reality, both processes occurred with the army sometimes expelling workers from self-managed estates in order to reconvert them into military cooperatives. See Clegg, *Workers' Self-Management in Algeria* (New York: Monthly Review Press, 1971), pp. 50-51.

4 Alain Marrill, "Buts Politiques Auxquels Répond l'Autogestion Algérienne," in d'Arcy et al, *Essais*, p. 177. Clegg gives the figure of 1,220,000 and 1,000 enterprises.

5 Ibid., p. 178.

6 Chaulet, *Mitidja*, pp. 49-56, especially workers' interviews. For instances of appropriation of commercial enterprises, see Monique Laks, *Autogestion Ouvrière et Pouvoir Politique en Algérie, 1962-1965* (Paris: E.D.I., 1970), pp. 138-140.

7 The first issue of the Union's paper, *L'Ouvrier Algérien*, did not, however, stress the role of the Union in self-management. On the contrary, it urged the government to appeal to French owners to reopen their enterprises within a new framework of labor/management relationship. See *L'Ouvrier Algérien*, 17 August 1962.

8 Chaulet, *Mitidja*, pp 50-51. *Ashur* tax is a 10% income tax.

9 *Journal Officiel de la République Algérienne Démocratique et Populaire*, No. 1, 1962.

10 It must be noted that the transitional government, *the Exécutif Provisoire*, which was established after the 19 March 1962 cease-fire, had already taken an ordinance on 24 August 1962 defining abandoned property as "vacant" property (*bien vacant*) and announcing that it would be temporarily taken care of until the return of its owners because its abandonment threatened the economy of the country.

11 Quoted in Chaulet, *Mitidja*, p. 57. See also Clegg, *Workers' Self-management*, p. 59.

12 This may be explained by the government's desire to respect the Evian Accords that concluded the colonial war. See Humbaraci, *Algeria: A Revolution That Failed* (New York: Frederick A. Praeger, 1966).

13 Laks, *Autogestion Ouvrière*, pp. 211-216.

14 For a discussion of the March decrees, see among others Laks, *Autogestion Ouvrière*, pp. 152-165; Alain Marrill, "Les Déviations du Système Prévu par les Décrets de Mars et les Efforts Entrepris pour les Pallier," in d'Arcy et al, *Essais*, pp. 193-200; Clegg, *Workers' Self-Management*, pp. 61-74; and Chaulet, *Mitidja*, pp. 146-157.

15 Chaulet, *Mitidja*, pp. 212-213.

16 Ibid., p. 149.

17 Ibid.

18 Ibid., p. 159.

19 Laks, *Autogestion Ouvrière*, p. 88.

20 Marrill, "Les Déviations du Système Prévu," in d'Arcy et al, *Essais*, p. 193.

21 Laks, *Autogestion Ouvrière*, p. 63.

22 Chaulet, *Mitidja*, p. 151.

23 Clegg, *Workers' Self-Management*, p. 163.

24 Recruitment of presidents of management committees was sometimes based on an appreciation of some individual's ability to command. For example, workers who were maintained in a subordinate position by the former colonists because of their "stubbornness" were promoted to the position of president. Conversely, where an individual did not display an outstanding character trait, his election to the presidency was always completed with an imputed "qualification" which enabled him to obtain material benefits. See Chaulet, *Mitidja*, pp. 165-167.

25 Clegg, *Workers' Self-Management*, pp. 162-170.

26 Chaulet, *Mitidja*, p. 150.

27 Laks, *Autogestion Ouvrière*, p. 69.

28 Ibid., p. 77.

29 Ibid., p. 80 and p. 83.

30 Clegg, *Workers' Self-Management*, p. 66.

31 Quoted in Laks, *Autogestion Ouvrière*, p. 171.

32 O.N.R.A. was apparently created on the recommendation of the French agricultural expert, René Dumont, who was hired by the Algerian Government to study the functioning of the self-managed estates. Dumont was in favor of increased state control over these estates. See Phillips Forster and Herbert Steiner, *The Structure of Algerian Socialized Agriculture* (College Park: University of Maryland, Department of Agricultural Economics, July 1964), pp. 22-23.

33 Quoted in Clegg, *Workers' Self-Management*, p. 67.

34 For examples of O.N.R.A.'s interference in self-management, see especially Clegg, *Workers' Self-Management*, pp. 144-145, 154-155, 161.

35 Ibid., p. 155.

36 The June 1964 decrees were taken as part of an effort to reorganize the Socialist Industrial sector. They called for a horizontal and vertical

concentration of enterprises by branches of activity. These centralized enterprises were then organized into district and national unions.

[37] Clegg reports that out of 400 applications only ten were granted a loan by the B.C.A. or the C.A.D. See Clegg, *Workers' Self-Management*, p. 155.

[38] The *Coopérative F. Fanon* went under in 1965, mainly because the government owed it 600,000 Dinars for painting and decorating jobs. Its committee was charged with inability to fulfill its obligations and was replaced with "experts" chosen by the Ministry of Finance and Industry.

[39] For an analysis of the role played by the B.C.A., see Laks, *Autogestion Ouvrière*, pp. 189-195.

[40] Bachir Boumaza, quoted in Laks, ibid., p. 192.

[41] For specific cases, see Clegg, *Workers' Self-Management*, pp. 156-157.

[42] Laks, Autogestion Ouvrière, p. 194.

[43] Clegg, *Workers' Self-Management*, p. 134.

[44.] Houari Boumédiène, in Ministère de l'Information et de la Culture, *Discours du Président Boumédiène, 19 Juin 1965-19 Juin 1970*, 2 vols., 1:704.

[45] Ibid., p. 330.

[46] Ibid., 2:318.

[47] Evaluations of the self-managed enterprises were based on their gross product and, therefore, were misleading. The point has been made that "as long as prices are not determined in terms of the social use of the product, financial results cannot help guide the management of the estates, nor can they inform those responsible for the policy of the country." See Chaulet, *Mitidja*, p. 143.

[48] *Clegg, Workers' Self-Management*, p. 152.

[49] Ibid.

[50] *Annuaire Statistique de l'Algérie*, Secrétariat d'Etat au Plan (Alger: Direction des Statistiques, 1972), p. 84.

[51] Ibid., p. 82.

[52] Boumédiène, *Discours*, 2:111.

[53] Ibid.

[54] *La Révolution Agraire*, (Alger: Présidence du Conseil), pp. 20-21.

[55] Ibid., p. 22.

56 The minimum daily wage for a rural worker is 7.54 Dinars ($1.07) and the maximum is 20 DA ($5.00). See Chaulet, *Mitidja*, pp. 110-113.

57 The ordinance gives the following breakdown of the land ownership:

16,500 individuals own	50 hectares	25% of all private lands
147,000 individuals own	10-50 hectares	50% of all private lands
114,000 individuals own	5-10 hectares	15% of all private lands
310,000 individuals own	less than 5 hectares	10% of all private lands

In other words, 3% of the population involved in agriculture own 25% of the cultivable land. The total arable land covers 6,800,000 hectares in northern Algeria for a rural population of 8,000,000. See Ordinance 71-73, 8 November 1971, p. 10.

58 Ibid., pp. 24-26.

59 In the absence of a male descendant who is of age, the cooperative to which the deceased was affiliated takes material care of his family.

60 Despite the limits put on the size of landed property, Egyptian landlords managed to increase their landholdings from 27,000 *feddans* in 1957 to 40,000 in 1964. Besides, they also managed to outnumber peasants at the cooperatives' boards, where by law peasants were to constitute 4/5 of all members, by placing in their own men. Quoted in Tami Tidafi, *L'Agriculture Algérienne et Ses Perspectives de Développement* (Paris: Maspéro, 1969), p. 158.

61 Volontariat des Etudiants pour la Révolution Agraire, Eté 1971 mimeographed (Alger: Ministère de l'Agriculture et de la Réforme Agraire, 22-24 Août, 1972).

62 Ibid., p. 16.

63 Ibid., p. 20.

64 Laks, *Autogestion Ouvrière*, p. 262.

65 Paul Blumberg, *Industrial Democracy: The Sociology of Participation* (New York: Schocken Books, 1969), p. 174.

66 Laks, *Autogestion Ouvrière*, p. 244.

67 Ibid., p. 250.

68 For a detailed report on workers' interventions, see Laks, *Autogestion Ouvrière*, pp. 219-231.

69 Ibid., p. 225.

70 Boumédiène, *Discours*, 1:21.

71 Boumédiène, *Discours*, 2:106-107.

72 For a good analysis of the U.G.T.A. Relationship with the government up to 1965, see Jeanne Favret, "Le Syndicat, les Travailleurs et

le Pouvoir en Algérie," *Annuaire de l'Afrique du Nord*, Vol. 3, 1964, pp. 44-62.

73 David Ottaway and Marina Ottaway, *Algeria, the Politics of a Socialist Revolution* (Berkeley and Los Angeles: University of California Press, 1970), p. 132.

74 The need to extend the union's activity to rural areas was imperative. The U.G.T.A. covered mostly urban centers. The creation of a *Fédération Nationale des Travailleurs de la Terre* aroused the hostility of the Ministry of Agriculture, who decided to get control of it through O.N.R.A. The latter listed some of its members as candidates to the Executive Committee of the F.N.T.T. on grounds that since they dealt with the rural sector of self-management they too could be considered rural workers. The F.N.T.T. tried to overcome the difficulty by stating that no O.N.R.A. official could also hold a position within the F.N.T.T. This was countered by the Ministry of Agriculture, who ordered O.N.R.A. candidates to resign their administrative posts, thereby becoming eligible to the F.N.T.T. See Ottaway, *Algeria*, pp. 136-138.

75 Ibid., p. 142.

76 Quoted in Clegg, *Workers' Self-Management*, p. 140.

77 Favret, "Le Syndicat," p. 62.

78 Jacques Berque, *Dépossession du Monde* (Paris: Editions du Seuil, 1964), p. 56.

79 Boumédiène, *Discours*, 1:86.

80 *Critères et Options de la Réforme des Sociétés* mimeographed (Alger: Ministère du Commerce, 20 May 1970).

81 *Le Code des Investissement*, (Alger: Ministère des Finances et du Plan, September 1967), p. 5.

82 Ibid., p. 11.

83 Ibid., p. 14.

84 *Critères et Options*, p. 8.

85 Ibid.

86 République Algérienne Démocratique et Populaire, *Industrie 1968* Vol. 3 (Alger: Direction Générale du Plan et des Etudes Economiques, Sous-Direction des Statistiques), p. 105.

87 Ibid.

88 These seem to be the assumptions underlying Chaliand's and Humbaraci's critical assessments of Algeria's "socialism."

[89] Secrétariat d'Etat au Plan, Direction des Statistiques, *Statistiques Financières*, (Alger, 1970), p. 12. This table does not include oil tax revenue. Direct taxes refer to income taxes, while indirect taxes relate to taxes collected on alcohols, tobacco, gas, matches, etc. Tariffs and taxes on registration of legal documents are also included in tax revenues. Note that foreign aid in 1970 covered only 7.2% of the total budget, or 61 million Dinars.

[90] Boumédiène, *Discours*, 2:108.

Notes
to
Chapter 6

[1] "Redressement" is the word used to preface administrative reports about the Algerian politico-economic situation since 1965. A double entendre is implied in this concept which may mean both correcting and making right.

[2] Quoted in Poulantzas, *Pouvoir Politique et Classes Sociales,* 2 vols. (Paris: Maspéro, 1971), 2:43. Poulantzas indicates that legitimacy refers to the ideological and political, that is, the political impact of the dominant ideology.

[3] For a discussion of Hegel's contribution to the concept of ideology, see George Lichtheim, *The Concept of Ideology and Other Essays* (New York: Random House, 1967), pp. 11-17.

[4] Ibid., p. 18.

[5] Ibid., p. 21.

[6] See, among others, David E. Apter, *The Politics of Modernization* (Chicago: The University of Chicago Press, 1965) and Kemal H. Karpat, ed., *Political and Social Thought in the Contemporary Middle East* (New York: Frederick A. Praeger, 1968).

7 See Daniel Bell, *The End of Ideology* (Glencoe: The Free Press, 1960).

8 For a critique of this particular conception of ideology, see Juan E. Corradi, "Cultural Dependence and the Sociology of Knowledge: The Latin American Case," *International Journal of Contemporary Sociology*, VIII, No. 1 (January, 1971), 37-54.

9 Karpat, *Political and Social Thought*, p. 3.

10 Lebjaoui, *Vérités sur la Révolution Algérienne* (Paris: Editions Gallimard, 1970), p. 170.

11 Ibid.

12 The history of the exact circumstances that led to the signing of the Evian Accords is still little known.

13 The Program of Tripoli, in Joachim Joesten, *The New Algeria*, (Chicago: Follett Publishing Co., 1964), p. 224.

14 Ibid., pp. 206-207.

15 Ibid., pp. 208-209.

16 Ibid., p. 209.

17 Ibid., p. 210. Emphasis added.

18 Ibid., p. 208.

19 Ibid., p. 212.

20 Ibid.

21 Ibid., p. 217.

22 Ibid., p. 219.

23 Ibid., p. 215.

24 André Mandouze, *La Révolution Algérienne par les Textes* (Paris: Gallimard, 1961).

25 Robert B. Revere, "Consensus in Independent Algeria" (Ph.D. diss., New York University, 1971), p. 119.

26 For a discussion of the origins of the Charter of Algiers, see Lebjaoui, *Vérités*, pp. 183-189. Lebjaoui makes the point that the 50-man commission failed to deal with issues such as democracy, workers' immigration to France, meaning of the concept of "counter-revolution" used on page 30 of the Charter.

27 F.L.N.—Commission Centrale d'Orientation, *La Charte d'Alger* (Alger: Imprimerie Nationale Algérienne, 1964), p. 40.

28 Ibid., p. 41.

29 Ibid., p. 42.

30 Ibid., p. 38.

31 Ibid., p. 39. The original text is very clumsy at this particular point and may lead to misinterpreting the "social stratum" and the bureaucratic bourgeoisie as two different entities. It says "une nouvelle couche sociale en formation accélérée risque *d'intervenir du côté* de la poussée instinctive anti-socialiste de la bourgeoisie bureaucratique qui se forme dans les appareils de l'administration." (Emphasis added.) The next paragraph is the text indicates that the bureaucratic bourgeoisie *is* the new social stratum referred to.

32 Ibid.

33 Ibid., p. 26.

34 Ibid., p. 61.

35 Ibid., p. 71.

36 Ibid., p. 70.

37 Ibid., p. 63.

38 Ibid., pp. 59-60.

39 Ibid., p. 110.

40 Ibid., p. 107.

41 Ibid.

42 Ibid., pp. 71-81.

43 Ibid., p. 71.

44 Ibid., p. 105.

45 Houari Boumédiène, in *Discours du Président Boumédiène, 19 Juin 1965-19 Juin 1970,* 2 vols. (Alger: Ministère de l'Information et de la Culture), 1:8.

46 Ibid., p. 20

47 For a perceptive discussion of whether Islam in North Africa is a crucial variable in understanding values and institutions, see Leon C. Brown, "The Role of Islam in Modern North Africa," in Leon C. Brown, ed., *State and Society in Independent North Africa* (Washington, D.C.: The Middle East Institute, 1966), pp. 97-120.

48 Boumédiène, *Discours*, 2:109.

49 *La Révolution Agraire,* pp. 20-21.

50 Ministère du Commerce, "Critères et Options de la Réforme des Sociétés," mimeographed (Alger, 20 Mai 1970), p. 12.

51 Ibid., p. 5. The number of national corporations increased from 12 in 1963 to 262 in 1968, the highest point being in 1966 when 105 corporations were created.

52 Revere, "Consensus in Independent Algeria," p. 126.

53 Joesten, *New Algeria*, "The Program of Tripoli," p. 210; also *La Charte d'Alger*, p. 44.

54 Maxime Rodinson, "Insuffisance Explicative du Rejet de la Dynamique des Contradictions Internes," in Maxime Rodinson, *Marxisme et Monde Musulman* (Paris: Editions du Seuil, 1972), pp. 282-283.

55 Khalfa Maameri, *Orientations Politiques de l'Algérie* (Alger: S.N.E.D., 1973), p. 103.

56 Rodinson, "Rapports entre Islam et Communisme," in *Marxisme et Monde Musulman*, pp. 154-180. Both Islam and Communism are defined as "militant ideological movements with a temporal socio-political program and aiming at building an all-encompassing community." See p. 154.

57 Boumédiène, *Discours*, 1:30.

58 Ibid., p. 280.

59 Karl Marx, *Writings of the Young Marx on Philosophy and Society*, Loyd D. Easton and Kurt H. Guddat, eds. (New York: Anchor Books, 1967), p. 408.

60 Ibid., p. 414.

Notes
to
Chapter 7

1 Some of the single-party non-proletariat states in Africa are: Algeria, Tunisia, Ivory Coast, Tanzania, Ghana, Uganda, Sierra Leone, Upper Volta and Sudan. In Asia: Cambodia.

2 Gwendolyn M. Carter, ed., *African One-Party States* (Ithaca: Cornell University Press, 1962), p. 3.

3 Ibid.

4 Immanuel Wallerstein, "The Decline of the Party in Single-Party African States," in Joseph LaPalombara and Myron Weiner, eds., *Political Parties and Political Development* (Princeton: Princeton University Press, 1966), p. 207.

5 Bedjaoui, *Law and the Algerian Revolution* (Brussels: International Association of Democratic Lawyers, 1961), p. 82 and p. 85.

6 Article 5, F.L.N., Commission Centrale d'Orientation, *La Charte d'Alger* (Alger: Imprimerie Nationale Algérienne, 1964), p. 86.

7 Ibid., Articles 9 and 10.

8 Ibid., p. 87.

9 Franz Schurmann, *Ideology and Organization in Communist China* (Berkeley: University of California Press, 1973), p. 110. Schurmann points out that the Chinese do not use the word "nation"(*Kuomin*) because the nation includes exploiting classes as well. This would indicate that the Chinese consider the revolution as still being in progress, whereas the Soviets seem to think that the revolution has already been achieved. In the Algerian case, the national character of the Party was meant to achieve as wide a consensus as possible in order to present a monolithic front to the colonial power structure which questioned the existence of an Algerian nation.

10 *Mudjahidine* are freedom fighters.

11 Bedjaoui, *Law and Algerian Revolution*, p. 43.

12 Ibid., p. 95.

13 *Le Programme de Tripoli*, published by La Tendance Révolutionnaire du Parti Communiste Français, pp. 9-10.

14 Mao Tse-Tung, "On Coalition Government," 24 April 1945, in Quotations from Chairman Mao (Peking: Foreign Language Press, 1968), pp. 126-128.

15 *Programme de Tripoli*, p. 11.

16 Ibid.

17 Ibid.

18 Deputy Abdennour Ali Yahia, quoted in Claude Estier, *Pour L'Algérie* (Paris: Maspéro, 1964), pp. 65-66.

19 Ali Mendjli, quoted in Estier, *Pour L'Algérie*, p. 66.

20 Articles 24 and 25 of the Constitution, quoted in Estier, *Pour L'Algérie*, p. 69.

[21] Ben Bella, quoted in Estier, *Pour L'Algérie*, p 76. The difference in opinion between Ben Bella and Khider is reminiscent of that between Lenin and the Mensheviks.

[22] La Charte d'Alger, p. 107.

[23] Ibid., p. 118.

[24] Quoted in Schurmann, *Ideology and Organization*, p. 118.

[25] *La Charte d'Alger*, p. 118.

[26] Ibid., p. 119.

[27] Schurmann, *Ideology and Organization*, p. 120.

[28] *La Charte d'Alger*, p. 123.

[29] Ibid., p. 124.

[30] William B. Quandt, *Revolution and Political Leadership in Algeria, 1954-1968* (Cambridge: The Massachusetts Institute of Technology Press, 1969), p. 228.

[32] François Buy, *La République Algérienne Démocratique et Populaire* (Paris: La Librairie François, 1965), p. 46.

[33] The failure of the Party to act as an active arbiter in situations of crises has been interpreted as a "symbolic function of maintaining national unity." The Party would perpetuate the image of a "faultless, unified power that cannot be affected by 'partisan' squabbles." See Jean Leca, "Parti et Etat en Algérie," *Annuaire de l'Afrique du Nord* (1968), 8:27-28.

[34] Quoted in Maschino and M'rabet, *L'Algérie des Illusions*, p. 168.

[35] Ibid., p. 169.

[36] Houari Boumédiène, *Discours du Président Boumédiène, 19 Juin 1965-19 Juin 1970*, 2 vols., ed. Ministère de l'Information et de la Culture (Constantine: El Baath, 1970), 2: 113.

[37] Ibid., p. 115.

[38] Ibid., p. 114.

[39] Ibid., p. 245.

[40] Maschino and M'rabet, pp. 176-177.

[41] Boumédiène, *Discours*, 2:273.

[42] Quoted in Maschino and M'rabet, p. 172.

[43] Ibid., p. 173.

[44] Ibid.

[45] Ibid., p. 171.

46 Mao Tse-Tung, *Quotations*, p. 104.

47 Ibid., p. 113.

48 Ibid., p. 124.

49 Ibid., p. 125.

50 Ibid., p. 131.

51 Quoted in Schurmann, *Ideology and Organization*, p. 164.

52 Ibid., p. 9.

53 D'Arcy et al, *Essais sur l'Economie de l'Algérie Nouvelle* (Paris: Presses Universitaires de France, 1965), pp. 1-91.

54 Mostefa Lacheraf, quoted in Chaliand, *L'Algérie, Est-Elle Socialiste?* (Paris: Maspéro, 1964), p. 108.

55 Mustapha Sehimi, quoted in Abderrahmane Remili, "Parti et Administration en Algérie," *Annuaire de l'Afrique du Nord* (1968), 7:47.

56 Remili, *Annuaire*, p. 48.

57 Ibid.

58 *La Charte d'Alger*, p. 118. The membership of the F.L.N. was estimated at 100,000 in 1964. See Chaliand, *L'Algérie, Est-Elle Socialiste?*, p. 107.

59 Boumédiène, *Discours*, 2:245.

60 Mao Tse-Tung, *Quotations*, pp. 118-119.

61 Chaliand, *L'Algérie, Est-Elle Socialiste?*, p. 108.

62 For a discussion of the relationship between Party and class, see Chris Harman. "Party and Class," in *Party and Class*, Essays by Toni Cliff, Duncan Hallas, Chris Harman and Leon Trotsky (London: Pluto Press, n.d.), pp. 47-64.

63 Ibid.

Notes
to
Chapter 8

1 Max Weber, *From Max Weber, Essays in Sociology,* eds., Mills, C. Wright and Gerth, Herbert H. (New York: Oxford University Press, 1958), pp. 232-235.

2 Ibid., p. 231.

3 Ralf Dahrendorf, *Class and Class Conflict in Industrial Society* (Stanford: Stanford University Press, 1959), p. 301.

4 Reinhard Bendix, "Bureaucracy and Power Relations," in *Bureaucracy,* ed. Robert K. Merton et al (New York: The Free Press, 1952), p. 129.

5 See Joseph LaPalombara, ed., *Bureaucracy and Political Development* (Princeton: Princeton University Press, 1963), especially selections by Fred W. Riggs, Merle Fainsod and J. Donald Kingsley.

6 For a comparison between Weber and Lenin, see Erik O. Wright, "To Control or to Smash Bureaucracy: Weber and Lenin on Politics, the State and Bureaucracy," *Berkeley Journal of Sociology* 19 (1974-75): 69-108.

7 Max Weber, *Max Weber and the Theory of Social and Economic Organization,* ed. Talcott Parsons, (New York: The Free Press, 1968), p. 154.

8 Lenin, *Essential Works,* p. 308.

9 Wright suggests that "Weber has an elaborate theory of organizational contradiction but an underdeveloped theory of social contradictions; Lenin has a relatively developed theory of social contradictions but no theory of organizational contradictions." See Wright, "To Control or to Smash Bureaucracy," p. 98.

10 Nicos Poulantzas, "The Problem of the Capitalist State," in *Ideology in Social Science*, ed. Robin Blackburn (New York: Vintage Books, 1973), p. 246.

11 Poulantzas, *Pouvoir Politique et Classes Sociales*, 2 vols. (Paris: Maspéro, 1971), 2:90.

12 This refers to William Kornhauser's "veto groups," as discussed in "Power Elite or Veto Groups?", in *C. Wright Mills and the Power Elite*, comp. G. William Domhoff and Hoyt B. Ballard (Boston: Beacon Press, 1968), pp. 37-59. It also refers to Robert Dahl's conception of power as being linked to the type of decision made in *Who Governs?* (New Haven and London: Yale University Press, 1961); and "A Critique of the Ruling Elite Model," in *C. Wright Mills and the Power Elite*, pp. 25-36. In fact, Poulantzas distinguishes between two theoretical trends: one that dissolves the political in the economic (e.g., veto groups) and one that has the economic "absorb" the political (e.g., theory of managerialism).

13 Poulantzas, *Pouvoir Politique*.

14 Marx, *The 18th Brumaire of Louis Bonaparte* (New York: International Publishers, 1969), p. 122.

15 Poulantzas is aware that Marx made a distinction between the parliamentary power of the French republic and the executive power of the bonapartist state, but he chose not to take that into consideration.

16 Ralf Miliband also makes this point in his rebuttal of Poulantzas' critique of *The State in Capitalist Society*. See Blackburn, *Ideology in Social Science*, pp. 253-262.

17 Poulantzas, *Pouvoir Politique*, p. 84.

18 Ibid., p. 114.

19 Miliband's analysis of *The State in Capitalist Society* is not included here because it is felt that it does not go beyond the conception according to which the state is an instrument of the ruling class.

20 Poulantzas, *Pouvoir Politique*, p. 164.

21 Ibid.

22 Ibid., p. 167.

23 Ibid., p. 168.

24 It must be noted, in this respect, that Djilas specifically points out that his "new class" is not a bureaucratic class.

25 Ian Clegg, *Workers' Self-Management in Algeria* (New York: Monthly Review Press, 1971), p. 113.

26 Ibid.

[27] Abderrahmane Remili, *Les Institutions Administratives Algériennes* (Alger: S.N.E.D., 1973), p. 189. The French baccalaureate is composed of two parts.

[28] Clegg, *Workers' Self-Management*.

[29] Quoted in Chaliand and Minces, *L'Algérie Indépendante* (Paris: Petite Collection Maspéro, 1972), p. 75.

[30] For a breakdown of these figures, see Remili, *Institutions* p. 186; also *Annuaire Statistique de l'Algérie, 1972*, p. 42.

[31] Remili, *Institutions*, p. 188.

[32] Ibid., pp. 192-213.

[33] Ibid., p. 119.

[34] Ibid., p. 125.

[35] Ibid., p. 118.

[36] Quoted from *Révolution Africaine*, No. 311, July 2, 1970, in Remili, *Institutions*, p. 148.

[37] Ibid., p. 151.

[38] Franz Schurmann, "Politics and Economics in Russia and China," in *Soviet and Chinese Communism: Similarities and Differences*, David Treadgold, ed. (Seattle: University of Washington Press, 1970), pp. 297-326.

[39] Houari Boumédiène, *Discours du Président Boumédiène, 19 Juin 1965-19 Juin 1970,* 2 vols. ed. Ministère de l'Information de la Culture (Constantine: El Baath, 1970, 1:15.

[40] Houari Boumédiène, *Discours du Président Boumédiène, 2 Juillet 1970-1 Mai 1972*, vol. 3, ed. Ministère de l'Information de la Culture (Alger: Ech-Chaab Press, 1973), p. 192.

[41] Ibid., pp. 192-94.

[42] This may also mean that non-Party members could counteract the centralizing effects of Party organization, thereby providing the government with an opportunity to denounce the anti-revolutionary character of the bourgeoisie. This was the case in China during the cultural revolution. It seems doubtful, however, that the same phenomenon is in process in Algeria. The Algerian dominant class is a petty-bourgeois class which has not yet solved its ambivalence toward the Party control of the bureaucracy.

[43] Remili, *Institutions*, p. 251.

[44] République Algérienne Démocratique et Populaire, *le Plan Quadriennal, 1970-1973, Rapport Général*, (Editions Populaires de l'Armée, Janvier 1970), p. 146.

45 Remili, *Institutions*, pp. 251-252.

46 Ibid., pp. 253-254.

47 Tami Tidafi, *L'Agriculture Algérienne et Ses Perspectives de Développment* (Paris: Maspéro, 1969), p. 160.

48 O. Sissani, "Le 1er Mai des Certitudes," *Révolution Africaine*, No. 532, May 3-9, 1974, pp. 6-7 and p. 10.

49 "Une Action Conséquente," *Révolution Africaine*, No. 533, May 10-16, 1974, p. 18. Reporting on the grievances the F.N.T.P.G.A. had concerning the promotion of skilled drillers who did not hold a diploma, the magazine wrote: "This problem seems to preoccupy the cadres of the Federation who told us about finding a solution to it in collaboration with the cadres of SONATRACH—*who are themselves* [emphasis mine]." SONATRACH is a state owned oil and gas corporation.

50 *El Moudjahid*, 14 February 1967, quoted in Remili, *Institutions*, p. 249.

51 Marx, *The 18th Brumaire* (New York: International Publishers), p. 122.

52 Maameri, *Orientations Politiques de l'Algérie* (Alger: S.N.E.D., 1973), p. 56. There were also 182 references to the Party and 134 to industrialization.

53 Ibid., p. 66.

54 Ibid., p. 75.

55 Frederick Engels, "Preface to the Peasant War in Germany," in Karl Marx and Frederick Engels, *Selected Works* (New York: International Publishers, 1969), p. 242.

56 Mostefa Lacheraf, *L'Algérie: Nation et Société* (Paris: Maspéro, 1965), p. 343. Originally published as "Reflexions Sociologiques sur le Nationalisme et la Culture en Algérie," in *Les Temps Moderns*, March, 1964.

Notes
to
Chapter 9

[1] *Le Programme de Tripoli* (Paris: Supplément au No. 84 "Le Communiste," n.d.), p. 3 and p. 5.

[2] Ibid., p. 9.

[3] *La Charte d'Alger* (Alger: Imprimerie Nationale Algérienne, 1964), p. 32.

[4] Karl Marx and Frederick Engels, *The German Ideology* (New York: International Publishers, 1972), Part One, p. 47.

[5] See Ahmed Akkache, *Capitaux Etrangers et Libération Economique: l'Expérience Algérienne* (Paris: Maspéro, 1971), pp. 89-97 and pp. 111-115.

[6] Ibid., p. 140.

[7] Ibid., p. 139.

[8] Algeria often launches international bids to investors, prescribing that the latter must reinvest 70% of their profits in Algeria and train Algerian personnel. In return, they may import 30% of the parts that are not available in Algeria, utilize the full capacity of their plants for producing various products, and ultimately obtain a concession to sell products of their own make. See Akkache, p. 106.

[9] Wallerstein, *L'Afrique et l'Indépendance*, trans. Arnelle de Lesquen (Paris: Présence Africaine, 1966), p. 80.

Notes
to
Postscript

1 *El Moudjahid*, June 22-23, 1975, p. 2, col. 2. The speech was not immediately reproduced in the French edition of the national daily paper.

2 Ibid.

3 Ibid., col. 7.

4 See Alfred Stepan, *The Military in Politics, Changing Patterns in Brazil* (Princeton: Princeton University Press, 1971).

5 *El Moudjahid*, col. 5.

6 POLISARIO Front stands for People's Front for the Liberation of Saguia El Hamra and Rio de Oro.

7 For an account of this event see *Le Monde*, March 14-15, 1976, p. 2. *Jeune Afrique*, March 26, 1976, pp. 18-19.

8 Ibid.

9 See Mahmoud Hussein, *Class Conflict in Egypt 1945-1970* trans. Michel Chirman et al (New York: Monthly Review Press, 1973).

Bibliography

Documents and Governmental Publications

Annex to the Program of Tripoli. Joachim Joesten. *The New Algeria*. Chicago: The Follett Publishing Co., 1964, Appendix B.

Collection de Documents Inédits sur l'Histoire de l'Algérie après 1830. Alger: Jules Carbonel, 1924.

Collection de Documents Inédits sur l'Histoire de l'Algérie. Paris: Editions La Rose, 1951.

Documents Algériens. Service d'Information du Cabinet du Gouverneur Général, January 1-December 31, 1948.

Programme de Tripoli. Edité par la "tendance révolutionnaire du Parti Communiste Français." Supplément au No. 84 *Le Communiste*, Paris, n.d.

République Algérienne Démocratique et Populaire (R.A.D.P.). *Plan Quadriennal*. Rapport Général. Editions Populaires de l'Armée, Janvier 1970.

R.A.D.P. Commission Nationale du Recensement de la Population d'Algérie. *Recensement de 1966*. Alger, 1970.

R.A.D.P. Commission Nationale des Investissements, *Le Code des Investissements*. Alger: Imprimerie Commerciale, September 1967.

R.A.D.P. F.L.N. *Charte et Code de la Gestion Socialiste des Entreprises*.

R.A.D.P. F.L.N. Commission Centrale d'Orientation. *La Charte d'Alger*. Alger: Imprimerie Nationale Algérienne, 1964.

239

R.A.D.P. Ministère de l'Agriculture et de la Réforme Agraire. *Communication sur le Déroulement du Volontariat de l'Eté 1972.* Alger, 19 February 1973.

R.A.D.P. Ministère de l'Agriculture et de la Réforme Agraire. *Coopération et Révolution Agraire.*

R.A.D.P. Ministère de l'Information et de la Culture. *Discours du Président Boumédiène*, 19 Juin 1965-19 Juin 1970. 2 vols. Constantine. 1970.

R.A.D.P. Ministère de l'Information et de la Culture. *Discours du Président Boumédiène*, 19 Juin 1970-1 Mai 1972. Alger: Ech-Chaab Presse. 1972.

R.A.D.P. Ministère de l'Information et de la Culture. *Discours du Président Boumédiène*, 5 Mai-19 Juin 1972. Documents.

R.A.D.P. Ministère d'Etat Chargé des Finances et du Plan. *Industrie 1968.* Vol. 3. Alger: Imp. Sous-Direction des Statistiques.

R.A.D.P. Ministère du Commerce. Critères et Options de la Réforme des Sociétés. Alger, 20 May 1970, mimeo.

R.A.D.P. Présidence du Conseil. *Révolution Agraire.* Ordonnance No. 71-73 du 8 Novembre 1971.

R.A.D.P. Secrétariat d'Etat au Plan. *Bulletin Trimestriel des Statistiques*, nos. 1 and 2. Alger, 1973.

R.A.D.P. Secrétariat d'Etat au Plan. A.A.R.D.E.S. *Enquête sur les Budgets Familiaux.* Alger, 1967-68.

Books, Monographs and Theoretical Studies

Abbas, Ferhat. *Guerre et Révolution d'Algérie*, I. *La Nuit Coloniale.* Paris: Julliard, 1962.

Ageron, Charles-Robert. *Les Musulmans Algériens et la France (1871-1919).* 2 Vols. Paris: Presses Universitaires de France, 1968.

————————. *Histoire de l'Algérie Contemporaine.* Paris: Presses Universitaires de France, 1966.

Akkache, Ahmed. *Capitaux Etrangers et Libération Economique: l'Expérience Algérienne.* Paris: Maspéro, 1971.

Ammour, Kader; Leucate, Christian; and Moulin, Jean-Jacques. *La Voie Algérienne.* Paris: Maspéro, 1974.

Bedjaoui, Mohammed. *Law and the Algerian Revolution*. Brussels: International Association of Democratic Lawyers, 1961.

Benoist, Charles H. *Enquête Algérienne*. Paris: Lecène, Oudin et Cie., 1892.

Ben Othmane Khodja, Hamdane. *Le Miroir*. Paris: Goetschy Fils et Cie., 1833.

Berque, Jacques. *Dépossession du Monde*. Paris: Editions du Seuil, 1964.

Berradi, Lhachemi; Bleuchot, H.; Camau, M.; Dubray, G.; Duchac, R.; Etienne, B.; Le Trouneau, R.; Martin, Y.; Michel, H.; Regnier, J.; Santucci, M-C.; Sraieb, N. *La Formation des Elites Politiques Maghrébines*. Aix-en-Provence: Centre de Recherches et d'Etudes sur les Sociétés Mediterranéennes, 1973.

Blackburn, Robin, ed. *Ideology in Social Science*. New York: Vintage Books, 1973.

Blumberg, Paul. *Industrial Democracy: The Sociology of Participation*. New York: Schocken Books, 1969.

Bottomore, Thomas B. *Elites and Society*. Baltimore: Penguin Books, 1964.

Bourdieu, Pierre; Darbel, A.; Rivit, J-P.; and Seibel, C. *Travail et Travailleurs en Algérie*. Paris: Mouton et Cie., 1963.

Bourdieu, Pierre, and Sayad, A. *Le Déracinement*. Paris: Editions du Seuil, 1964.

Brown, Leon C., ed. *State and Society in Independent North Africa*. Washington, D.C.: The Middle East Institute, 1966.

Burnham, James. *The Managerial Revolution*. London: Putnam and Co., 1943.

Buy, François. *La République Algérienne Démocratique et Populaire*. Paris: La Librairie François, 1965.

Carter, Gwendolyn M., ed. *African One-Party States*. Ithaca: Cornell University Press, 1962.

Chaliand, Gérard, and Minces, Juliette. *L'Algérie Indépendante*. Paris: Petite Collection Maspéro, 1972.

Chaliand, Gérard. *L'Algérie Est-Elle Socialiste?* Paris: Maspéro, 1964.

Chaulet, Claudine. *La Mitidja Autogérée*. Alger: S.N.E.D., 1971.

Clark, Michael. *Algeria in Turmoil*. New York: Grosset and Dunlap, 1960.

Clegg, Ian. *Workers' Self-Management in Algeria*. New York: Monthly Review Press, 1971.

Cliff, Toni; Hallas, D., Harman, C.; and Trotsky, L. *Party and Class*. London: Pluto Press, n.d.

Confer, Vincent. *France and Algeria: The Problem of Civil and Political Reform, 1870-1920.* Syracuse: Syracuse University Press, 1966.

Dahl, Robert. *Who Governs?* New Haven and London: Yale University Press, 1961.

d'Arcy, François; Krieger, A.; and Marill, A. *Essais sur l'Economie de l'Algérie Nouvelle.* Paris: Presses Universitaires de France, 1965.

Domhoff, William G., and Ballard, Hoyt, eds. *C. Wright Mills and the Power Elite.* Boston: Beacon Press, 1968.

Douence, Jean-Claude. *La Mise en Place des Institutions Algériennes.* Paris: Centre d'Etudes de Relations Internationales, Etudes Maghrébines, No. 2, 1964.

Emerit, Marcel. "L'Algérie à l'Epoque d'Abd-El-Kader." Gouvernement Général de l'Algérie. *Collection de Documents Inédits sur l'Histoire de l'Algérie*, Vol. 4. Paris: Editions La Rose, 1951.

Engels, Frederick. *Socialism: Utopian and Scientific.* New York: International Publishers, 1969.

Estier, Claude. *Pour l'Algérie.* Paris: Maspéro, 1964.

Fanon, Frantz. *The Wretched of the Earth.* New York: Grove Press, 1966.

Forster, Phillips, and Steiner, Herbert. *The Structure of Algerian Socialized Agriculture.* (University of Maryland Miscellaneous Publication No. 527). College Park: Department of Agricultural Economics, Agricultural Experiment Station, July, 1964.

Guérin, Daniel. *L'Algérie Caporalisée.* Paris: December, 1965.

––––––––––. *L'Algérie Qui Se Cherche.* Paris. 1964.

Gurvitch, Georges. *Etudes sur les Classes Sociales.* Paris: Editions Gonthier, 1966.

Gramsci, Antonio. *The Modern Prince and Other Writings.* New York: International Publishers, 1972.

––––––––––. *Prison Notebooks.* New York: International Publishers, 1972.

Heggoy, Alf A. *Insurgency and Counterinsurgency in Algeria.* Bloomington: Indiana University Press, 1972.

Humbaraci, Arslan. *Algeria: A Revolution That Failed.* New York: Frederick A. Praeger, 1966.

Hussein, Mahmoud. *Class Conflict in Egypt: 1945-1970.* Translated by Michel Chirman et al. New York: Monthly Review Press, 1973.

Isnard, Hildebert. *La Réorganisation de la Propriété Rurale dans la Mitidja.* Alger: Imprimerie Joyeux, 1947.

Jameson, Frederic. *The Prison House of Language.* Princeton: Princeton University Press, 1972.

Joesten, Joachim. *The New Algeria*. Chicago: Follett Publishing Co., 1964.

Julien, Charles-André. *Histoire de l'Afrique du Nord*. Paris: Payot, 1964.

——————. *L'Afrique du Nord en Marche*. Paris: René Julliard, 1952.

Karpat, Kemal H., ed. *Political and Social Thought in the Contemporary Middle East*. New York: Frederick A. Praeger, 1968.

Lacheraf, Mostefa. *L'Algérie: Nation et Société*. Paris: Maspéro, 1965.

Lacoste, Yves, and Prenant, André. *L'Algérie Passé et Présent*. Paris: Editions Sociales, 1960.

Laks, Monique. *Autogestion Ouvrière et Pouvoir Politique en Algérie (1962-1965)*. Paris: E.D.I., 1970.

LaPalombara, Joseph, and Weiner, Myron, eds. *Political Parties and Political Development*. Princeton: Princeton University Press, 1966.

LaPalombara, Joseph, ed. *Bureaucracy and Political Development*. Princeton: Princeton University Press, 1963.

Laroui, Abdallah. *L'Histoire du Maghreb*. 2 vols. Paris: Maspéro. 1975.

Lebjaoui, Mohammed. *Vérités sur la Révolution Algérienne*. Paris: Editions Gallimard, 1970.

Lenin, Vladimir I. *Selected Works of Lenin*, ed. Henry M. Christman. New York: Bantam Books, 1966.

Lichtheim, George. *The Concept of Ideology and Other Essays*. New York: Randam House, 1967.

Maameri, Khalfa. *Orientations Politiques de l'Algérie*. Alger: S.N.E.D., 1973.

Mandouze, André. *La Révolution Algérienne par les Textes*. Paris: Gallimard, 1961.

Marx, Karl. *The Class Struggles in France, 1848-1850*. Moscow: Progress Publishers, 1972.

——————. *The 18th Brumaire of Louis Bonaparte*. New York: International Publishers, 1969.

——————. *Capital*. Vol. 3. New York: International Publishers, 1972.

——————. *Grundrisse*. London: Penguin Books, 1973.

——————. *Pre-Capitalist Economic Formations*. New York: International Publishers, 1972.

——————. *Writings of the Young Marx on Philosophy and Society*. Easton, Loyd, and Guddat, K., eds., New York: Anchor Books, 1967.

Marx, Karl and Engels, Frederick. *The German Ideology*. Part One. New York: International Publishers, 1972.

_____. *Selected Works*. New York: International Publishers, 1969.

Maschino, Tariq and M'rabet, Fadéla. *L'Algérie des Illusions*. Paris: Editions Robert Laffont.

Mao Tse-Tung. *Four Essays in Philosophy*. Peking: Foreign Languages Press, 1966.

_____. *Quotations from Chairman Mao*. Peking: Foreign Languages Press, 1966.

Merle, Robert., ed. *Ahmed Ben Bella*. Paris: Gallimard, 1965.

Miliband, Ralf. *The State in Capitalist Society*. New York: Basic Books, 1969.

Mills, C. Wright, and Gerth, Herbert H., eds. *From Max Weber: Essays in Sociology*. New York: Oxford University Press, 1958.

Nouschi, André. *Enquête sur le Niveau de Vie des Populations Rurales Constantinoises de la Conquête jusqu'en 1919*. Paris: Presses Universitaires de France, 1961.

_____. *La Naissance du Nationalisme Algérien: 1914-1954*. Paris: Editions de Minuit, 1962.

Opperman, Thomas. *Le Problème Algérien*. Paris: Maspéro, 1961.

Ottaway, David, and Ottaway, Marina. *Algeria: The Politics of a Socialist Revolution*. Berkeley and Los Angeles: University of California Press, 1970.

Perroux, François, ed. *L'Algérie de Demain*. Institut d'Etudes de Développment Economique et Social. Paris: Presses Universitaires de France, 1962.

Perroux, François. *Problèmes de l'Algérie Indépendante*. Institut d'Etudes de Developpment Economique et Social. Paris: Presses Universitaires de France, 1963.

Poulantzas, Nicos. *Pouvoir Politique et Classes Sociales*. 2 vols. Paris: Maspéro, 1971.

Quandt, William B. *Revolution and Political Leadership in Algeria, 1954-1968*. Cambridge: The MIT Press, 1969.

Remili, Abderrahmane. *Les Institutions Administratives Algériennes*. Alger: S.N.E.D., 1973.

Revere, Robert B. "Consensus in Independent Algeria, 1962-1965." Ph.D. Dissertation, New York University, 1971.

Rodinson, Maxime. *Marxisme et Monde Musulman*. Paris: Editions du Seuil, 1972.

Ruedy, John. *Land Policy in Colonial Algeria*. Los Angeles: University of California Press, 1967.

Schurmann, Franz. *Ideology and Organization in Communist China*. Berkeley: University of California Press, 1973.

Silvert, Kalman H. *Expectant Peoples. Nationalism and Development*. New York: Vintage Books, 1967.

Stepan, Alfred. *The Military in Politics*. Princeton: Princeton University Press, 1971.

Tiano, André. *Le Maghreb Entre Les Mythes*. Paris: Presses Universitaires de France, 1967.

Tidafi, Tami. *L'Agriculture Algérienne et Ses Perspectives de Développement*. Paris: Maspéro, 1969.

Van Vollenhoven, Joost. *Essais sur le Fellah Algérien*. Paris: Arthur Rousseau, 1903.

Viratelle, Gérard. *L'Algérie Algérienne*. Paris: Editions Economie et Humanisme, 1970.

Wallerstein, Immanuel. *L'Afrique et l'Indépendance*. Translated by Arnelle de Lesquen. Paris: Présence Africaine, 1966.

Walsin-Esterhazy, *De la Domination Turque dans la Régence d'Alger*. Paris: Librairie Charles Gosselin, 1840.

Yacono, Xavier. *La Colonisation des Plaines du Chélif*. 2 vols. Alger: Imprimerie Imbert, 1955.

——————————. *Histoire de la Colonisation Française*. Paris: Presses Universitaires de France, 1969.

——————————. *Les Etapes de la Décolonisation Française*. Paris: Presses Universitaires de France, 1971.

Yver, Georges. *Documents Relatifs au Traité de la Tafna*. Gouvernement Général de l'Algérie, II. Collection de Documents Inédits sur l'Histoire de l'Algérie après 1830. Alger: Jules Carbonel, 1924.

Articles

Ashford, Douglas E. "Political Aspects of Rural Development in North Africa," *State and Society in Independent North Africa*. Edited by Leon C. Brown. Washington, D.C.: Middle East Institute, 1966.

Balbus, Isaac. "Ruling Elite Theory vs. Marxist Class Analysis." *Monthly Review*, May 1971.

Bendix, Reinhard. "Bureaucracy and Power Relations." *Bureaucracy*. Edited by Robert K. Merton et al. New York: The Free Press, 1952.

Berque, Jacques. "L'Idée de Classe." *Cahiers Internationaux de Sociologie*. 38 (1965): 169-184.

Brown, Leon C. "The Role of Islam in Modern North Africa." *State and Society in Independent North Africa*. Edited by Leon C. Brown. Washington, D.C.: Middle East Institute, 1966.

Bourdieu, Pierre. "De la Guerre Révolutionnaire à la Révolution." *L'Algérie de Demain*. Edited by François Perroux. Paris: Presses Universitaires de France, 1962.

Carlo, Antonio. "Lenin on the Party." *Telos*. 17 (1973): 2-40.

Corradi, Juan E. "Cultural Dependence and the Sociology of Knowledge: The Latin American Case." *International Journal of Contemporary Sociology*. 8 (January 1971): 37-54.

Dahl, Robert. "A Critique of the Ruling Elite Model." *C. Wright Mills and the Power Elite*. Edited by William G. Domhoff and Hoyt B. Ballard. Boston: Beacon Press, 1968.

Debbash, Charles. "Les Elites Maghrébines devant la Bureaucracie." *Annuaire de l'Afrique du Nord*, Vol. VII. Editions du Centre National de la Recherche Scientifique. Aix-en-Provence and Paris, 1968.

Destanne de Bernis, Gérard. "L'Industrialisation en Algérie." *Problèmes de l'Algérie Indépendante*. Edited by François Perroux. Paris: Presse Universitaires de France, 1963.

Djilas, Milovan. "The New Class." *Structured Social Inequality*. Edited by Celia Heller. London: The Macmillan Co., 1969.

Dumont, René. "Des Conditions de la Réussite de la Réforme Agraire en Algérie." *Problèmes de l'Algérie Indépendante*. Edited by François Perroux. Paris: Presses Universitaires de France, 1963.

Fainsod, Merle. "Bureaucracy and Modernization: The Russian and Soviet Case." *Bureaucracy and Political Development*. Edited by Joseph LaPalombara. Princeton: Princeton University Press, 1963.

Favret, Jeanne. "Le Syndicat, les Travailleurs et le Pouvoir en Algérie." *Annuaire de l'Afrique du Nord*, Vol. III. Editions du Centre National de la Recherche Scientifique. Aix-en-Provence and Paris, 1964.

Galissot, René. "Classification Sociale en Système Précapitaliste. L'Exemple Algérien." *Cahiers du Centre d'Etudes et de Recherches Marxistes*, 60, 1968.

Haykal, Muhammad H. "Communism and Ourselves: Seven Differences Between Communism and Arab Socialism. History Does Not

Unfold on a Closed Path." *Political and Social Thought in the Contemporary Middle East*. Edited by Kamal H. Karpat. New York: Frederick Praeger, 1968.

Harman, Chris. "Party and Class." *Party and Class*. Essays by Tony Cliff, Duncan Hallas, Chris Harman and Leon Trotsky. London: Pluto Press, n.d.

Helie, Damien. "L'Autogestion Industrielle en Algérie." *Autogestion*. Cahier no. 9-10. September-December, 1969, pp. 37-57.

Kingsley, J. Donald. "Bureaucracy and Political Development, with Particular Reference to Nigeria." *Bureaucracy and Political Development*. Edited by Joseph LaPalombara. Princeton: Princeton University Press, 1963.

Kornhauzer, William. "Power Elite or Veto Groups?" *C. Wright Mills and the Power Elite*. Edited by William G. Domhoff and Hoyt B. Ballard. Boston: Beacon Press, 1968.

Leca, Jean. "Parti et Etat en Algérie." *Annuaire de l'Afrique du Nord*, Vol. 8. Editions du Centre National de la Recherche Scientifique. Aix-en-Provence and Paris: 1968.

Lewis, William H. "The Decline of Algeria's F.L.N." *The Middle East Journal* 20, no. 2 (Spring 1966): 161-172.

Luben, Dusan. "Les Bases du Système Socialiste en Yugoslavie." *Autogestion*. Cahier no. 9-10 (September-December, 1969), pp. 155-189.

Michel, Hubert. "Chronique Politique." *Annuaire de l'Afrique du Nord*, Vols. IX. X. and XI. Editions du Centre National de la Recherche Scientifique. Aix-en-Provence and Paris, 1970 to 1972.

Miliband, Ralf. "Reply to Nicos Poulantzas." *Ideology in Social Science*. Edited by Robin Blackburn. New York: Vintage Books, 1973.

Poulantzas, Nicos. "The Problem of the Capitalist State." *Ideology in Social Science*. Edited by Robin Blackburn. New York: Vintage Books, 1973.

Remili, Abderrahmane. "Parti et Administration en Algérie." *Annuaire de l'Afrique du Nord*. Vol. VII. Editions du Centre National de la Recherche Scientifique. Aix-en-Provence and Paris, 1968.

Riggs, Fred W. "Bureaucrats and Political Development: A Paradoxical View." *Bureaucracy and Political Development*. Edited by Joseph LaPalombara. Princeton: Princeton University Press, 1963.

Salah Beh, Anisse. "L'Assemblée Nationale Constituante Algérienne." *Annuaire de l'Afrique du Nord*, Vol. I. Editions du Centre National de la Recherche Scientifique. Aix-en-Provence and Paris, 1962.

Sissani, O. "Une Action Conséquente." *Révolution Africaine*. May 10-16, 1974, pp. 18-19.

Schurmann, Franz. "Politics and Economics in Russia and China." *Soviet and Chinese Communisms. Similarities and Differences*. Edited by David Treadgold. Seattle: University of Washington Press, 1970.

Wallerstein, Immanuel. "The Decline of the Party in Single-Party States." *Political Parties and Political Development*. Edited by Joseph LaPalombara and Myron Weiner. Princeton: Princeton University Press, 1966.

_____. "Class and Class Conflict in Africa." *Canadian Journal of African Studies* 7, no. 3 (1973): 375-380.

Wright, Eric O. "To Control or to Smash the Bureaucracy: Weber and Lenin on Politics, the State and Bureaucracy." *Berkeley Journal of Sociology*, Vol. 19 (1974-75): 69-108.

Glossary

Aga (also spelled agha): the Captain General of the Turkish militia. The term was later used as an honorary title given by the French to Algerians who helped them administer rural areas.

A.L.N.: *Armée de Libération Nationale*, the Algerian army that fought the French from 1954 to 1962.

A.M.L.: *Amis du Manifeste et de la Liberté*, a political association sponsored by Ferhat Abbas in 1944.

A.N.P.: *Armée Nationale Populaire*, the Algerian army formed after independence was obtained in 1962.

Arsh: refers to both tribal land and a form of property based on the actual labor invested in the land. *Arsh* property may be inherited but cannot be alienated.

Azel: Turkish public domain which was also used as spoil. The *azel* can also refer to the permission given by the Turkish government to the local Algerian notables to collect taxes.

Autogestion: Workers' management of the enterprises they work in. Also referred to as self-management.

Bey: representative of the Turkish government at the provincial level.

Beylik: domain or jurisdiction under the *Bey*. Also used in the popular language to refer to the Turkish state as a whole.

B.C.A.: *Banque Centrale d'Algérie*, Central Bank of Algeria appointed to hold the funds of industrial enterprises under self-management.

249

B.N.A.: *Banque Nationale d'Algérie*, National Bank of Algeria created in 1966 to handle the finances of the various management committees.

B.N.A.S.S.: *Bureau National d'Animation du Secteur Socialiste*, an institution created in April 1963 to integrate all branches of the socialist economy.

Caid: local administrator used by both the turks and the French at the beginning of the colonization of Algeria.

C.C.A.A.: *Conseil Communal d'Animation d'Autogestion*, a council of presidents of management committees and representatives of the army and the administration created to decentralize control over workers' managed enterprises.

C.C.E.: *Comité de Coordination et d'Execution*, the first executive organ of the F.L.N.

C.N.R.A.: *Conseil National de la Révolution Algérienne*, the highest structure of the F.L.N. It was created in 1956 and acted as a parliament.

C.O.G.E.H.O.R.E.: *Comité de Gestion des Hôtels et Restaurants*, a committee for the management of nationalized hotels and restaurants. It was dismantled in 1966.

C.O.R.A.: *Coopératives de la Réforme Agraire*, institution for marketing agricultural produce at the provincial level.

C.R.C.: *Caisses Régionales de Crédit*, credit institution that handled the accounts of self-managed enterprises after O.N.R.A. was dismantled in 1966.

C.R.U.A.: *Comité Révolutionnaire d'Unité et d'Action*, a group of about thirty men who were responsible for the starting of the armed struggle against the French on 1 November 1954.

Dey: literally, maternal uncle. Title of the commanding officers of the Janissaries who from the 18th century onward became governors of the Regency of Algiers.

Duar: literally, dwelling arranged in a circle. Close equivalent of a hamlet. Refers to the smallest functioning tribal unit.

E.N.A.: *Etoile Nord-Africaine*, a political organization formed in Paris in 1922 among Algerian workers. It was led by Messali Hadj.

Fellah: small farmer.

F.F.F.L.N.: *Fédération de France du Front de Libération Nationale*, the F.L.N. chapter in France during the war of national liberation.

F.L.N.: *Front de Libération Nationale*, the Algerian party that led the Revolution.

G.P.R.A.: *Gouvernement Provisoire de la République Algérienne,* the provisional government formed in 1958 with headquarters in Tunis.

Gurbi: small dwelling of a poor peasant, similar to a shack.

Haush: a privately owned estate bearing the name of its founder. This is a typically North African institution. Since owners of *haush* could exercise their right to alienate their portion, one *haush* was divided up among several owners.

Habus: pious donation of property for the benefit of a foundation devoted to religious activity or a charitable and cultural institution.

Kasma: F.L.N. Party Council at the commune level.

Khammes (plural Khamamis): farm tenants who received, in return for their labor, land, tools, seed, animals and one-fifth of the harvest.

Makhzen: refers to tribes who, in return for their allegiance to the Turkish government, received land and tax compensations.

Melk: private property similar to the European freehold. However it was less easily alienated than the freehold.

Métayer: sharecropper who pays his rent in kind.

M.N.A.: *Mouvement National Algérien,* a movement formed by Messali Hadj in 1955 as an alternative to the F.L.N.

M.T.L.D.: *Mouvement pour le Triomphe des Libertés Démocratiques,* a nationalist movement founded by Messali Hadj in Algeria after World War II.

Mudjahid: freedom fighter.

Odjak (also spelled udjak): refers to the Turkish military corps.

O.N.A.C.O.: *Office National de la Commercialisation,* institution in charge of the exportation and importation of agricultural produce.

O.N.R.A.: *Office National de la Réforme Agraire,* supervisory body of the system of self-mangement. It was created in March 1963.

O.S.: *Organisation Spéciale,* the underground organization formed by the M.T.L.D. in the 1940's to prepare for an armed struggle.

P.P.A.: *Parti du Peuple Algérien,* a nationalist party formed by Messali Hadj after the E.N.A. was banned in 1937 by the French government.

Rais: leader, chief.

R'ya (also spelled raya): tribes half subdued by the Turks.

U.D.M.A.: *Union Démocratique du Manifeste Algérien,* a moderate party formed by Ferhat Abbas after World War II.

U.G.E.M.A.: *Union Générale des Etudiants Musulmans Algériens,* Algerian students' organization before independence.

U.G.T.A.: *Union Générale des Travailleurs Algériens*, the Algerian workers' union founded during the war.

Ulema (plural of the Arabic *Alem*): refers to the Algerian scholars who undertook to reform the Islamic malpractices in the 1930's.

Umma: the community formed by those who practice Islam as a religion.

Taifa of Rais: organized body of corsair leaders who competed for power with the *odjak*.

Wali: head of administration at the district level.

Wilaya: military zone during the Algerian war. There were six wilayas— Aures, North Constantine, Kabylia, Algiers area, Oran area and Sahara. Today the term refers to an administrative district.

Zawia: religious center for learning.